ALL TOGETHER NOW

THE
PROGRESSIVE ALLIANCE
AND THE 2017 GENERAL ELECTION

ALL TOGETHER
NOW

BARRY LANGFORD

Biteback Publishing

First published in Great Britain in 2017 by
Biteback Publishing Ltd
Westminster Tower
3 Albert Embankment
London SE1 7SP
Copyright © Barry Langford 2017

ISBN 978-1-78590-286-4

10 9 8 7 6 5 4 3 2 1

A CIP catalogue record for this book is available from the British Library.

Set in Minion Pro

Printed and bound in Great Britain by
CPI Group (UK) Ltd, Croydon CR0 4YY

MIX
Paper from
responsible sources
FSC® C020471

CONTENTS

FOREWORD BY ZOE WILLIAMS

The idea of a progressive alliance started to solidify and become irresistible in 2010. Before that, there had long been a sense that first past the post (FPTP) was a blunt tool and that it fostered disengagement and shut out difference, but it worked. It delivered decisive and stable victories for parties who could then act upon their promises or face the consequences. Once you accept that voting system, you accept that alliances basically mean a massacre for the smaller party: the best tactic for left and leftish parties, large or small, was to annihilate one another in order to consolidate the progressive vote. This seemed to get into the bloodstream of the political culture, which led to the bizarre spectacle, in every election post-'97, of Greens and Labour, Labour and the Lib Dems, appearing sincerely to hate one another with a greater passion than any of them mustered for the Conservative Party.

Post-2010, all that changed: FPTP no longer delivered, Lib Dems were no longer necessarily left-wing, and most importantly to my mind, the potential damage the Conservatives could do was actually intensified, rather than mitigated, by a weak hand. The slimmer their majority, the more concerned they were with placating those at the extreme edges of their own party, and the less responsive they were to the opposition. Arguably there is much more flexibility and compromise possible from a party with a landslide than there is from a precarious one. But that's for the birds: landslides are starting to look very last-century.

This shock awakening to the gravity of a Conservative-dominated hung parliament, or a weak Tory government, gave urgency and purpose to the idea of progressive alliance, but it was a slow build. It required a radical shift, most of all for the Labour Party, whose driving purpose was to become monolithic again; just as weak governing parties deliver extreme agendas, so weak opposition parties become very risk averse. It wasn't until 2016, post-Brexit, that experiment and innovation became allowable elements of the 'whither-the-left' debate; possibly because, until that point, politics didn't look broken enough for radical fixes to compete with old certainties. There was only one certainty by September, when the Greens discussed a progressive alliance at their conference: the old way was certainly broken.

It was then that we had a few conversations about the name – whether or not 'progressive alliance' sounded too wholemeal and mushy, and whether or not it was too late to change it – and they come up now as light relief in the progressive alliance story, the bit where we tried to jazz it up (rebel alliance), inject some comedy (coalition of the losers), focus on an enemy (anti-Tory alliance). But, looking back now, I think of this as not a trivial matter, but something at the very heart of the challenge, both what stood in its way and gave it its energy. It doesn't sound very sexy, does it? What do you believe in? A progressive alliance. What gets you out on the streets, waving banners, congregating, knocking on doors? Well, the idea of working constructively with people I don't always agree with, of course. Duh. Because I kept circling and constantly landing on this phrase, I had to think seriously about what that actually means, sexy politics. It sounds like a way to turn a social movement into a *Cosmo* article, but it's shorthand for something important.

Politics has to exhilarate and it has to do so authentically; it isn't something you can fake with self-righteousness and closed circuits of mutually-enforced boosterism. To paraphrase Henri Bergson, the Protestants didn't turn Catholics by persuading them; new religions break through a closed moral and intellectual atmosphere by exuding vitality, seeing in their mind's eye a new social atmosphere, an environment in which life would be more worth living, so that if people tried it they would refuse to go back to old customs. This takes certainty, dynamism, confidence, single-mindedness and, above all, a sense that one has genuinely discovered some wellspring, some generative theory of change, to which one can return infinitely for energy, solidarity, ideas and solutions. It cannot be a platitude, something everyone from Cameron to Corbyn would sign up to – social justice, equality, sustainability. It has to be more precise than that, yet nor can it be ashamed of pursuing those ends.

A progressive alliance makes new demands: certainty has to be tempered with flexibility; dynamism cannot build up such momentum that it crushes dissent; confidence has to be humble if it's to forge meaningful rather than instrumental allegiances; single-mindedness must find a way – and this is pushing at the boundaries of the language – to be open-minded. Stating these qualities in the abstract is infuriating; the more necessary each sounds, the more impossible it is to dovetail them. It is only when you see them enacted in people – like-minded but never

identical, purposeful but never rigid, passionate but never or-
thodox – that you begin to understand how single-mindedness
and open-mindedness cannot just co-exist but are precon-
ditions for one another. A progressive alliance always made
sense, but it was only in its flesh-and-blood iteration – the
meetings on the ground, the actions, the sacrifices, the energy,
the optimism – that it found its pulse. It was considered a huge
shame that a snap election precluded so much planning and
organisation, but in retrospect, I think it was a blessing. It was
the catalyst that fired the alliance's neurones. We could have
spent a decade wondering what would animate the idea of a
progressive alliance, and not realised that it was the human act
of allying that brought it to life.

   This doesn't mean its progress has been without frustration:
there was never any question what a victory would look like,
for those fighting a new battle on old terrain. It would deliver
a much less bad than expected defeat for the Labour Party; an-
nihilation for the Green vote-share; nothing terribly significant
for the Lib Dems. It would be eminently deniable by the Labour
Party and, consequently, bruising for everyone else. Yet, all
that having come to pass, it has overturned a miserable status
quo, and turned the unbeatable Conservatives overnight into a
zombie government. It has made the impossible seem possible,
and the gatekeepers of possibility look very confused. It has
made engagement seem purposeful again. And it has, after all,
only just begun.

AUTHOR'S NOTE

Everyone knows that beginning any book with a negative is a false move. Still, it seems sensible to make it clear that this book is not a comprehensive account of the 2017 UK general election. The story of that election – which began as apparently a foregone conclusion only to deliver one of the most unexpected and consequential outcomes of recent times – is of course well worth telling and will be told, many times, by journalists and scholars alike, in the months and years to come. But while the overall arc of the election naturally unfolds alongside the narrative recounted here, my focus in these pages is, so to speak, akin to that of the military historian who seeks to explore in careful detail one particular theatre of operations in a larger conflict. I have sought to tell the story of how one small, non-aligned and under-resourced group, for whom Theresa May's decision to call a snap election presented both a daunting challenge and a thrilling opportunity, sought to open an entirely new front – one that if successful promised to change not only the outcome of this election but, potentially, the entire direction of travel of British politics for this generation and beyond. The Progressive Alliance ultimately neither realised the success they had dreamed of, nor suffered the failure they feared at the outset of the campaign. The story of what they sought to achieve and why, the obstacles and opportunities they encountered and the lessons of their experience may prove to have sown the seeds of future progressive politics in this country.

Most campaign narratives tend to focus on personalities and processes: stories of *how* things happened, that is, rooted in highly individualised accounts of *who* was responsible (for confirmation, see any of the recently published 'insider' accounts of Hillary Clinton's 2016 US presidential campaign). My own narrative, by contrast, perhaps unfashionably places a greater emphasis on ideas than on personalities. Of course the motivations and characters of individuals play a part in what they decide to do in the public and political spheres, the choices they make and the decisions they take. But the team that coalesced around the Progressive Alliance in 2017 – none of whom was running for office, or stood to gain in any way personally from their efforts (almost all of them, in fact, were volunteers and in several cases effectively placed productive professional careers on hold for the duration of the campaign) – were acting from conviction, not from ambition or the murky depths of political rivalry. What held them together and drove them forward was their shared belief in the value and validity of what they were doing. So, in this book, while paying due attention to both the motivations and the reactions of individual participants, I have striven also to give as much life and oxygen as possible to the views and internal dialogues and debates (for no one involved in the Progressive Alliance was a zealot, or in any way convinced that they more than anyone else had a monopoly on wisdom) that impelled and animated them.

All Together Now is structured as a broadly chronological

account of the Progressive Alliance campaign, starting with the seminal experience of the Richmond Park by-election of December 2016 and progressing towards the climactic events of election day (and night) itself, 8 June 2017. This narrative is, of course, written with the benefit of hindsight but proceeds basically in the present tense: that is, the reader's knowledge of the outcome of the election is taken as a given, but (with the exception of the section dealing with the distinctive election campaigns in Scotland and Northern Ireland) analysis of the result and its implications is held back until the final chapter, Postscript and Afterword. The intention has been as far as possible to preserve the immediacy of the choices and problems facing the Progressive Alliance activists (who of course did not have the benefit of advance knowledge, and would have acted in some important respects very differently had they done so) as events unfolded over the weeks and months covered in the book. The chapters in the main narrative sequence, which are the spine of the book, are subdivided into sections dealing with the different practical and conceptual challenges faced by the Progressive Alliance team. They alternate with chapters that address, respectively, the core ideas behind the Progressive Alliance (Chapter Two); some of the many contrasting experiences of electoral pacts and alliances worldwide, both historical and contemporary, and the lessons to be drawn from them (Chapter Four); and a detailed discussion of the two most relevant examples of such collaborative arrangements in recent UK political history, the SDP–Liberal Alliance of the 1980s and the Blair–Ashdown 'compact' before and during the 1997 general election (Chapter Six). The final chapter offers an extended analysis of the outcome of the 2017 general election, assesses the achievement of the Progressive Alliance, and offers some tentative routes forward for the future.

• • •

All Together Now was written and researched at speed in the weeks immediately following the general election of 8 June 2017. I am immensely grateful to the following people for giving generously of their time, insight and experience during the sometimes hectic preparation of this book: Neal Lawson, Frances Foley, Mike Freedman, Roger Wilson, Georgia Amson-Bradshaw, Ian Lovering, Luke Walter, Jana Mills, Barnaby Marder, Cath Miller, Steve Williams and Robert Park. The professionalism and expertise of the editorial staff at Biteback Publishing, especially Iain Dale, Olivia Beattie and Alison Mac-Donald, ensured that the expedited publication process was managed with grace and efficiency. My thanks also to Rakib Ehsan of the Department of Politics and International Relations at Royal Holloway, University of London, for his invaluable research assistance with Chapter Four. It goes without saying that the responsibility for the opinions and any factual errors herein is entirely mine, and that I will be happy to correct any of the latter in future editions of this book.

Barry Langford
Richmond, July 2017

PROLOGUE

'I WOULDN'T START FROM HERE'

It was a lectern moment.

Nobody in the Westminster press corps seems sure when exactly Prime Ministers acquired the habit of making major announcements from behind a portable lectern in front of the doors of 10 Downing Street. Older hands couldn't remember Major or Blair or Brown gripping the sides of a wooden stand. Scratchy archive footage of premiers from Neville Chamberlain onwards showed UK leaders content to address the nation – when not speaking as they more usually did in stilted fashion from behind a leather-topped Downing Street desk – either impromptu or from a sheaf of notes casually retrieved from an inside pocket (or in Mrs Thatcher's case, her ubiquitous handbag). It seemed to have been David Cameron who acquired the lectern habit – and he had had plenty of opportunities in his brief and inglorious final term for historic announcements. There was general agreement that the lectern's arrival on the political stage reflected the growing 'presidentialisation' of British politics, as well as the age-old rivalry of British leaders with national leaders who, unlike their UK equivalents, combined the roles of head of government and of state and enjoyed the rich panoply of honorific props and regalia that came with their quasi-regal role. In any event, the appearance of the lectern had become the signal to the press that something special was afoot.

On this sunny spring Tuesday, 18 April, the first day back at work following the long Easter weekend – which Prime Minister Theresa May had spent on a walking holiday in Wales with her husband Philip – the lectern once again materialised. That it was devoid of the coat of arms that accompanied an announcement in the name of Her Majesty's Government indicated May would be speaking as Conservative Party leader rather than as Prime Minister. This dramatically narrowed the range of possibilities of what was to come. There were few major statements a Prime Minister could make in their capacity as party leader that could justify a lectern moment. John Major's dramatic 1995 announcement that he was resigning as Conservative Party leader (but not as Prime Minister) to fight a leadership election against the Eurosceptic 'bastards' in his own party who had been undermining his administration was one such moment (though Major – he of the soapbox – never used a lectern). But no one believed that May, elevated to the leadership less than a year previously in the tumultuous weeks following Britain's narrow vote to leave the European Union and David Cameron's ensuing resignation as PM, and enjoying, as it seemed, unquestioned authority over her party, would be following Major's lead.[1] Fashioning a workable Brexit was the stuff of Prime Ministerial nightmares, but May seemed almost eerily untroubled by its complexities. Her infuriatingly opaque

---

1 In the moments before May spoke, Foreign Office sources apparently spread a rumour that she was indeed resigning – which may testify to the department's marginalisation under Boris Johnson.

but apparently sincere assertion that 'Brexit means Brexit, and we're going to make a success of it', however, was starting to morph into the grimly determined insistence that 'no deal is better than a bad deal' (a claim that left most economists slack-jawed in horrified stupefaction). That left only one option to explain this lectern moment … she was going to call a general election. And sure enough, she did just that.

She declared that, as it approached the Brexit negotiations, the country faced 'a moment of enormous national significance'. She painted a rosy picture of the prosperous future an 'independent' free-trading Britain could look forward to outside the EU (again, a view altogether at odds with those of leading economists) and declared her readiness to lead the nation to those broad sunlit uplands. But then she got to the real meat of her announcement. There was one major obstacle standing between Britain and its post-EU destiny. The problem was not, as one might have imagined, the EU's Brexit negotiating team, the twenty-seven remaining members of the EU or the EU Parliament, all of whom had to agree to the terms of Britain's departure and who, in the opinion of the experts so reviled by Michael Gove, would be unlikely to want Britain to exit the EU with a better, or indeed a comparable, deal to the one it had enjoyed as a member for forty-five years. No, the problem was here at home. The problem was that some – elected representatives, no less – dared to disagree with the Prime Minister. 'There should be unity here in Westminster, but instead there is division', May warned ominously. 'The country is coming together' (which country did she mean? some listeners wondered; surely not the country which the EU referendum had divided like no issue since Suez, or even perhaps since appeasement?), 'but Westminster is not.' She darkly listed the sins of all the opposition parties, whose positions, variously opposing or even qualifying the stark 'hard Brexit' May's government seemed increasingly to favour, she characterised as 'political game-playing' that would jeopardise Britain's security. 'Division in Westminster will risk our ability to make a success of Brexit and it will cause damaging uncertainty and instability to the country.' So that was the reason for calling this election – the early election she had promised the country repeatedly she wouldn't call, and which she professed to have triggered 'reluctantly': to extinguish the opposition she had already determined to be illegitimate.

Not a few of those who heard this speech felt a little queasy at the characterisation of democratic disagreement and opposition scrutiny as specious game-playing. It seemed to border on authoritarianism. There were echoes of Margaret Thatcher's 'enemy within'. Just as Leave's narrow victory in the referendum result was now asserted to be 'the will of the [*the*, not some or even most of the] people,' so May would take the emphatic victory she clearly anticipated as an unquestionable endorsement of whatever it was the government was planning to do. (Exactly what the government's Brexit plan was, if there even was one – many doubted it – had been carefully shielded from the public gaze on the grounds of 'not giving away one's bargaining hand'.) Anyone harbouring such concerns wouldn't have been even slightly reassured by the following day's coverage of May's announcement on the ever-shriller front pages of the adulatory Tory press: 'Crush the Saboteurs' ranted the *Daily Mail* (which before Christmas had chillingly denounced as 'Enemies of the People' the High Court judges who ruled that Parliament should vote on Brexit), day by day transforming the self-proclaimed voice of middle England into something like a Rotarian edition of *Der Stürmer*.

This wasn't supposed to be happening. Set aside May's repeated assurances since taking office – the most recent less than a month before[2] – that there was no prospect of an early election; the Fixed-Term Parliaments Act, passed at the start of the Conservative–Liberal Democrat coalition government in 2010, had in any case supposedly stripped the Prime Minister of the day of the power s/he had always hitherto exercised under royal prerogative to call an election at a time of his/her own choosing (that is, his/her own best political advantage). To hold an election before the expiry of the full five years required a two-thirds Commons majority. But May knew she would get her way. Having denounced the government for two years and demanded its departure, the Labour Party could hardly refuse the opportunity now to put its case before the people. To vote to avert an election would seem, in Mrs Thatcher's memorable word, 'frit'. And it wouldn't make any real difference: if push came to shove, the Tories could simply use their majority to repeal the Fixed-Term Parliaments Act to which they had only assented in the first place as a sop to their Lib Dem junior coalition partners (who rightly feared that, without it, David Cameron would dump them as soon as the political climate favoured the Tories winning an outright majority). As ever in British governance, a Commons majority – even one as relatively narrow as the twelve seats enjoyed by May – gave the executive virtually unlimited power. The election was on, because Theresa May wanted one.

For the underlying reasons that explain why the country's self-styled serious and sober leader had performed a 180-degree turn on those frequent reassurances there would be no early

---

2 On 20 March, the Press Association quoted May's spokesperson insisting there was 'no change in our position on an early general election … there isn't going to be one … It is not going to happen.'

election, you needed look no further than the opinion polls, which showed Labour lagging 20 per cent or even more behind the government. Since its disastrous showing in the 2015 general election, the official Opposition, already reduced to its fewest MPs since the mid-1980s, had been in a state of perpetual crisis. In the Labour leadership contest precipitated by Ed Miliband's instant post-election resignation, the mass membership's overwhelming preference for leftist perpetual backbencher Jeremy Corbyn had been greeted by the parliamentary party (of whom barely a handful actively supported him)[3] with mutinous incredulity; since his elevation, Labour's big parliamentary beasts (in truth, in the party's shrunken circumstances, none of them really all that big) had mostly pursued a policy of passive-aggressive non-co-operation with the lunatics who, in their view, had stormed the asylum. The referendum result – and the perception that Corbyn, like his political mentor Tony Benn a lifelong Eurosceptic, had lent at best lukewarm support to Labour's official Remain campaign – tipped Labour MPs from internal exile into outright insurgency. In the days immediately following the referendum, even as the Conservatives were smoothly transitioning from Cameron to May, the anti-Corbyn majority in the PLP proceeded to stage one of the most inept putsch attempts in recent political history, following up a slow-motion would-be palace coup – in the form of a weekend of serial resignations from Corbyn's shadow Cabinet – with a leadership challenge by one of those former frontbenchers, Owen Smith, which could

---

3   Famously or infamously, depending on your point of view, Corbyn secured the thirty-five PLP nominations he needed to enter the race courtesy of a number of votes 'lent' by (mostly London) MPs on the basis that the party's left should be included – and, it was assumed, vanquished – in the ensuing debate. Following Corbyn's astonishing victory a number of these MPs – most prominently former Foreign Secretary Margaret Beckett – publicly regretted the gesture.

charitably be described as quixotic. The outcome was that Corbyn was re-elected with an even greater majority from the party membership, and the party's warring and unreconciled factions returned to their miserable pre-existing condition of alienated cohabitation. Labour's lamentable performance in a series of by-elections – embarrassingly losing its deposit in Richmond Park in December, then in February much more seriously surrendering Copeland (Labour-held since 1935) to the Tories and, on the same evening, narrowly holding off UKIP's preposterous leader Paul Nuttall in proverbially Labour Stoke Central – pointed to existential problems that went beyond a divided party with, as polls indicated, a deeply unpopular and unpersuasive leader. Brexit seemed to have levered open a gaping fissure between the party's liberal metropolitan voters – overwhelmingly and forcefully Remain – and its traditional white working-class base in the former industrial regions of the English Midlands and the North (Scotland had, as it were, already gone south for Labour in its 2015 wipe-out at the hands of the Scottish National Party), who had voted heavily to Leave.

In the months following the referendum, a new received wisdom set in that the referendum had licensed a large-scale rejection of the political and cultural priorities of metropolitan Britain – foremost amongst them, an embrace of free-market globalisation and large-scale immigration – by communities in regions already traumatised by the loss of traditional manufacturing and extractive industries. These areas, the consensus held, had been 'left behind' by the neoliberal economic orthodoxy enthusiastically embraced by Tony Blair and Gordon Brown; and once Conservative austerity policies withdrew the life-support mechanism of public-sector expansion by which such declining regions had been sustained under New Labour,

the fraying connection between these traditional Labour heartlands and a remote Labour elite focused on yet further economic liberalisation simply broke. Already in 2015, safe Labour seats
in the north-east had shown an unexpectedly strong surge in
support for UKIP (hitherto regarded as principally an electoral
threat to the Tories' Eurosceptic flank), while conversely London
and other large metropolitan districts supplied Labour's only
real success stories in that election. In the referendum, some
of the biggest majorities for both Remain (Hornsey & Wood
Green and Vauxhall)[4] and Leave (Stoke on Trent and Hull) alike
were found in Labour seats. Paralysed by the conundrum as to
how to preserve an electoral coalition binding together both of
these vital yet contradictory and mutually hostile blocs, Labour
under Corbyn seemed unable to put forward a remotely convincing or even coherent policy on the overriding issue of the
day. His three-line whip in March on triggering Article 50 (the
UK's formal notice to the EU of its intention to withdraw) provoked widespread dismay amongst Labour's urban voters (and
was defied by forty-seven Labour MPs, including the great majority of Corbyn's fellow London MPs) while apparently doing
little to persuade Leavers that Labour were 'sound' on Brexit.

Most commentators of every political stripe saw Labour
heading for an electoral calamity as unprecedented in scale as
it was inevitable. The only disagreement was on the dimensions
of the impending disaster: a car-crash as bad as or worse than
1983 when, under Michael Foot, the party slumped to its poorest result since the 1930s, just 203 seats (but then still buoyed
up by its forty-one Scottish MPs, now all but annihilated by
the 2015 SNP tsunami); or even apocalyptic 'Pasokificiation', a

---

4 Ironically, Vauxhall is represented by Labour maverick Kate Hoey, one of only a
   handful of Labour MPs campaigning for Leave.

near-total nationwide wipe-out like that suffered by Labour's Greek social-democratic sister party, which went from governing majority to just thirteen seats in only six years.

Theresa May was in no doubt that she had been handed a historic opportunity to demolish Labour for a generation – if not for ever – and had started making her pitch for disaffected Labour voters as early as her announcement of her bid for the Conservative leadership. The rhetoric of her speeches then and since (though not the accompanying policies, such as they were) had acknowledged the exclusion of large sections of working-class Britain from the prosperity enjoyed by much of London, the south-east, and some other metropolitan centres – while never failing to feed them what she believed they wanted above all: the red meat of a hard-as-nails Brexit. With little sign of any threat from the Liberal Democrats, still flat-lining below 10 per cent in the polls, May's radar was unflinchingly focused on Labour, which she intended to depict as unpatriotic, extremist, economically incompetent and fatally unable or unwilling to deliver the 'people's will' of an unequivocal Brexit. The *Daily Mail* and *The Sun* had already anointed her Thatcher's second coming: now the grammar-school educated PM believed she could regenerate the blue-collar Toryism that Thatcher had corralled but that her successors (especially the cosmopolitan public-school smoothies grouped around David Cameron) had failed to connect with. In fact, she would go one better than Thatcher, by winning support for Conservatives in parts of the Midlands and the North that had been tribally and ineluctably Labour since time immemorial. Well aware that unelected Prime Ministers lacked the personal authority of those who had fought and won an election, mindful of Gordon Brown's fate when in 2007 he havered and hesitated and finally shied away from calling an election he would almost certainly have won, and conscious that the majority of just twelve she had inherited from Cameron was not robust enough to sustain the government through the impending turmoil of Brexit, May's self-imposed goals were to put the mortally wounded Opposition out of its misery and proceed to govern with a vastly increased majority (the word 'landslide' was on everyone's lips) and an unchallengeable mandate.

The announcement of the election took the political world largely by surprise. May's denials had been frequent and persuasive enough that most had believed her, however irresistible the political calculus. (As it turned out, the damage her vicar's-daughter integrity 'brand' suffered from the U-turn – and the transparent partisan political opportunism driving it, however much Tory ministers prated about the 'national interest' – would be just the first of May's many missteps in the campaign.) Especially after the deadline passed to be able to hold an election on 4 May, when much of the country was already going to the polls for local elections, many observers convinced themselves there wouldn't be an election that year after all. A minority, however, had long believed in the sheer weight of the advantage May and the Tories stood to gain from fighting an election now – not least, before entering the purgatory of the Brexit negotiations proper, scheduled to begin just a week after the election now scheduled for 8 June. And it was this group – which included the leaderships of both the Greens and Labour – who had been proved right.

Not that they could take much comfort from their predictions coming true. For most on the British left, the prospect of an election provoked a sickening sense of impending doom. Reading the same polls as May and her advisors (and every

political commentator), most Labour MPs drew identical conclusions: that the best – the very best – they could hope for
was to fight a sufficiently strong campaign to stand a chance of
preserving their own seats, probably at local constituency level.
(Because they overwhelmingly believed that the more voters
saw of Corbyn, the less likely they would be to vote Labour, the
best option seemed to be to run a semi-independent campaign
emphasising one's individual achievements as a constituency
MP and relying on the advantages of incumbency and the traditional, not Corbynite, Labour 'brand'.) There was next to no
talk of targeting marginal Tory seats as possible Labour gains:
on the contrary, Labour MPs with small majorities – especially,
though far from exclusively, those representing strong 'Leave'
seats in the Midlands and North – glumly prepared for an attri-
tional defensive battle they fully expected to lose.

For one small, non-party-aligned organisation on the left,
however, the election presented not only a hugely daunting
challenge but a historic opportunity. Since the debacle of the
2015 election, the think tank/pressure group hybrid Compass –
usually characterised as 'soft-left' and certainly neither Blairite
nor Corbynite, but both more radical and much less readily
pigeonholed than the 'soft-left' tag suggested – had been the
most prominent and consistent advocate of a 'progressive alliance' of centre-left parties as the most effective means of ending
prolonged Conservative rule. Amidst the manifest disarray and
ideological evacuation of traditional social democracy following its wholesale capitulation to neoliberalism, and with the
neoliberal settlement itself now in serious question following
the 2008 financial crisis, Compass saw an opportunity: to create
a new left sufficiently pluralist, generous, principled and, at the
same time, ideologically flexible to meet the challenge of new

and difficult times. For Compass, headed by a former aide to Gordon Brown, Neal Lawson, and since 2011 a non-aligned organisation open to members of all political parties and none, it had become axiomatic that Britain's established parties, arisen as they were from the vanished social-economic context and mass movements of the twentieth century, were no longer fit for the political purposes of the twenty-first. Sustained long beyond their sell-by date by the rigid exoskeleton of the first-past-the-post voting system, they were wedded to ways of thinking and doing politics that were both unsuitable and irrelevant to the needs of contemporary society.

Gazing upon the wreckage of the 2015 election – when, not for the first time, a divided centre-left vote handed a Commons majority to a Conservative government returned with a minority of popular support (in 2015, just 37 per cent of the nationwide vote) – Lawson became convinced that only by forging a functional alliance between those parties whose common values, notwithstanding important differences of both policy and philosophy, set them all apart from Conservative ideology, could the left find a way out of the cul-de-sac into which it had been led by New Labour's uncritical embrace of neoliberalism and the Party's subsequent befuddled response to the post-financial crisis Great Recession. A progressive alliance (PA) could be both a tactical means and a strategic end. As a means of winning elections by pooling progressive votes behind a single mutually agreed candidate in elections fought under first-past-the-post, PA was an effective tactic to combat prolonged Tory hegemony and all that would entailed: a hard Brexit, the real prospect of Scottish independence and the disappearance of its mostly progressive bloc of MPs from Westminster, boundary changes institutionalising the Conservatives' grasp on power even as the party itself became increasingly indistiguishable from UKIP, and the continuation of austerity policies devastating public services and exacerbating inequality. A shattered and rudderless centre-left would be frozen out of government for a generation, maybe many. The UK would become part of the international problem, not part of the solution to our civilisation's most urgent and important issues.

A strategy born partly out of desperation, the Progressive Alliance was, unashamedly, a way of gaming a system that structurally inhibited innovative, radical thinking while hobbling progressive forces by fragmenting the centre-left vote. But winning electoral contests, though vital, was in itself only the most obvious and functional aspect of PA. Lawson's conviction was that the very process of breaking down the habitual barriers of suspicion and winner-takes-all thinking between Britain's warring progressive tribes in electoral politics would incubate the more diverse, responsive, risk-taking, intellectually and ideologically promiscuous, relevant politics he believed modern society desperately needed. 'The old order is dying and the new cannot yet be born: meanwhile a variety of morbid symptoms emerge': to Lawson, this famous aphorism of the pre-war Italian Communist leader Antonio Gramsci (originally a comment on the rise of fascism) remained deeply relevant today. The financial crisis, austerity, Brexit, Corbyn, May, even PA itself: all in their different ways could be seen as symptoms of the death throes of the neoliberal era. But uniquely, PA had the capacity to help carve a path out of the morass towards a new political and intellectual environment founded on principles of social solidarity, collaboration and sustainability. Whereas the piecemeal and marginal adjustments to the post-Thatcher settlement undertaken by New Labour, where Lawson had cut his own political teeth, had as he always feared proven all too frail and vulnerable once the Tories reclaimed power, PA could enable a deeper-rooted, broader-based, more intellectually robust and genuinely radical politics and thus a more enduring reorganisation of British society. If, that is, it got the chance.

The December 2016 by-election in Richmond Park in south-west London, where the Liberal Democrat candidate had overturned a Tory majority of over 23,000 with support from the Green Party, who stood down their candidate to give the Lib Dems a free run, amidst the collapse of the Labour vote – massive tactical voting saw the Labour candidate lose his deposit – had supplied a controlled experiment under laboratory conditions of how PA might work as a matter of practical politics. Compass had convened a public meeting early in the campaign to kick-start the idea of a progressive alliance, and Compass volunteers from parties – including local Labour members – campaigned for the Liberal Democrat candidate on an explicit PA basis (i.e. urging a tactical vote in this particular contest while not endorsing the Lib Dems in general). Since then, the campaign had gathered pace. The Greens' spring conference just a month before had overwhelmingly passed a motion supporting the principle of PA and authorising Green parties nationwide to explore such arrangements with other parties in light of their local circumstances. Well-attended Compass-sponsored public meetings on PA from Birmingham to Godalming and Lancaster to Truro pushed the idea further into the mainstream of political debate on the British left. Meanwhile, a small working group about a dozen strong – including several volunteers who had entered Compass's orbit during the by-election – had met on a handful of occasions to start plotting what was then envisaged as a three-year national campaign to build public awareness of and support for a progressive alliance, to agitate within Labour, the Liberal Democrats and the Welsh and Scottish nationalist parties, and ultimately to secure their buy-in to the idea ahead of the next scheduled general election in 2020. In fact, a major London launch event had been provisionally scheduled for the first week of June … best-laid plans now scuttled by Theresa May's announcement.

Of course, amongst the PA working group, the question had already been asked how – or, indeed, whether – the campaign should respond if there was indeed an early election: all hands to battle stations to achieve what could be achieved under the circumstances; or, faced with the sheer impossibility of making progress on such a colossal transformation of generations-old political cultures, to fold Compass's tents for the duration and reconvene in the undoubtedly dismal aftermath? The general preference had been to hope it wasn't a choice they'd have to face. But now the choice was upon them, nobody seriously suggested walking away from the battle. The fight was here, it was now, and it would have to be fought with the imperfect tools, resources and time available.

'Men make their own histories,' Karl Marx reminds his readers in *The Eighteenth Brumaire of Louis Bonaparte*, 'but not under circumstances of their own choosing.' Or, as the old joke goes, a man travelling from Galway to Dublin takes the scenic route and becomes hopelessly lost. Stopping at a crossroads, he asks a local for directions. Having pondered the question, the fellow advises him soberly: 'If I were headed for Dublin, I wouldn't start from here.' The Progressive Alliance – which, with the onset of the election, morphed from concept to campaign and became an entity in its own right (hence the capital letters) – hadn't intended or hoped to fight the forthcoming election at this time with so little preparation, so few contacts on the ground, or so few human or financial resources in the face of an obdurately defended tribal political culture whose walls they had hardly begun to scale. But everyone on the nascent PA team was convinced that this was the right cause to fight for, however imperfect the timing and unfavourable the terrain. The specific circumstances of the election made it all the more vital: PA promised not only a more humane, intelligent politics but – if the polls were right – perhaps the best chance to avert or at least mitigate a defeat whose dimensions might set the British left back for a generation.

So they would give it their best shot. What nobody could yet know was whether it would make any difference.

CHAPTER ONE

AUTUMN LEAVES, RICHMOND REMAINS

Insect-like, the news helicopter hovered in the grey December skies over Richmond town centre in prosperous south-west London. In the streets below, shoppers and pram-pushing mothers glanced upwards with mild curiosity, wondering what the copter's presence might portend. A couple of years previously, Richmond had garnered some unwanted publicity when a frozen stowaway on a London-bound flight from Johannesburg tumbled from his ill-advised hiding-place amidst the landing-gear onto the roof of the offices of the internet homewares consolidator Not On The High Street as the plane started its descent into nearby Heathrow Airport. Happily, the reassuring absence of wailing sirens today argued against anything comparably sinister: perhaps instead a member of the royal family was paying a visit to this gracious riverside town rich in royal associations?

Not exactly. The real object of the media's interest was to be found just the other side of George Street, Richmond's main commercial drag, standing on the well-tended grass of Richmond Green. Gathered in front of the Grade-I-listed red-brick

Victorian facade of Richmond Theatre was a small crowd of perhaps three dozen mostly white, mostly middle-aged, uniformly middle-class-looking people bundled up against the onset of winter. A light breeze scuffed fallen leaves against their legs and a couple of dogs bounced about energetically. Their owners matched their pets' enthusiasm, if not their physical dexterity, as they waved rhombus-shaped tangerine placards for the benefit of a gaggle of print and television journalists, earthbound counterparts of their airborne colleagues still whirring overhead. From the God's-eye perspective of the news copter it must, in truth, have seemed a fairly unimpressive gathering (the shots on that evening's television news broadcasts would confirm it); even at ground level it rated no more than a passing mildly curious glance from passing pedestrians. There were no royals, no celebrities as most would understand the term, nobody and nothing very obviously newsworthy at all. Nonetheless, the media interest wasn't misplaced. For this modest assembly, instantly recognisable as a herd of what the novelist Michael Frayn once called Britain's 'herbivores' – tolerant, well-meaning, well-mannered, easily marginalised – had gathered to celebrate a political earthquake: one they themselves had helped set off.

At the centre of all the activity stood a wiry, rather geeky-looking forty-something-year-old man, his hair an indeterminate shade somewhere between sandy and outright ginger and prematurely receding in classic male-pattern-baldness formation, a beaming, slightly lopsided smile permanently fixed onto his apple-cheeked, rather boyish face. At his shoulder, beaming a million-watt smile beneath dark eyes and strikingly arched eyebrows, a grey-blazered, raven-haired woman outdid him for cheeriness.

The man was Tim Farron, leader of the Liberal Democrat Party, the ebullient woman beside him was Sarah Olney, the newest member of his parliamentary caucus – and they had much to celebrate. Just hours previously, shortly after midnight on 2 December 2016, Olney had been confirmed victorious in the Richmond Park by-election precipitated by incumbent Conservative MP Zac Goldsmith's resignation in protest at his own government's decision to greenlight the construction of a third runway at Heathrow – a decision Richmond residents believed would further blight their leafy, picturesque suburb, already afflicted by noise pollution from the airport's flight path. At the previous year's general election, as the Lib Dem vote collapsed, Goldsmith had increased almost six-fold the modest majority by which in 2010 he had recaptured the seat (held by the Liberal Democrats for the previous thirteen years) to an enormous 23,000 – making Richmond Park, on paper at least, one of the safest Tory seats in the country.[5] And yet, less than eighteen months later, Goldsmith – running as an 'Independent' Conservative ostensibly without endorsement or support from the Conservative Party (which nevertheless chose not to field an official Conservative candidate against him) – saw his huge majority evaporate and Sarah Olney – a political neophyte who had only joined the local party the previous year – elected with a majority of just under 2,000 on a colossal 22 per cent swing. This was a genuinely sensational result. An opinion poll midway through the by-election campaign had predicted a Goldsmith win by a whopping 27 per cent. The day before the election, he remained the bookmakers' one-to-three odds-on favourite. It was by some way the Liberal Democrats' most

---

5   Goldsmith's 2015 majority was 23,015 – thirty-second largest of the 331 Conservative MPs elected that year.

eye-catching by-election victory since the mid-2000s, when the party became a refuge for disaffected Labour supporters revolted by the Blair government's role in the disastrous Iraq invasion, and the Conservatives' worst defeat at Lib Dem hands since it surrendered true-blue Newbury and Christchurch in the dog days of John Major's moribund administration in the mid-1990s.

Farron's glee was turbo-charged by sheer relief, for the Liberal Democrats had had precious little to cheer in several mortifying years. The party's 2010 decision to enter government in coalition with David Cameron's Conservatives following the inconclusive outcome of that year's election, their (as it seemed to many) overly enthusiastic collusion in that government's public-sector austerity programme in the aftermath of the 2008 financial crash, and their reversal of an apparently iron-clad and iconic manifesto pledge to abolish university tuition fees (which on the contrary trebled on the Lib Dems' watch) had trashed the Lib Dems' reputation as a straight-talking, progressive party of the centre-left. But it was precisely this reputation, carefully fostered during the 2000s under the then leader, the late Charles Kennedy, on which a substantial proportion of their growing national support – reaching 23 per cent of the vote in 2010, inflated by 'Cleggmania', an ephemeral bubble of public enthusiasm for Kennedy's successor Nick Clegg[6] – relied. In the 2015 election, left-leaning voters fled the Liberal Democrats in droves – not least in seats such as Richmond Park, where anti-Tory tactical voting by Labour supporters in this perennially

---

6 After Kennedy was forced out as leader in 2006 by his MPs' concerns over his chronic alcoholism, he was briefly succeeded by Menzies Campbell, who in turn stepped down when his age became a perceived issue – he was sixty-five upon taking the post – and gave way to Clegg.

unwinnable seat for Labour had long sustained the Lib Dems
as the Conservatives' main challengers, helping to elect Lib
Dem MPs in three successive elections from 1997. The party's
numbers in the Commons collapsed from a robust fifty-seven
seats in 2010 to a pitiful eight in 2015 (in the process relegating
them from their traditional berth as the third party of British
politics to joint fourth, far behind the triumphant Scottish National Party which all but swept the board north of the border,
winning fifty-six of Scotland's fifty-nine Westminster constituencies – including ten formerly held by the Lib Dems – and
level on seats with the hard-line Northern Irish Democratic
Unionist Party). Notwithstanding Farron's conservative social
views grounded in his evangelical Christian faith on issues such
as gay marriage and abortion, which made him a somewhat
awkward match for the majority of his party's educated, heavily
metropolitan remaining supporters, he was subsequently elected leader of a rump party whose entire Westminster cohort,
as wags liked to point out, could fit into a family-sized people
mover.

Following the trauma of electoral meltdown in 2015, the
fortunes of the humiliated and marginalised Lib Dems had, if
anything, deteriorated further, obstinately flat-lining below 10
per cent in the polls and reaching a nadir with the Leave victory
in the 2016 EU referendum, a body-blow to this most avowedly
and deeply pro-European of the Westminster parties.

So it's small wonder the Lib Dems hailed their staggering
victory in Richmond Park as a political resurrection befitting
the party's longstanding, perpetually optimistic emblem, the
phoenix bird. True, Richmond had offered them unusually
propitious terrain. The seat was familiar campaign turf for the
party, in its millennial pomp part of a bastion of suburban

south-west London Westminster seats and local authorities
(in an arc running from Richmond's immediate neighbours
Twickenham to the west, southwards through Kingston &
Surbiton, Sutton & Cheam and Carshalton & Wellingborough
– in all of which, bar the last, Lib Dem MPs were ousted in
the 2015 debacle) where the Lib Dems had long traded power
with the Conservatives, with Labour all but invisible. Notwithstanding Goldsmith's enormous majority, his rancorous and
unsuccessful run for the London mayoralty earlier that year
had incurred a good deal of ill-will. The campaign, devised
for him by the Tories' election Svengali Lynton Crosby was
accused of 'dog-whistle' racism in its unsubtle and distasteful
(and resoundingly unsuccessful) attempt to tar the impeccably
centrist Labour candidate Sadiq Khan, a British Muslim, with
improbable extremist associations. Voters tend to dislike stunt
elections (in this case being called to the polls for the third time
in barely eighteen months). And Goldsmith's supposed trump
card, his opposition to Heathrow expansion, was neutralised
by the simple fact that every other candidate in the contest was
just as vehement about the issue: given the misery the flight
path's proximity had inflicted on locals for years, taking any
other position would be electoral suicide. So with Heathrow
– Goldsmith's stated reason for resigning his seat and calling
the election in the first place – a non-issue, the campaign was
free to focus on other things. Austerity, for example, even in
such a wealthy area: shockingly and shamingly, four food banks
had opened their doors across the borough of Richmond since
2010. But one central issue would dominate the campaign, to
the virtual exclusion of everything else: Brexit.

The country's narrow decision to leave the EU in the referendum less than five months previously had carved (or perhaps

just revealed) deep new fissures in the British political land-scape, divisions that threatened to fracture historic patterns of party identification and redraw the political map. For example, Labour's traditional white working-class vote in the former industrial Midlands and the North, having already desert-ed the party in significant numbers to vote for UKIP in 2015, followed through by ignoring Labour's official exhortations to vote Remain and instead voted heavily for Brexit. The aftermath of the referendum found Britain's old pitted against its young, its educated and affluent against its underskilled and underem-ployed and, perhaps most notably of all, its most metropolitan and cosmopolitan citizens – the inhabitants of most of Britain's largest cities and its university towns – against those in rural areas and smaller towns and cities. The Brexit map of England and Wales (both Scotland and Northern Ireland voted strongly to remain in the EU) showed a broad carpet of more thinly pop-ulated Leave-voting regions pockmarked by splotches of dense, urban Remainers like an angry rash on the Eurosceptic body politic. London as a whole was the most furious and unrecon-ciled Remain patch of all, with its diverse, youthful, mobile, educated and globalised population voting 60:40 to stay in the EU and several London boroughs returning the most lopsided winning margins for either camp: 78 per cent Remain in Lam-beth and Hackney, 76 per cent in Haringey (amongst London's most diverse boroughs though, interestingly, not by any stretch its most affluent) and so on. Leave's victory – predicted by almost no poll or pundit – provoked an emotive outpouring of Europhilia rarely seen during Britain's more than four decades of often querulous EU membership. If, as Malcolm reports to Duncan, nothing so became the Thane of Cawdor's life as the leaving it, much the same was true of the UK and the EU. Tears were shed openly on London's Tube the morning after the night before on behalf of a democratically challenged, overly bureaucratic multi-national trading bloc to which in all honesty few people bar the obsessive Europhobes of UKIP and Conservative Party fringe meetings, and the even smaller band of professional British Eurocrats, had given a great deal of thought, let alone feeling, for most of the previous forty-five years.

Richmond Park[7] voted almost 73 per cent Remain, with an exceptionally high 82 per cent of its voters defying torrential rain on the day of the referendum to turn out and vote. Richmond's highly educated, affluent residents, boasting a higher proportion than anywhere else in the country of professionals and workers in certain sectors of the British economy – the City, the creative industries, the learned professions – potentially most vulnerable to Brexit, reacted in near-universal dismay, even horror, to the outcome. A mood of mutinous denial characterised many households who simply refused to accept the legitimacy of what some scathingly referred to as a 'plebiscite' and – given the Leave campaign's glaring porkies about £350 million per week for the NHS, Turkey's imminent EU accession, and the like – a mendacious one at that. And it was in this cussed, angry state of mind that Tim Farron saw his opportunity.

Without question, no party was ideologically better suited to the task of channelling Remainers' rage than the Lib Dems. Although the party's most senior Coalition ministers Clegg and Vince Cable (Coalition Business Secretary and Richmond

---

7 The London Borough of Richmond upon Thames incorporates most of two parliamentary seats: all of Twickenham and most of Richmond Park; the remaining section of the latter seat falls across the boundary with the Royal Borough of Kingston upon Thames (which voted 62 per cent Remain).

Park's neighbouring MP in Twickenham until he too lost his seat in 2015, the highest-profile and least expected of his party's hecatomb), perhaps nervously sensing the temper of the times, had made some mildly Eurosceptic or at least Euro-critical noises about Brussels during their period in government, an almost reflex Europhilia was written into Lib Dem DNA. The party had opposed a referendum on EU membership: in fact, it was widely believed in Westminster that David Cameron had included the proposal of an in–out vote in his 2015 manifesto largely as a sop to his more carnivorously Europhobic backbenchers and UKIP-inclining Tory voters, in sanguine expectation of again falling short of a majority and re-entering a coalition with the Lib Dems. For the latter the referendum would undoubtedly be a red-line matter and at their insistence Cameron could duly cancel the vote he had never wanted to hold in the first place, while shifting the blame (a Cameron speciality) onto the smaller party. Cameron, in this regard, ultimately fell victim to his own success, having cannibalised his erstwhile coalition partners to win an unexpected majority, and was thus compelled to hold the referendum whose loss precipitated his own immediate resignation. In the aftermath of the (from the Lib Dems' perspective) disastrous outcome – and with Labour busily engaged in internecine warfare as its overwhelmingly Remain MPs angrily blamed defeat on Jeremy Corbyn's manifestly tepid support for 'their' (and most, but critically far from all, of their voters') cause – the Lib Dems were both well-placed politically and virtually to a man and woman united around the principle of fighting Brexit tooth and nail. From early in the immediate aftermath of the referendum, alone of the major party leaders Farron had publicly urged a second referendum, in the hope of rallying 'the 48 per cent' – the near-half of the country that voted Remain, a cause that narrow defeat, he hoped, would rather energise than deter – en bloc to Lib Dem colours.

Investing so much of the Liberal Democrats' scant political capital in such a divisive cause was a risky move – not least given the implications for the party's hopes of recovering electoral ground in their traditional strongholds in the (strongly Leave) south-west of England, all annihilated in the 2015 rout. But in the party's present extremity, Farron had little to lose. The opportunity was in Remain Richmond, not Leave Cornwall; that would have to be a battle for another day.[8] And there were straws in the wind to give him grounds for optimism that his great gamble would indeed pay off. The most substantial wafted in from the only other post-referendum by-election so far, held just five days before Zac Goldsmith triggered the Richmond Park poll, in Witney – David Cameron's erstwhile constituency which, after he resigned the premiership, he abandoned with what seemed to many fairly indecent haste as he glided smoothly into lucrative early retirement on the international lecture circuit. Here, in a classic Tory-shire seat which had never elected anyone but a Conservative[9] – but which had voted 56 per cent to remain – and without seriously campaigning to win, the Lib Dem candidate had increased her vote by over 23 per cent (on a 19 per cent swing), cutting the majority of Cameron's successor Robert Courts by 20,000 votes. Now the new Conservative Prime Minister Theresa May, though a Remainer herself in the referendum campaign (albeit with no

---

8   During the 2017 general election campaign, Farron would claim unconvincingly in a BBC interview to be 'a bit of a Eurosceptic'.

9   Bar a brief and somewhat bizarre interregnum when Shaun Woodward crossed the floor and represented the seat for two years as a Labour MP before being parachuted (in what Labour MP and diarist Chris Mullin called 'one of New Labour's vilest stitch-ups') into the safe Labour seat of St Helens South.

greater enthusiasm, and far less visibility, than Jeremy Corbyn), was ignoring the 48 per cent as assiduously as Farron sought to make himself their tribune, apparently bent on steering the country towards what pundits had come to call a 'hard Brexit' (out of the single market and customs union, withdrawing from the European Court of Justice and curbing freedom of movement). On far more congenial and familiar political ground than rural Oxfordshire, Farron saw an opportunity he was determined to grasp.

Over the five weeks of the ensuing campaign, the Lib Dems never strayed far from the golden vote-mining seam (as Farron hoped) of Brexit. Admittedly, they were fortunate in their opponent. Not only did Zac Goldsmith's own support for Leave (a conviction he seemed to have inherited along with his millions from his late father, tycoon James Goldsmith, whose 1990s anti-EU Referendum Party was UKIP's direct ancestor) instantly alienate swathes of his natural Conservative supporters, but his languid, unfocused personal style also seemed to many to encapsulate the air of entitlement and plutocratic chumocracy under whose sway the nation had fallen during the ascendancy (now abruptly terminated) of fellow Old Etonian David Cameron. Although no one was fooled by Goldsmith's supposed 'independence' (the lack of an official Conservative candidate spoke volumes), the absence of the formidable professional resources of CCHQ[10] inevitably showed, even with the resources a multi-millionaire could pour into his own campaign. But, after all, you can only play the opposition you get – and having got the Brexit bit between their teeth, the Lib Dems never relaxed their jaws. Their candidate Sarah Olney, a local accountant who

---

10 Conservative Campaign Headquarters.

had only joined the party after the 2015 general election, campaigned on a firm commitment to vote against the triggering of
Article 50 (the once obscure, never hitherto invoked, but now
internationally famous section of the Lisbon Treaty that sets
out the process for withdrawal from the EU) if elected. With
Labour's equally pro-EU candidate, the transport historian
and campaigner Christian Wolmar, irrelevant and side-lined
(of which more later), the campaign rapidly became – and was
treated by the attendant national media as – an effective replay
of the referendum itself. In the small hours of 2 December, Farron's gamble paid off big-time. A 22 per cent swing brooks no
argument. 'The people of Richmond Park & North Kingston
have sent a shockwave through this Conservative Brexit government,' announced Olney in her victory speech, Goldsmith
looking shell-shocked beside her, 'and our message is clear –
we do not want a hard Brexit.' The following day on Richmond
Green, a triumphantly validated Farron insisted that 'this result
might change the direction of British politics'. Richard Dawkins
wrote to *The Guardian* hailing the Lib Dems as the champions
of 'the swelling 48 per cent' (surely a triumph of hope over expectation) and suggesting that, to seal the deal (and expunge
toxic memories of the coalition), the party should change its
name to 'The European Party'.

But hold the phone (as they might say in California, where
the ousted Zac Goldsmith spent part of his gilded youth): if
the Lib Dem resurgence were the only story here, it would –
with all due respect to Tim Farron and Sarah Olney – hardly
be worth the telling. After all, 'Liberal [Democrat] revivals' are
an enduring and much-loved feature of British political life
dating back at least as far as the old Liberal Party's celebrated
capture of Orpington from the Conservatives in 1962. Over

the past century, it was the party's handsome parliamentary representation in the late 1990s and 2000s under Paddy Ashdown, Charles Kennedy and Nick Clegg (peaking at sixty-two seats in the post-Iraq War 2005 election) and still more its five years in government from 2010–2015, that were exceptional – not its subsequent reduction to a derisory and irrelevant single-figures rump, duly followed by sensational and unexpected by-election success and renewed hopes of national revival. Lib Dem by-election victories are the tornadoes of British politics; a recurrent phenomenon whose dramatic appearances are guaranteed, sometimes significant, with the capacity to cause meaningful damage, but unpredictable and rarely sustained. Nor was Brexit quite the only story in town. The same *Guardian* letters page that showcased Richard Dawkins's Europhiliac paean to the Lib Dems also ran a number of other letters that drew quite different conclusions from the result. Several noted the humiliation suffered by Labour's Wolmar, whose derisory 1,515 votes not only totalled barely a quarter of the vote share taken by Labour's candidate in the 2015 general election and lost him his deposit, but – in a widely noted statistic – won fewer votes than there were registered Labour Party members in the constituency at the time. The inescapable and obvious conclusion (publicly confirmed by several letters from Labour members) was that Labour voters had abandoned their own party's candidate *en masse* in this altogether unwinnable seat for Labour in favour of Sarah Olney, the only plausible winner – though, at the start of the campaign, it looked a tremendously big ask – against Goldsmith.

In itself, such behaviour by Labour supporters in Richmond Park wasn't such terribly big news either. Jenny Tonge's successes in 1997 and 2001, and Susan Kramer's in 2005, all owed much to tactical voting – tacitly colluded in, even encouraged, by Labour in 1997 at least.[11] Winning 12.5 per cent of the vote in 2015 marked a twenty-year high for the party[12] – undoubtedly the result of Labour supporters reclaiming their 'loaned' votes to protest and punish the Lib Dems for their role as the Tories' junior partners in the coalition, even if by doing so Zac Gold-smith's re-election was ensured (in the event, Goldsmith's huge margin of victory rendered the consequences of Labour 'tactical unwind' quite irrelevant). Having said that, however, the scale of the Labour-to-Lib Dem tactical vote in 2016 was striking and unprecedented. It denoted a massive and concerted effort to unite the anti-Conservative vote behind a single electable can-didate. What's more, this hadn't happened spontaneously or by what ageing political pundits like to think of as the mystical os-mosis of popular democracy. Still another *Guardian* letter came from Andrée Frieze, who had originally put herself forward as the Green Party's candidate in the by-election only to withdraw on behalf of Sarah Olney. Frieze argued that Olney's victory happened only because voters of the anti-Conservative parties pooled their differences and made common cause against their common foe. She called it a 'progressive alliance.' What she didn't add is that none of this had happened of its own accord. Ultimately, it all happened because Tim Farron hadn't been the only one to spy – and seize – an opportunity to change the po-litical weather in Richmond Park that autumn.

•   •   •

---

11 See Chapter Six.
12 The present author was Labour's candidate in Richmond Park in 2001, polling 5,541 votes (11.3 per cent).

Fresh from a Master's in Political Science at the University of Birmingham, Glasgow-born, Oldham-raised, Oxford-educated Frances Foley had been working for the left-wing pressure group Compass – one-third of a team comprised of Compass chair Neal Lawson, herself and just one other (soon-to-depart) staffer – for slightly over a fortnight when, early on the morning of Saturday 4 November, Lawson called her in a considerable state of excitement. The Greens had announced they were standing down their candidate in the by-election and Lawson wanted to hold a public meeting in Richmond to promote the cause of a united front – a progressive alliance – against Zac Goldsmith. In just three days' time.

Compass, as its official history proudly proclaims, started out 'like many good organisations do – with a letter to *The Guardian*' in September 2003. Alongside other prominent New Labour-era thinkers, including the Fabians' Michael Jacobs and Tony Blair's newly appointed policy unit head Matthew Taylor,[13] former Gordon Brown aide Neal Lawson warned that in the wake of the Iraq War Blair's government risked 'losing its way' and failing to seize a historic opportunity to create a more equal, democratic and sustainable society in Britain. Out of the letter materialised Compass, initially as a pressure group within Labour seeking as its name suggested to keep the Labour government on course towards a better – a more egalitarian, democratic and pluralist – party and society. In the coming years the organisation became a prominent campaigning voice, clearly to the left of the New Labour consensus but not identified with any Labour factions, old or new. As the New Labour era drew to a close, Lawson came to feel that Compass' vision

---

13 His new position required Taylor to remove his name from the letter – but he never denied having co-drafted it.

– which had always embraced ideas from a plurality of sources –
was incompatible with excluding members of other progressive
parties. What justification could there be for Peter Mandelson,
say, to be entitled to join Compass (he didn't) when someone
outside Labour like the Greens' Caroline Lucas, who had already
spoken at Compass events and whose views chimed with Compass values, was excluded because her party membership card
was a different colour? In 2011, Compass voted to open itself up
to members of other political parties. Going forward, this crucial (and at the time not uncontroversial) decision shaped both
the organisation's direction of travel and the increasingly pluralist tenor of its internal culture. It wasn't without cost: having
disaffiliated from the party, Compass lost its voice in Labour's
policymaking bodies at just the time when, under Ed Miliband,
the left was finally better placed to gain a receptive hearing. But
it has become an article of faith for Compass as an open and
democratic space for people who want to develop a new form
of politics that, while Labour inevitably remains the principal
vehicle for social and political transformation in Britain, no
single party can claim a monopoly on political wisdom or can
alone usher in a Good Society. And Compass's wholesale commitment to first the principle and ultimately the delivery of the
Progressive Alliance would have been impossible (not to say
disallowed under Labour Party rules) had the party not already
actualised pluralist democracy in its own internal structures.

The wreck of Ed Miliband's uncertain and conflicted attempt
to plot a new path for Labour prompted the seismic upheaval
amongst the party mass membership that with the election of
Jeremy Corbyn buried New Labour once and for all. But Neal
Lawson was as unpersuaded by Corbyn's old-time-religion faith
in the power of the centralised state as he was by the Blairites'

dogmatic faith in the free market. He saw a larger, tectonic shift underway in which the 'vertical' bureaucratic, mechanistic top-down solutions proposed by parties moulded in the same hierarchical image could no longer adequately speak to, let alone address the needs of, a 'horizontally'-oriented society – one animated by mobility and change more than permanence, individualism and localism more than the nation state, and increasingly vexed by the patent inadequacy of market-based economic models to deliver the basic security, freedom from want, and opportunity for self-actualisation that people (but not markets) regarded as a human right.

The new horizontal politics – empowering and enabling rather than directive and paternalist – would still need the resources of the old vertical politics: not least to combat the regressive forces that would inevitably combat the profound threat to their own vested privilege and power posed by a self-confident, modernised left. Hence Lawson's coinage of '45 Degree Politics': the Archimedean point of leverage where the organisational ability of the vertical combines with the some-times unformed and inchoate yet creative and transformative energy of the horizontal. As the idea of the Progressive Alliance started to concretise during 2015–16, it sought to embody this idea – a highly practical (some would say, borderline cynical) effort to game a broken system that, at the same time, required creative lateral thinking and inventive, quicksilver moves going well beyond the blinkered outlook and sclerotic pace of con-ventional political manoeuvring.

Meanwhile, in the realm of very practical politics Frances Foley had a public meeting to organise at seventy-two hours' notice. Her first instinct was that it was a pretty tall order. But she was, after all, projects and campaigns co-ordinator: a less grand role than it

might sound in a staff of three, but still. So she located a suitably
ecumenical venue in Richmond for that Tuesday evening – the
surprisingly grand redbrick Unitarian Church – and began calling around. Top of her list, naturally, were the local candidates:
Andrée Frieze, the Green candidate who was standing down, and
Sarah Olney, who would be the beneficiary of the Greens' bold
gesture. What about Labour? Christian Wolmar had been nominated that very same Saturday morning as Labour's candidate
at an ill-tempered Constituency Labour Party (CLP) selection
meeting. To Wolmar's credit, he requested the opportunity to
appear at the Tuesday meeting and defend his decision to stand,
and Foley was happy to include him. But the many local Labour
supporters who felt their party was dead wrong as strongly as
Wolmar apparently felt he was right would also have a voice, in
the trim, pugnacious form of Mike Freedman.

A born fixer with a challenging gaze beneath bushy grey
eyebrows, Freedman boasted proudly of having once been
called 'a leather-jacketed thug' by the widely reviled former
Tory minister David Mellor. Freedman had a long history in
Labour politics, having stood as a parliamentary candidate as
far back as 1974 and later using his professional experience in
management consultancy to help Tom Sawyer, Tony Blair's ap-
pointee as General Secretary, modernise party structures ahead
of New Labour's 1997 triumph. Recently retired, Freedman had
stepped back from Labour, disillusioned like so many others by
the later New Labour years, and, though a long-time Richmond
resident, had taken no interest whatsoever in the workings of
the perennially unelectable Richmond Park CLP – until the
previous weekend, when he had awoken in a spirit of quiet
fury. Like all CLP members Freedman had received word of the
candidate selection meeting scheduled for that morning. He

was utterly convinced that, given the gravity of the post-Brexit crisis and the urgency of sending an unmistakeable message to Theresa May's government that 'the people's will' did not as she maintained provide a mandate for destructive separation from Britain's European neighbours and partners, for Labour to risk siphoning off votes that would hand the Tories a victory they would undoubtedly claim as validating their course was little short of madness. Three prominent Labour MPs – Clive Lewis, Lisa Nandy and Jonathan Reynolds – had already published a joint statement calling on Labour to consider standing aside in the by-election. But there was no sign that the party leadership had any inclination to do so. So Freedman betook himself to the candidate selection meeting at a Sheen secondary school determined to speak out as a voice of sanity.

As soon as the CLP chair opened the meeting, Freedman got to his feet and raised a point of order (the universal procedural cover for trying to talk about matters that aren't on or contradict the agenda): namely that the decision to select a candidate should be subject to a democratic vote by members as to whether or not they wished to run any candidate at all in light of the local and national political situation. This intervention clearly ruffled feathers – as Freedman had intended it to – and the platform took a few minutes to formulate a response, during which Freedman's proposal received both support and opposition from the floor while the seven (!) aspiring candidates cooled their heels in the vestibule outside, innocent of the ructions within. Finally, the senior party representatives present – Andy Slaughter, MP for neighbouring Hammersmith, who had been tasked with 'shepherding' the eventual candidate through his/her campaign, and a representative from Labour's governing National Executive Committee (NEC) – came down clear and hard: the meeting had been called to select a candidate; it was not at liberty under party rules not to do so; should members refuse to nominate a candidate one would be imposed upon them.

It was hard to miss the glaring irony that the CLP was being hobbled in this way under the leadership of Jeremy Corbyn, of all people – who, throughout his thirty-year career as a backbench refusenik and serial rebel, had been identified with the Labour left's longstanding campaign to democratise the party and in particular to empower constituency parties at the expense of the NEC and leadership. But this being Richmond, no one was ill-mannered enough to mention it. Thus gagged, Freedman led a small walkout from the meeting which duly proceeded to select Christian Wolmar (by another irony, not a local resident but in fact a constituent of Corbyn's in Islington) as the by-election candidate. Freedman nursed his grievance at Labour's blinkered idiocy but wasn't sure what more, if anything, he could do bar urging his friends to vote, as he fully intended to, for the Lib Dems. Neal Lawson's call the following morning inviting him to speak at Compass's meeting that Tuesday came as a complete surprise – Freedman had never met Lawson, wasn't even a Compass member and was entirely unaware of the evolving campaign for a progressive alliance. But he knew good sense when he heard it and unhesitatingly agreed to come.

Having lined up party voices, Foley proceeded to tap up Compass's established list of public supporters of cross-party collaboration. Since the 2015 election, Compass had been holding public and private meetings to test the level of interest in and support for a progressive alliance. Over time, a number of high-profile politicians and commentators started to become, in differing degrees, visible advocates and spokespeople for cross-party collaboration: Caroline Lucas of the Greens, Clive Lewis from Labour, Tommy Shepherd of the SNP, the Liberal Democrats' Vince Cable and Dick Newby (Lib Dem Leader in the Lords) and Sophie Walker, leader of the Women's Equality Party, alongside centre-left writers and commentators such as Zoe Williams, John Harris, Owen Jones and Paul Mason. Lucas, Williams, Walker and Newby were available to address Tuesday's meeting. In short order, Foley had a programme of speakers. The question was, would anyone come?

They came: 300 of them, packed into the pews and aisles and doorways of the Unitarian Church, fizzing with indignation at Goldsmith's temerity and arrogance in calling the election and itching for a chance to get payback for what everyone present felt as the almost personal injury of Brexit. They enthusiastically applauded the media pundits, especially John Harris, who insisted that the terrifying rise of the nationalist right and the threat it posed to liberal and democratic culture amounted to a national emergency, and that at such moments, people had to be willing to put aside tribal and personal interests. They listened in polite but deeply sceptical silence as Wolmar offered a painfully thin defence of his party's insistence on fielding a candidate in this unwinnable contest (one of his principal arguments was the party's need to maintain a local profile ahead of local council elections the following year – a position that would have more force had Richmond elected a single Labour councillor since 1998.) They urged on their designated standard-bearer Sarah Olney. And they rose to their feet and cheered Andrée Frieze, the progressive hero of the hour, to the rafters.

And then the evening ended, as evenings do, and everyone went home. And everything might have played out as it did, or equally it might not: for rousing heated passions at a cathartic, energising meeting is one thing; channelling them effectively into the drudgery of weeks of campaigning in what remained – after all was said and done – a pretty improbable cause is, as any organiser will tell you, quite another. Which is where history, in the most God-awful way, lent a hand. For the Richmond Progressive Alliance meeting was held on the evening of Tuesday 8 November. And people left invigorated by the novelty of the idea of a new politics and fired up to help Sarah Olney on her way. Doubtless a few – maybe more than a few – would have followed through anyway. But then they woke up the following morning to find that as unthinkable as the EU referendum result had been, thousands of miles away across the Atlantic something more unthinkable still had happened. The election of a pathological liar, narcissist, fraud and sexual predator to the presidency of the United States, following a campaign that pandered to his nation's basest traits of untrammelled racism, sexism, xenophobia and bestial ignorance, persuaded anyone who still needed convincing that these were indeed new, different, and very dangerous times.

Trump's election prompted Neal Lawson to pen one of his most impassioned and eloquent open letters, which arrived in Compass subscribers' inboxes before lunchtime that day. He didn't pull any punches:

When will we ever learn? Brexit, as terrible as it was, was not the wake up call to the progressive sentiment. Now we have Brexit × 10. The victory of Donald Trump. But what do we expect when we stand establishment candidates who helped create the conditions for Trumpism? Clintonism and Blairism, as we keep saying, are finished.

A politics that attempts to humanise neo-liberalism and only ends up embedding it was doomed to fail. Elections are no longer won from the centre and the slide into the abyss cannot be defeated by triangulation. The only thing that can win is a genuine alternative, created with and by our fellow citizens, that makes our country much more equal, sustainable and democratic.

He warned that 'left behind' British voters, too, 'ground down by a system that doesn't work for them and doesn't care about them,' could in their desperation be conned into supporting a reactionary movement like Trump's in the US. And he built to a harrowing peroration, worth quoting in its entirety:

A generation of politicians has failed our country. The seeds of this terrifying shift have been sowed long ago and run very deep. The capitulation to financialisation and free markets by the mainstream centre-left has reaped a social and now political whirlwind. People feel so alienated and humiliated that they will vote for Brexit here and for Trump in the USA. What bit of 'it's our fault' does the old progressive establishment not get? [...]

So this is still not the worst it can get. Things are now moving so fast that our political opponents could yet emerge in uniforms. 1930's [sic] parallels are easy to make but that doesn't make them wrong. The victory of Trump will unlock another wave of hatred. People have been lost, let down, bewildered and marginalized for so long that they are turning to a dark side. Just think what has been said in the UK in the last few days about electing our judges. Think about the rise in hate crime since Brexit. And we have to say that Labour, thus far, is not stemming this tide or showing signs of being able to. And even if they did, they cannot hope to do it alone. The moment calls for unity amongst everyone who cherishes a liberal, more egalitarian, sustainable and democratic society.

Compass is a small organisation, but not so small we didn't see this coming and not so small that we can't play a key role in digging the deep intellectual, cultural and structural basis for the fight back. We, like the progressives we fight alongside, understand this moment, why it's happened and what we do about it. And we know that everything that gave rise to Brexit and Trump can and must be countered. It is all about who is best at politics. It's now imperative that we show it's all of us.

There were those on Compass's mailing list who were in tears by the time they reached the end of Lawson's letter. Nobody at that moment doubted that the stakes, high enough before, had now grown existentially higher. Nor that the work to save the future started now, and started of all unlikely places in Richmond Park – Lawson's email itself identified the previous night's meeting as a flame of hope amidst the gale of disaster, and found room too to denounce the tragic 'folly' of Labour's 'narrow tribalism in the face of such a terrible threat'. It was a call to action, and the ensuing showing and success of the Progressive Alliance in Richmond – and beyond – may have owed much to the electrifying power of Lawson's words at this critical moment.

•   •   •

Over the next seven months, the Green Party would frequently find themselves portrayed – not least by their co-leader Caroline

Lucas and by Compass, with which Lucas had long been closely allied – as the heroically selfless pathfinders of the Progressive Alliance, the only party to follow through on the principles of pluralism and openness to which in various ways most parties of the centre-left paid lip service (remember Jeremy Corbyn's promise as Labour's newly elected leader to build 'a kinder politics'?), but did little to deliver. And in many ways, they were just that. But the story of how the Greens came to turn the idea of a progressive alliance, long bruited in discussions on the British centre-left, into a concrete reality is also a reminder that nothing in politics ever happens from sheer altruism or principle, outside the realities of the politically possible and desirable, or indeed without a strong dose of hard-headed political calculation.

When Zac Goldsmith precipitated the stunt election in Richmond Park, far more than any other party the Greens were abreast of the idea of a progressive alliance. The election of Caroline Lucas and Jonathon Bartley as the party's co-leaders just the previous month, with PA as a principal plank of their platform, gave the green light to local Greens (who under the party's highly devolved constitution enjoy a striking degree of functional autonomy – certainly compared to the centralised administrative structures of the Labour Party) to consider such arrangements in forthcoming contests. The Witney by-election called just days after Lucas and Bartley's election by an overwhelming 86 per cent of Green members probably came too soon to be able to give the idea a test run, and in any case struck nobody as a viable prospect for a progressive victory. The surprising, and from a progressive perspective frustrating, result that failed only by a relatively narrow margin to inflict a hugely embarrassing reversal on Theresa May's still-infant administration, ensured the next opportunity, wherever it occurred, would be taken very seriously. Even so, the party's initial position was that unless Labour was willing to join forces, the Greens would be obliged to stand in Richmond Park. In that spirit, the party's candidate in the 2015 general election, Andrée Frieze, was adopted. The eventual reversal of this decision came about through a classic combination of high principle and low politics.

The Greens had done exceptionally well in Richmond Park in 2015, with Frieze increasing the party's vote share by 600 per cent on its 2010 result (and in the process saving the party's deposit for the first time in the constituency's history). Like Labour that year, the Greens benefited from the 'tactical unwind' of centre-left voters repatriating their tactical Lib Dem votes from previous elections. But when the by-election came around, Frieze along with the co-chair of the Richmond & Twickenham party, Richard Bennett, felt the Greens could be on a hiding to nothing. The Witney result and Brexit's continuing consumption of the political oxygen made it a near-certainty that the contest would in large part be – and would certainly be treated by the national press, notoriously uninterested in local issues, as – a referendum rerun. In such a scenario, which would likely compound the general tendency in by-elections to concentrate votes behind one anti-government candidate, the Greens could expect their vote, like Labour's, to be squeezed as the Lib Dems (past masters at pavement politics and targeted one-off contests) poured resources into the seat and voters at least temporarily forgave them their coalition sins in the wider and pressing context of national near-emergency. Frieze knew that at national leadership level Jonathon Bartley shared her concerns. It was very possible the Greens would lose their deposit. And that mattered because the reputational damage the party would in that case incur could have knock-on effects for its credibility as a player in future elections: specifically, in the local elections scheduled for May 2018 where the Greens were in serious discussion with the local Liberal Democrats about the possibility of fielding a joint slate in one or two key wards – that is, the Lib Dems running only two candidates in a three-member ward and endorsing a Green for the final berth. A dismal showing for the Greens in the by-election might undo the hard-won achievement of the recent general election (in 2010, the Green candidate had won just 572 votes) and reduce their bargaining power in those discussions. So the party's long-term strategy – which centred on maximising elected Green representatives at any level – could be better served in this case by letting the local election tail wag the Westminster dog. In addition, the Greens would gain a tremendous amount of both publicity and good-will by taking a stand that could be presented as courageous, principled and putting national before party interest.

The analysis was sound and had the backing of the party's national leadership. Briefly, there was some heady talk of a high-profile 'unity' candidate uniting all the anti-Tory parties on a Remain platform. When this predictably failed to materialise, however, and the Lib Dems nominated the earnest, but certainly not high-profile, Sarah Olney, Richmond Greens agreed their best bet was to go ahead and blaze a path for a progressive alliance. Richard Bennett sounded out members about the idea of standing aside and found considerable support.[14] It instinctively felt like the right thing to be doing – unlike persuading Green

---

14 One member replied it would be 'brave and wonderful' – prompting Bennett to recall that Sir Humphrey in *Yes, Prime Minister* characteristically used 'brave' as a mandarin euphemism for 'unwise'.

Party volunteers to campaign hard to get Green votes that might well help Zac Goldsmith get re-elected. And whatever the Lib Dems' failings (as one Green Party member said to Gareth Roberts, Leader of the Lib Dem group on Richmond Council), 'we have significant ideological differences, and we hate you for what the coalition did, but you support PR, are pro-Remain, are anti-Heathrow expansion, the country is facing a crisis, and most of all you are not Conservatives.'

But geography then created an unexpected pitfall.

Because a large chunk is occupied by 955 hectares of Richmond Park itself, the constituency's boundaries extend south of the park into parts of south-west London that are in truth neither geographically nor culturally contiguous with the majority of the seat: New Malden and some northern parts of Kingston. This smaller part of the constituency falls within the Royal Borough of Kingston-upon-Thames. Because Green parties (unlike Labour and the Conservatives) are organised solely on a local authority rather than a constituency basis – reflecting the party's much greater prospects of winning local council seats than returning MPs to Westminster, and the practical difficulty with fewer members of staffing multiple overlapping local organisations – that meant two, not one, local Green parties needed to agree on the proposed stand-aside in the by-election. And the Kingston Greens didn't really feel like playing ball.

Dominated by a younger and aggressively anti-Lib Dem cohort with connections to the Corbynite Labour group Momentum, the Kingston Greens felt strongly that the Greens should fight for every available vote – especially given Goldsmith's ostensible *casus belli* of Heathrow expansion, an issue on which the Green voice, they felt, had to be heard. At the very least, the Kingston group refused to agree to support a progressive alliance unless Labour did the same. And there was no suggestion that Labour would. Despite the growing support for a stand-aside in the Richmond party, the Kingston Greens – secure in the protection afforded them by the party's disaggregated structures – stood firm. At a contentious summit meeting in the upper room of the Old Ship pub in central Richmond, the Kingston crew raised the ante still further: unless they could see a tangible benefit to themselves, they threatened to nominate and run their own Kingston-based candidate – who would have the status of an official Green Party candidate on the ballot paper, despite representing in effect only four of the constituency's eleven wards. Extraordinarily, it seemed that under Green Party rules this would actually be constitutionally possible. Meanwhile, Andrée Frieze had been advised by former Lib Dem council leader David Williams (who had a well-earned reputation as a tough political operator) that any prospect of an electoral alliance for the 2018 local elections would be doomed should she, or any other Green candidate, be unwise enough to stand.

In the end it took urgent phone calls between Caroline Lucas, Frieze and senior Kingston Liberal Democrat councillor Liz Green to broker a sellable deal whereby in return for a free run against Zac Goldsmith the Lib Dems agreed to stand aside candidates in Kingston borough wards in 2018. Armed with this assurance, the two local Green parties were able to come to an agreement and on Friday 4 November Frieze publicly announced the party's decision to withdraw her candidacy – the declaration that prompted Lawson's breakfast-time démarche to Frances Foley. Of course, the Greens' official announcement didn't mention the back-room deals or the internal divisions. And the party duly received praise for its 'grown-up' approach from commentators such as *The Guardian*'s John Harris (a long-time Compass ally) – while the same voices showered Labour's boneheaded, blinkered tribalism with opprobrium.

But not everyone, even in the Greens, was apparently quite as grown-up as all that. The party's official, slightly contorted position – designed in part to keep the Kingston Greens onside – was that, although it had chosen to stand down its candidate, it was not endorsing the Lib Dems; rather, it encouraged its supporters to vote for 'the candidate best capable of beating Zac Goldsmith'. This remained the official Green position throughout the campaign. But it may been that the still-unreconciled Kingston Green cohort – including the local party chair, the Greens' 2015 candidate in Kingston & Surbiton, and a member of the party's national executive – were looking for an excuse to break ranks. When Caroline Lucas took to the Richmond streets in the last weekend of November to explain the party's position to local residents, word seems to have reached Kingston Greens that she had joined Sarah Olney and Tim Farron on the campaign trail and effectively endorsed Olney's candidacy after all. In any event, this was certainly the assertion the Kingston cohort made in an inflamed letter they fired off to *The Guardian* denouncing the 'regressive' Lib Dems, declaring the progressive alliance in Richmond Park dead in the water ... and endorsing Labour. Unsurprisingly, this fit of pique, though ultimately doing nothing to affect the result of the by-election, saw the carefully brokered local election co-operation from Kingston Lib Dems swiftly withdrawn.

And then there was the mysterious affair of the £250,000 'bung'. Sometime after the by-election, the Kingston Greens – or rather, that portion who had opposed the alliance – assembled a 'report' making the explosive claim that an anonymous high-value donor had offered the Greens £250,000 to stand aside. The report was then leaked to right-wing blogger Guido Fawkes, who gave it plenty of oxygen. This charge – which, if true, would not only have violated the Greens' own rules on anonymous donations, but would certainly have been a criminal offence under election law – was strenuously denied by Caroline Lucas who at once started disciplinary proceedings against the party members responsible (most of whom subsequently jumped ship to the Labour Party). It became apparent that money had indeed been offered to the party around the time the by-election was called, but the exact timeline was murky and, according to Caroline Lucas, the offer was declined by the party before the by-election was announced. She also insisted that the donation had never been conditional on standing down. As the £250,000 never materialised and nor were any smoking-gun emails or texts uncovered, the claim ultimately failed to gain a great deal of traction outside Guido Fawkes's feverishly conspiratorial imagination. In fact, as Andrée Frieze herself first heard of the proposed donation several weeks after the decision about her candidacy was taken, the claim that her own decision was in any way affected by it quickly falls apart. If nothing else, it showed how seriously the regressive alliance and Conservative supporters took potential progressive alliances, and helped reassure many PA supporters that they were doing the right thing. But lingering questions about the affair continued to dog Caroline Lucas into the general election campaign the following year – and to some, at least, knocked a bit of the shine off the Greens' unique claims on civic virtue.

But that was OK, too. Politics can be a grubby business and it isn't always best to be seen as above sin. In the coming months, the Greens would have ample opportunity to reflect – not always happily – on the idea that virtue is its own reward.

•   •   •

Back on the ground in Richmond, as the brief by-election campaign rushed towards polling day the progressive alliance (not yet capitalised, and lacking a logo or a clear brand identity) started to move from aspiration to slightly chaotic reality. Lawson, Foley and Freedman were on the forecourt of Richmond Station on the Saturday morning following the public meeting with fresh leaflets promoting cross-party co-operation in the by-election. In the coming weeks, progressives mobilised both within and outside the Liberal Democrat campaign operation. Those who worked with the Lib Dems found themselves part of an effective machine honed over decades: even in this winter of their general discontent, the Lib Dems still knew how to fight a by-election and benefit by harvesting protest votes against the government of the day. Those who preferred a role as supportive outsiders or fellow travellers embarked on a basically improvisational journey whose shape might change from one day to the next. Without access to the electoral register and even more importantly previous years' canvass returns (which tell you where the voters you want to persuade – primarily Labour in this case – might live), it was all but impossible to undertake canvassing in the traditional sense: so people just did what they thought best. Mike Freedman wandered up and down streets in his own neighbourhood of East Sheen, knocking on doors and seeing who wanted to engage in a conversation about the principles of a progressive alliance. A surprising number did, whether they approved of it or not.

None of the data could be collated or wrangled as it would have been had Compass been geared up for fighting elections; but just as important, or maybe more so, was the confirmation its handful of activists received from their impressionistic, unorganised door-knocking and leafleting – that people were hungry for a political conversation in which they were approached and engaged as rational, thoughtful adults, not functions in a party organiser's algorithm. This would be a key lesson for the fully fledged Progressive Alliance going forward. And although, over the months ahead, the Progressive Alliance would of necessity take on a more directed, professional tenor and approach, much of the improvisational, plate-spinning, make-it-up-as-you-go-along flavour of the PA's first election would persist – not least because everyone, including those who had most experience of the airless, chanceless, risk- and thought-free zone of contemporary professional campaigning, liked the way this felt and didn't want to lose it.

There was a lot of energy associated with Compass's effort in Richmond Park, and for those involved it was an eye-opening, even revelatory experience. Everyone recognised that it was a ramshackle and unorganised (if not positively disorganised) affair – but that was part of what made it so intoxicating and inspiring. There was a palpable sense that the old rules no longer applied (even if they often did: for example, even had they wished to – in fact it wasn't seriously considered – the Greens would have largely been unable to campaign actively on Sarah Olney's behalf because the UK's unusually restrictive election laws dictate strict and low spending limits on organisations not standing candidates, and that any joint campaigning between parties, for instance any printed publicity benefiting a named candidate, becomes chargeable to that candidate's campaign, even if they haven't explicitly authorised it – so third-party campaigning risks throwing off campaign budgets). Over the campaign, individuals from different political backgrounds were drawn into the Compass/PA orbit. Like all small organisations, Compass was constantly hungry for volunteers and whoever made themselves available was not only welcomed, but in all likelihood immediately charged with key tasks. Those who would go on to play key roles in the Progressive Alliance campaign in 2017 included local Green Party and Compass members Roger Wilson and Chuck Dreyer, former Labour veteran Stephen Clark from Ealing, and from far out in deepest-blue Tory Surrey Steve Williams, a transplanted Liverpudlian now living in Godalming, where he had helped set up a thriving Compass chapter. Frances Foley remembers feeling as she worked alongside Greens and renegade Labour members that 'this was it, the Progressive Alliance, coming into being before my eyes'.

So did it all make a difference? Almost certainly. One rarely gets the same granular analysis of individual by-election results to which general elections are subjected, so inevitably there's a lot of speculation involved. The Lib Dems poured all their effort, resources and expertise into fighting for Richmond Park. One resident (who fully intended to vote for Olney) reached breaking point as the umpteenth piece of personally addressed Lib Dem propaganda came through his letterbox and found himself swinging open the door angrily to beg for a little respite … coming face-to-face with Vince Cable, one of the best-known politicians in the country. But this was nothing new. Nor were the leaflets insisting that 'Labour can't win here', complete with diagrams showing Labour's puny local vote share (not to scale). Any Richmond resident – anyone who'd ever lived in any Lib

Dem target seat – would have been familiar with these tactics. The Lib Dems had been successful in harvesting tactical votes over many years, but never before on the scale seen in Richmond that Thursday in December.

Beyond the shock of the result itself, Labour's near-death experience was the most eye-catching aspect of the vote. Most commentators took it as a further index of Labour's post-Brexit paralysis, as well as reflecting the polarised, which-side-are-you-on political climate. (The novelist Linda Grant tweeted pithily that 'Richmond residents insisted on voting on the defining issue of our time. Unfortunately we don't have a policy on that.') Of course, this was a Brexit election (and the salience of the issue, and above all the intractable problems it seemed to pose for Labour, would be crucial in Theresa May's opportunistic, fateful decision to call an early general election a few months later). But for Compass, as delighted and surprised as everyone was by the result, how they had got there mattered at least as much. For Neal Lawson, Richmond Park had delivered 'proof of concept' under controlled, localised conditions. The challenge now would be to take PA onto a bigger stage and show that what had been achieved in the crucible of the by-election could be replicated at a national level.

Richmond Park had opened up immense, exhilarating opportunities. The progressive alliance had moved from concept to experimental prototype. The next stage would be to try to start up mass production.

CHAPTER TWO

TOGETHER FOR A CHANGE: THE PROGRESSIVE ALLIANCE MANIFESTO 2017

The Progressive Alliance never got around to producing a 'manifesto' for the 2017 general election. It lacked the time and the resources to do so. More to the point, it hurled itself into the fray, brokering deals, targeting seats and supporting progressive candidates. It kept its slogans snappy – 'Build a Progressive Majority', 'Say No to One-Party Rule' – and its statements terse. There were hundreds of thousands of words pouring from the press, the parties and the blogosphere through the campaign – so why add yet more when the crucial point was so simple and simply understood: 'vote smart, vote tactically, vote collaboratively, vote progressively to stop the Tories'?

But one of the major surprises of the 2017 election (a campaign not short on surprises) was that manifestos – those old-fashioned, cumbersome, implausible documents, part-polemic, part-prospectus, part-fantasy, a burden to governments, a bore for voters and an easy target for journalists and pundits – mattered. People read them (or least read the summaries of them on television or online). They cast their votes, in part, because of the ideas and the values that, in their typically style-free leaden prose, they somehow nonetheless embodied and communicated. 2017 was an election where ideas, unexpectedly, mattered.

One of the frustrations for Compass was that the longer they campaigned, and the more traction PA got, the more difficult it was to remind people that at bottom this wasn't about tactical voting – or a Labour victory, or even just 'getting rid of the Tories'. It was about an idea of a better society. The PA was a way of bringing that society a step closer and – maybe – could in itself embody some of its values. Amidst the sound and fury and sheer busy-ness of an election campaign, that could easily get lost. But the truth was that the Progressive Alliance was an unusual combination of high ideals and low tactics, and where the one ended and the other began was often hard to tell. So let's imagine the PA had somehow found the time to bequeath a manifesto for the political historians of the future to retrieve: what might that document have looked like?

• • •

What is the Progressive Alliance?
The Progressive Alliance aims to maximise the voting power of the centre-left at UK elections held under first-past-the-post. In the Progressive Alliance, progressive – that is, centre-left – political parties co-ordinate their electoral efforts, pool resources and campaign to concentrate their supporters' votes towards the most electable centre-left candidate (of whichever party) on a constituency-by-constituency basis. By working together, we aim to secure the election of as many centre-left candidates as possible. In England and Wales, the core participants in the

Progressive Alliance will be the Labour Party, the Liberal Democrats, the Green Party and Plaid Cymru.

But aren't all these political parties quite different from one another? Don't they often campaign against one another in both local and national elections?
Of course, and quite rightly so. Political parties exist for a reason. Each party has its own distinct history, its own culture, its own political philosophy and its own set of priorities. The Liberals were the great reformist party of the nineteenth century, challenging the dominance of the old landed aristocracy. The Labour Party came into being to give representation to the industrial working class of the twentieth century. The roots of the Green Party lie in the heightened environmental consciousness of the 1960s counterculture. These histories of commitment and struggle continue to inform the values and policies of the modern-day parties. Together they make up the democratic mosaic we all rightly value and cherish.

These parties have sometimes co-operated; for example, in the first decade of the twentieth century, the Liberal Party entered a secret pact with the Labour Representation Committee to ensure the election of the first Labour MPs in 1906. Much more recently, Tony Blair's New Labour and the Liberal Democrats under Paddy Ashdown co-operated closely at the 1997 general election to maximise the anti-Tory vote.[15] More usually, they have competed for votes, often fiercely. While there have been numerous instances of Labour–Lib Dem (and/or sometimes Green, Plaid, etc.) coalitions in regional and local government, as well as many examples of excellent personal relations between

---

15 For more on both of these, see Chapter Six.

individual politicians, in general relations between the different progressive parties are often far from fraternal.

But the position of the Progressive Alliance is that alongside these differences, and notwithstanding the history of competition – which our adversarial political culture encourages and exacerbates – on many core issues there is consensus across the parties of the centre-left, for example:

- on building a fairer, more humane, more sustainable economy;
- on supporting excellent non-selective state education;
- on preserving the NHS, free at the point of use and unthreatened by creeping privatisation;
- on delivering constitutional reforms to modernise and improve our democracy;
- on protecting civil liberties;
- on pursuing a multilateral and consensual approach to foreign relations, defence, and disarmament;
- on combating climate change and safeguarding our planet for future generations;
- on building the closest possible relationship with our friends, neighbours and most important trading partners in the EU.

These shared values reveal another core truth: however real our differences, they are a good deal smaller than the gulf that divides all of us from the Conservatives. Across the centre-left spectrum, it's understood that prolonged Conservative rule will only make our society less equal, less tolerant, less open, less liberal, less generous and less sustainable. If progressives want to stop that happening, they will need to recognise who their real adversaries are and turn their fire not on each other but on them.

The idea of the Progressive Alliance – and we need to say

this as loudly and clearly as possible – is not, and has never been, that parties should dissolve themselves or abandon the programmes they have agreed and that their supporters wish to see implemented. That's not how democracy works, nor how alliances work. You make alliances with those who are different from you not because your differences don't matter but because, right now, other priorities matter more.

Why is this necessary? And why now?

There's a history here. Every pundit will tell you that the Conservative Party is the most successful election-winning machine in European politics. Yet, as measured in actual numbers of votes cast, there has never been a Conservative majority in Britain as a whole. In fact, the largest Conservative majorities in post-war history have been achieved despite a steadily shrinking proportion of the national vote: Mrs Thatcher won a smaller vote share in 1983 and 1987 than in 1979.

What has made this possible is the fragmentation of the centre-left vote. In 1983, the centre-left opposition won more than half the votes cast – but because those votes were almost equally divided between Labour and the SDP–Liberal Alliance, Mrs Thatcher won mountainous landslide victories then and again in 1987: victories that changed the face of British society for ever. Despite the real differences and often poisonous hostility between the SDP and Labour in the 1980s, neither party supported the divisive, destructive or callous policies of the Thatcher governments, nor the kind of society they brought about. But by fighting one another as hard as they ever fought Thatcher – maybe harder – they made Thatcherism's victory possible. We're still living with the legacy of those choices and those defeats.

To label the different parties of the centre-left 'progressive' is not to take a position on how 'progressive' a particular party, let alone a given policy, might be. We suspect that anyone for whom 'progressive' is a positive concept will tend to see their own position, and that of the party they support, as more 'progressive' than others. Nor do these progressive parties compete for exactly the same voters; there are Green voters who would not normally support either of the other parties, there are certainly many Liberal Democrats who see their political philosophy as fundamentally different from that of Labour and Labour voters who cannot forgive the Lib Dems' participation in the Tory-led coalition (or, if they are older, who cannot forgive the 'betrayal' of the SDP, one of the Lib Dems' two predecessor parties). As Monty Python indelibly reminded us in *Life of Brian*, the left has never flagged in pointing the finger at renegades, backstabbers and faint-hearts in its own ranks. But the centre-left parties are all fishing in the same limited pool of progressive votes, whereas the Conservatives (until the advent of UKIP, which in any case has proved at least as big a threat to Labour as to Tories, if not more so) benefit from a lack of alternatives or competition on the right.

The centre-left's dilemma today is starker still than in the 1980s. With even less claim to a democratic mandate than Mrs Thatcher, having won just 36 per cent of votes cast in 2015 in an election where barely two-thirds of Britons cast a ballot, the Cameron government pursued policies that devastated public services and fractured the bonds of civil society. Since the EU referendum, under Theresa May's premiership, this has become ever more clearly a government enacting the programme of the radical right, borne up by a broken political system.

So, how can those of us who yearn to change the economic and social models that gave us the financial crisis, endless austerity and Brexit continue to collude in the perpetuation of extremist Tory governments? For by insisting on chasing down votes for our own political tribe without regard to this bigger picture, that is exactly what we are doing. In our view, this is no time to persist with 'politics as usual'. It is anything but.

At present, the Tories have a slim and potentially fragile minority in the Commons. When it comes to current polling, they seem certain to increase that majority enormously at the coming election. But across England and Wales, there are dozens of marginal seats where, based on 2015 results, bringing together the votes cast for centre-left parties could prevent the election of Conservative MPs – either by winning back Tory seats or by making it easier to defend seats currently held by the parties of the centre-left. In the great majority of these it's brutally clear that only one party (most often Labour or Liberal Democrat) stands a realistic chance of winning. By running candidates and actively campaigning in such constituencies, the other centre-left parties succeed only in fragmenting the anti-Tory vote and siphoning off votes from the sole electable progressive candidate.

The Progressive Alliance accepts this electoral reality and asks others to do the same. We aim to encourage centre-left parties to find ways of working with, rather than against, one another and to prevent the needless sacrifice of seats to the Conservatives.

How will it work?
In theory, there's a wide range of different options for how political parties might co-operate. At one end of the spectrum would be some kind of 'Popular Front' (or, closer to home, the SDP–Liberal Alliance in the 1980s) with a common programme, joint manifestos and candidates and unified campaign strategies. We don't believe this is remotely realistic in the present context or

necessarily (because it would blur and blend the richly varied colours of the progressive rainbow) even desirable. Another possibility is for partly open primaries (partly, because these would not be open to all members of the public, but only to members of the parties involved) in which an internally selected candidate from each local progressive party in a constituency runs in a plenary competition for the nomination as the single agreed progressive candidate to fight the Conservatives at the general election. In principle, this might be a good option, provided that primary voters genuinely cast their ballots on the basis of their chosen candidate's qualities and programme. If instead they vote simply on a basis of party loyalty, it will ensure that the party with the largest membership – in almost every case, likely to be Labour – will carry the nomination. Such tyranny of the partisan majority might make matters worse than they are now – by not only eliminating most Green and indeed Lib Dem candidates, but by in all probability delivering many nominees who would lack sufficiently broad appeal outside their party base. In any case, such structures have very little precedent in the UK – which is not in itself a reason for discounting them, but means they are not realistic 'runners' for the immediate future, and are utterly unachievable in the compressed timeframe now forced upon us by this snap election.

At the other end of the spectrum, we find variations on the familiar idea of tactical voting – which should remind us we've (almost) been here before: in 1997, semi-open co-ordination by Labour and Liberal Democrat campaign strategies, mounting only token campaigns in unwinnable seats while turning a blind eye to each other's supporters voting, or even working for, their centre-left rivals, routed the Conservatives and reduced them to a rump opposition for the next thirteen years.

1997 proved that co-operation trumps competition. But since then, the progressive vote has splintered once again with Labour's decline, the Liberal Democrats' catastrophic partnership in the Tory coalition, and the rise of the Green Party. The conversations between Labour and other progressive parties that sowed the seeds of such a fruitful, if sadly ephemeral, partnership in 1997 have largely ceased for many years. And once again, the Tories are profiting from our divisions.

Something bolder and braver than old-style tactical voting is needed to seize the present moment. So today we offer an effective, straightforward and practical road map for a progressive alliance leading the way to a progressive victory at the next general election. We have already identified those marginal parliamentary seats where the centre-left stands a clear chance of winning. The Progressive Alliance campaign – a cross-party movement with no sectarian or factional agenda – will provide the forum for centre-left parties in those key constituencies to reach out to one another, with the stated aim of reaching an agreement to stand only one candidate amongst them. With representation from all Britain's progressive parties in our own ranks, we are happy to act as an honest broker in such discussions. The agreed candidate would campaign under his or her own party's banner but with the official and explicit endorsement of the other local centre-left parties – who, crucially, would then actively campaign (within the legal limits imposed by UK electoral law) to mobilise their vote for the agreed candidate.

Local deals between progressive parties may well be necessary to make such arrangements workable and palatable to the parties that are standing down their own candidates. For example, the party of the agreed 'progressive champion' in the general election could offer reciprocity either in the form of

standing their own parliamentary candidate down in a neighbouring or nearby seat, or offering the other party/parties
uncontested runs in some wards in future local elections.

But let's not lose sight of the wood for the trees. Ultimately,
this isn't about delivery mechanisms. Much more fundamentally, it's about being prepared to do politics differently. It's about
making a radical break with competitive winner-take-all – or,
for progressives, more often, beggar-my-neighbour – politics.
It's about working with, not against, the grain of history to make
the twenty-first century, unlike the last, a progressive century.

**But isn't this anti-democratic? Shouldn't people be able to
cast their vote for whichever party or candidate best reflects
their views, if they so wish?**
Naturally, our opponents – seeing their grasp on power under
threat – and the Tory press will denounce our efforts as a
'stitch-up'. They will profess an outraged defence of democratic
principles belied at every step by their own record of political
manipulation and deceit.

Of course, the Progressive Alliance could indeed become a
stitch-up if it's treated as a means of preserving politics as usual
rather than ending it. If, for example, we try to instrumentalise
centre-left voters – that is, treat them as a homogeneous bloc of
votes, deliverable to the agreed candidate at the stroke of a pen
– then, frankly, we deserve to fail. That's not the way. Instead, we
want to promote ongoing open and democratic debate within
and between centre-left parties at every level, national and local,
top to bottom – making our campaign a genuinely democratic,
participatory exercise in which all our supporters get to debate
and understand our proposed arrangements and the reasons
behind them. There will doubtless be cases where, once all the

arguments for an alliance have been heard, local parties will nevertheless determine that they still want to run candidates. That is their democratic right and it must be honoured.

But what about the most obvious and heartfelt objection of all: that every voter has the right to cast her ballot for the party whose values best reflect her own? After all, isn't that the very essence of democracy?

The truth is that voters are way ahead of us. In 2016, the Progressive Alliance burst into spontaneous life on the streets of Richmond Park during the post-Brexit by-election. There was a palpable popular demand to send an unmistakeable message to Theresa May's doctrinaire UKIP-lite government, trumping recent political history (which in the previous year's general election saw progressive voters desert the Liberal Democrats to punish their collusion with the worst excesses of the Tory-led coalition), sentiment and tribalism alike. The local Green Party heard and understood this demand and chose not to stand a candidate. The Labour Party, however, foolishly and despite the urgings of some high-profile Labour MPs, did. We all know what happened. Progressive Richmond voters ignored the irrelevant Labour candidate – who lost his deposit – and unseated the racist Leave millionaire Goldsmith. Labour members not only voted but openly campaigned for the Liberal Democrats' Sarah Olney.

Voters are far more mature and sophisticated than pundits usually recognise. Votes are rarely if ever cast under perfect laboratory conditions where your chosen candidate or party perfectly reflects your values and beliefs – least of all under first-past-the-post. Just ask any of the countless voters who held their noses and voted for Tony Blair in 2005 or Gordon Brown in 2010 because the alternatives were so much worse.

Even so… Isn't the PA manipulating the electoral system by trying to force all progressive votes into a single box, regardless of what voters want?

The lesson of Richmond Park is that the Progressive Alliance isn't a ruse dreamed up by political elites to defraud the people of democratic rights. It's what centre-left voters want. They know all too well where the real fault lines in our politics lie. And, as society grows ever more networked, ever more diverse in the associations and connections people make across cultures, across traditional identities and tribal loyalties, so centre-left voters have been quite literally voting for change.

The Progressive Alliance is in the first place a means, not an end, designed to tackle a dysfunctional and obsolete electoral system that actively penalises centre-left voters for supporting smaller parties that reflect their own views and values. The immediate aim of the Progressive Alliance is the election of a centre-left coalition government that can roll back the calamities of Tory rule while preparing for new elections on a genuinely democratic, proportional system.

But at the same time, the Progressive Alliance will itself demonstrates the possibility for co-operation between political parties that underpins our larger aims. It's our premise that no party has a monopoly on truth, that pluralism is essential to a flourishing democracy, and that wisdom can be gleaned from many different traditions. In this respect, even as a 'means' the PA embodies the kind of politics we are trying to achieve.

What's the connection between a progressive alliance and proportional representation?

To be precise, PA (the Progressive Alliance) doesn't necessarily = PR (proportional representation, of which there are in any event several different models). The Progressive Alliance doesn't take a firm view on which particular kind of electoral system should replace the one we currently have, although it does take the view that the one we have is no longer fit for any kind of purpose. In fact, the very need for the Progressive Alliance in the particular form we are proposing proves it.

We see this version of the Progressive Alliance, ideally, as a concept that, if successful, will put itself out of business. We don't want to carry on having to 'game' a broken system. We don't think that it is sustainable for voters to be denied real choice at the ballot box in perpetuity. Under a proportional system, there would be no need for arrangements of the kind we are arguing for as every party, large and small, would have the opportunity to make its case to the electorate confident that they would secure parliamentary representation in broad proportion to the strength of their popular support (subject, most likely, to a minimum threshold). In all likelihood, voter behaviour would change radically under such a system. The progressive vote would probably redistribute itself, perhaps dramatically. Free from having to worry about 'wasting' their vote, citizens could support the candidate of their conviction, not of their convenience or necessity. Smaller parties – particularly on the left – would no longer face accusations of 'letting the Tories in' by splitting the progressive vote. Larger parties, rather than being able to rely (as Labour has done in many areas for many years, to its increasing cost) on a mass of votes cast in their favour because there has been no realistic local alternative, would have to campaign with equal intensity and integrity everywhere, in the knowledge that every vote counts.

In principle, therefore, PA and PR are intimately connected. In practice, too, one is indivisible from the other. Consider the implications if no changes were made to the UK's existing first-past-the-post system: it would mean that the allocation of candidacies arrived at in the very first progressive alliance would be set in stone. Labour would remain the overwhelmingly dominant party; the Greens might never be invited to stand another candidate in a winnable seat. It would mean the smaller progressive parties taking an endless hit for, effectively, the benefit of a Labour, or Labour-led, government. Clearly any progressive government will be led by Labour: its support in England and Wales far outstrips that of the other progressive parties. But it cannot be right that those smaller parties should be asked to accept a perpetual silencing of their own voice.

The truth is that, for a progressive alliance of the kind we envisage to come into being, Labour will need to make a meaningful move towards electoral reform. Even a clear statement short of a firm manifesto commitment to introducing a proportional system (there is a substantial and growing body of support for PR within Labour, but the party is some way from embracing electoral reform, let alone making it a legislative priority), would make it vastly easier for the Lib Dems and Greens, for both of whom electoral reform is an absolute priority, to sell the idea of alliances to their members. In any case, as a democratic socialist party, Labour ought to recognise that an electoral system that so grossly and consistently delivers an elected legislature bearing little resemblance to the popular vote is democratically insupportable. This has to go beyond narrow questions of party self-interest. Just as first-past-the-post has historically discriminated against the Liberal Democrats (including the SDP–Liberal Alliance), there have been occasions where it has greatly exaggerated the electoral performance of the Labour Party – particularly during the New Labour years.

Put simply, because of the geographical distribution of the two parties' votes, it takes many more voters to elect a Lib Dem MP than it does a Labour MP (the Greens' position is even worse: effectively, it takes every Green vote in the entire country to elect a single Green MP.) This must not be a stumbling block when it comes to co-operation between progressive parties in the event of a future hung parliament where they could command a parliamentary majority. As Labour's grip on voters declines in its traditional densely populated heartlands in the former industrial regions of the North of England, Labour's advantage under first-past-the-post will in any case probably reduce. But this should be a choice made from principle, not necessity. And such a choice is politically possible: in Scotland, despite the extraordinary victory delivered them in 2015 under first-past-the-post (when they all but annihilated the other three parties, winning fifty-six of Scotland's fifty-nine seats on 'only' 50 per cent of the vote), the SNP has consistently supported a proportional system.

While it would undoubtedly be easier for Labour internally to 'sell' a basically non-proportional system like the Alternative Vote – which would also have the advantage of retaining the UK's single-member constituencies – from a progressive perspective such a compromise would necessitate the perpetuation of something like the 2017 progressive alliance. Labour voters would need to be encouraged to place the Liberal Democrats as their second choice over the Conservatives and vice versa. In other words, parties would still be compelled to 'work' the system rather than trust it to work for the electorate, whose servants they are supposed to be.

Our view in the Progressive Alliance is clear: we believe that a move towards an electoral system where every vote counts, and where elections can accordingly be fought on the basis of programmes created to reflect parties' governing philosophies, rather than catering to the views of a hundred-thousand-odd (by definition atypical) swing voters in a handful of marginal seats, is absolutely necessary. We see the Progressive Alliance itself as a necessary intermediate step towards such a system (because the Tories, facing as Mrs Thatcher foresaw prolonged or even permanent exclusion from government under a proportional system, will never introduce one).

Beyond that, a proportional electoral system, which will make coalition governments the norm in the UK as they are in most developed nations, will help foster the emergence of the more collaborative, intersectional politics we want to see. We have said that that we want to move to a system where there is no longer a need for the particular kinds of electoral alliances proposed in this manifesto (instrumental, tactical, contractual), and we do. But under that new system, conversations, relationships, collaborations and, yes, alliances will be an integral part of forging the progressive consensus underpinning a more sustainable, equal and democratic society. Beyond its immediate task of defending and expanding the progressive vote in the upcoming election, by forging relationships and building bridges across party divisions the Progressive Alliance aims to open up the new spaces of political activism, debate and encounter that we so urgently need to address the challenges of our times. Ours is a rapidly changing, often bewildering world in which relationships, identities, ways of working and ways of being are all more fluid and interactive than ever before. Hidebound political conventions and blinkered tribalism offer no path to building a good society in this changed landscape. Only by talking to one another, working together, accepting that no one party or philosophy has all the answers, guided by progressive principles rather than hardened dogma, will we be able to build the better world that in our hearts we all believe is possible.

We believe passionately in both the principles and the practical methods of the Progressive Alliance outlined here. We call on all progressive voters – everyone who wants that better, more equal, more just, more sustainable world – to set aside their differences and join each other as part of this alliance.

No one should pretend any of this can be willed or wished into being. We're talking about a sea-change in our adversarial political culture. Getting there will be hard work. But ultimately, together we can make the Progressive Alliance work if we want it to – if the willingness is there.

Together for a change. On 8 June, vote to build a progressive majority.

CHAPTER THREE

THE CAMPAIGN PART I:
18 APRIL – 5 MAY

The War (and Peace) Room

On the morning of Monday 24 April, as a ballot-weary Britain braced itself for the third (or if you were in Scotland, fourth) nation-defining festival of democracy in as many years, the Progressive Alliance, relocating from Compass's offices in vibrant but out-of-the-way Bethnal Green, moved into its temporary campaign headquarters. The 'War Room', as it was immediately labelled by volunteers, was a large open-plan office hard by Ludgate Circus at the St Paul's end of Fleet Street, a stone's throw from the iconic Art Deco façade of the old *Daily Express* building. The PA team (not least Neal Lawson, himself the son of a newspaper printer) were fully aware of the ironies of their location, close to London's ceremonial and financial heart, nestled by the bleached bones of the old media behemoths – *the Express, the Telegraph, The Times* – all long relocated to their de-unionised digital fortresses in Docklands and beyond: from this spot super-saturated with British political history and power, like a Greenpeace skiff tacking dangerously across the path of an Exxon oil tanker, the Progressive Alliance was setting out to break the mould of British politics.

For the uninitiated, the martial tenor of the War Room – Frances Foley subsequently led a peacenik insurgency that saw it rebranded the 'War (and Peace) Room' – might have conjured up visions of Ken Adam's grandiosely apocalyptic set designs for Stanley Kubrick's *Dr Strangelove*; or perhaps less fancifully, the White House situation rooms glimpsed in occasional official photographs and imagined in countless political thrillers, where braided generals clutching dossiers and sweaty shirt-sleeved politicians with ties at half-mast tensely determined the fate of the Western world. The War Room would absorb its fair quota of perspiration in the weeks to come, but the comparisons ended there. The single large first-floor room overlooking Fleet Street, featureless but for the three large whiteboards on each of the facing walls, was obstinately un-glamorous and unmemorable.

If your fondly held image of politics is of a relentlessly dramatic trade conducted by charismatic individuals striding on urgent business from one well-appointed interior to the next, you've probably been bingeing too many box-sets of *The West Wing*. Whatever the reality in the corridors of power in Washington, DC, however, day-to-day political work in the UK is a much more workaday affair: and, notwithstanding the Progressive Alliance's grand ambitions to shape the new politics, the War Room was much like all the other pop-up rented office spaces from which Election 2017 would largely be contested. To call it functional would be flattering. But any political hack, regardless of ideological orientation, would have felt right at home here. Apart from the whiteboards, the room's only fur-nishings were a handful of landline phones, three large tables and a cluster of cheap, lumbar-hostile caster chairs on which volunteers glided Dalek-like from one desk to another. The most important fixed furniture, of course, was invisible: the wi-fi on which every modern campaign, like every modern business and every modern individual, is utterly reliant. A campaign worker transported, say, from the pioneering New Labour days when so much of the contemporary campaign was reinvented, would find much that was familiar: above all, the whiteboards which from Day 1 were cross-hatched in multi-coloured marker into the 'grids' of daily and weekly events, every modern political campaign's lifeblood since the heyday of Peter Mandelson. But our time traveller would be struck by the absence of the gleaming heavy-duty hardware in which Mandelson in his pomp took such pride: no fixed terminals or mainframes nowadays, of course, just the ubiquitous mobile devices and laptops via which the messages hatched in the campaign hive are – ideally – zipped seamlessly to pavement-pounding worker bees dispersed around the country.

The cliché would be that this was a most unlikely setting for a political revolution. The truth is it wasn't that unlikely at all – it was simply nondescript, and in its very mundanity typical of the spaces in which contemporary political battles are fought. Once upon a time, the values vested in political actors were powerfully expressed in architecture. During the 1980s, the titanic, if one-sided, battles between a Labour Party still unabashedly committed to building a socialist Britain and Margaret Thatcher's unfettered red-in-tooth-and-claw market individualism were encapsulated in the contrast between their respective party headquarters: Labour's Victorian redbrick building in Walworth Road in working-class south London, a perpetual stream of traffic grinding past towards the Old Kent

Road, on the one hand; and on the other, the gracious Georgian frontage of Conservative Central Office in Smith Square, just south of the Palace of Westminster, from whose windows Thatcher and, later and more unexpectedly, John Major saluted their triumphant supporters at election after winning election. Since when, the demands of modern IT-driven campaigning and (in Labour's case, at least) tightening financial constraints have seen both parties relocate to a succession of more-or-less interchangeable and unremarkable office spaces. The offices on Millbank occupied by Labour from 1997 to 2005 became briefly synonymous with the frenzied 'modernisation' of the Blair years – Blair, Mandelson and their cronies and gophers were not-so-affectionately labelled the 'Millbank Mafia' – but the force of the image lay as much in the symbolic contrast between steel-and-glass Millbank and the tatty surroundings of the Elephant and Castle as in any aesthetic qualities of the utterly bland Millbank Tower itself. (It is rarely remarked that, following Labour's departure in 2005, Millbank became Conservative Campaign HQ under David Cameron. Such are the unsentimental transactions and transitions of modern political business.)

As the PA team settled into their workaday new home – the space they would occupy weekdays, weekends and bank holidays (two of them in May) alike – a daily clutter of post-its, scribbled notes-to-self, drafted and redrafted leaflets, poster designs and website ideas began to amass, visible spoor of the team's efforts and the only paper trail of this largely virtual smart campaign. In the wake of the paper washed up another daily scurf of coffee cups, packets of biscuits, pizza boxes and takeout food containers (our New Labour time traveller would recognise the unhealthy eating habits but probably be struck by the globalised cuisine – Thai, Korean, Scandinavian – now supplanting, at least in mass-produced simulacrum, the white-bread sandwiches of yore), all vanished during the watches of every night by the usual invisible squadron of migrant-worker cleaners on zero-hour contracts.

Everyone involved with the Progressive Alliance campaign knew they faced a Sisyphean task: to dismember, in seven short weeks, a starkly oppositional British political culture that had been calcifying for generations and assemble in its place a co-operative network of bridges and alliances. But the very steepness of the challenge infused the team with a sort of giddy, manic determination. Neal Lawson spoke for many of the PA team when he confessed a perverse relief upon realising that the Alliance's originally-planned long march to a 2020 election would be so drastically foreshortened: 'Three years of organising seemed like a slog, really. Hard to sustain. Seven weeks to change the world felt like the kind of ridiculous challenge everyone would rise to.'

The nucleus of the PA team had been formed in the Richmond by-election campaign: circumstances which meant that generally un-radical south-west London was wildly over-represented in the PA's inner circles. Mike Freedman brought his businessman's strategic acumen (one often had the sense that Freedman yearned for just a little more structure and a little less fertile creative anarchy). Thoughtful, quietly passionate Roger Wilson, who in civilian life ran a change management company, revealed a capacity for the detailed seat-by-seat analysis of majorities, swings, vote shares and the like that would be vital for the PA when the time came to identify the key target seats, and ultimately to make voter recommendations. Wilson formed a core number-crunching partnership with Chuck Dreyer that would underpin the PA's detailed work over the course of the campaign. Steve Williams and Stephen Clark, well connected to Labour, started working the phones to try to find people – MPs, MEPs, councillors, CLP officers, party organisers – around the country in that obdurate organisation who were sympathetic to PA and, just as importantly, willing to say so. Theirs would prove to be the most gruelling and frustrating task of anyone's in the PA.

The beating heart of the team throughout the campaign was always Lawson and Foley. Though everyone on the PA team was a veteran of political work dating back in some cases to the 1960s, only Lawson had served time close to the top level of a national campaign. He drew on his experience of working for Gordon Brown in the run-up to the 1997 general election and modelled the office routine closely on the New Labour play-book (fully aware of the irony, but you didn't have to agree with them to learn from them). This involved daily morning con-ference calls with the principal stakeholders (soon including SmallAxe, the creative and communications consultancy team who quickly became an integral part of the PA team), key tasks being allocated and mapped onto the daily grid and, underpin-ning it all, a consistent sense from the top down of movement, progress, advance – even when, as would often enough be the case, each forward step seemed to be followed by two back.

Quite apart from being the only woman in what was – prior to a serious and very welcome injection of diversity once Small-Axe were integrated into the campaign - a lamentably white, male (not to mention southern) environment, Frances Foley was also by far the youngest member of the team, just four years out of university. Hers would be the steepest learning curve of all as she took upon herself, effectively (though the role was never formalised – it wasn't that sort of workplace), the job of campaign director. With Lawson driving strategy, working his considerable list of contacts to get media coverage and political traction and generally supplying the public face of the Progressive Alliance, it fell to Foley to translate strategic aims into immediate tactical tasks, to prioritise and intervene when necessary to redirect the energy and skills of Compass volunteers – many of them far older and more experienced than she – into the areas where the campaign needed them, rather than where their own personal enthusiasms and bright ideas took them. Her northerner's mien of slight scepticism seemed appropriate given the size of the challenge the PA was taking on.

Very quickly, it became apparent that forging a progressive alliance for Election 2017 would pose additional challenges beyond the ingrained resistance of Britain's tribal political traditions. The EU referendum result, which had put so much else into play, also sheared through the whole notion of a broadly consensual centre-left on which PA strategy was centrally predicated. In particular, Labour's contortions on Brexit as it struggled to hold together its own fundamentally riven coalition – with many of its northern MPs, overwhelmingly Remainers themselves, representing constituencies that voted as heavily to leave the EU as their colleagues' seats in London, metropolitan centres like Bristol and Manchester and university towns like Cambridge voted to remain – were painful to behold. Labour's inability to articulate a distinctive or even coherent position on the overriding issue of the day had opened up a gulf between the party and its notional centre-left allies, above all the Liberal Democrats, who since their Richmond Park triumph had amped up their 'party of the 48 per cent' riff even more stridently while covetously eyeing swathes of Labour Remain votes in London, Bristol, Manchester and the university towns (though odd voices within the party fretted about the risk of becoming a single-issue outfit, not least when the issue was as divisive as Brexit).

Lawson, who has a taste for mixed sporting metaphors, observed that 'you never a get a perfectly rolled pitch … the lines aren't drawn straight and the wind's catching the ball and the goalposts are wonky … but you just have to get out there and play'. The unexpected Henry Newbolt overtones notwithstanding, this cheerfully bloody-minded, seize-the-day attitude seemed to speak for most in the PA team, who appeared energised rather than dispirited by the obstacles they faced, and the new ones that each week seemed to throw up. For the 1960s American New Left, an ideal of the 'Beloved Community' supplied the image of its own organisational structures and practices: democratic, participatory, supportive, non-hierarchical and dialogic. Lawson and Foley were too pragmatic, too modest and far too bullshit-wary in a very 21st-century way ever to invoke such a lofty ideal. But those were the nonetheless the principles for which the PA stood and, bar the odd expletive, they were the principles by which they operated. Throughout a gruelling campaign, the War (and Peace) Room remained a happy ship.

On the map
Knowing how under-prepared the Progressive Alliance was for a snap election, Frances Foley's first response to hearing of May's announcement, by her own account, was to yell, 'Fuck! Fuck! Fuck!' for a solid minute. Her second act was to carry on with her German cycling holiday and try to ignore the hectic torrent of emails from increasingly agitated Compass members flooding her inbox. Her third, upon returning to the UK and

moving Compass operations for the duration into the War (and Peace) Room, was to stick on the wall a Parliamentary map of the UK marking out all 650 Westminster constituencies, from St Ives in the south-west to Ross & Skye reaching from the tip of Scotland far out into the Atlantic. As well as a practical tool, the map inescapably symbolised both the literal and metaphoric challenge facing the PA as it shaped itself into an embryonic election-fighting – and, hopefully, election-changing, maybe even (whisper it) – winning-machine. Concretely and metaphorically, the question was the same: how to get on the map?

As Foley Blu-Tacked the map onto the wall, her gaze skimmed across the towns and shires, counties, cities and islands of the electoral landscape. There were so many of them. And, in most of them, the Progressive Alliance was barely a rumour. The great thing about being a small, effectively start-up outfit was being able to fight a guerrilla campaign – to move fast, step lightly, react sharply to changing conditions. The downside, however, was also pretty obvious: not enough resources, not enough know-how and not enough boots on the ground. When planning the anticipated three-year campaign leading up to the 2020 election-that-would-never-be, establishing a network of sympathetic party and unaffiliated activists in key constituencies had been an obvious priority. Working the phones, building on the scattered contacts who had made themselves known to Compass one way or another around the country in recent months, following up further leads on potential influencers – PA-friendly constituency and regional party officers, MPs who might be willing to put their heads above the party parapet, local supporters of closely related non-party campaigning organisations like Make Votes Matter – was the scheduled task of the early summer. Now the whole process was absurdly foreshortened as the PA team effectively set about trying to will a nationwide grassroots campaign into being at a stroke. Both philosophically and practically, everyone knew that an 'astroturf' movement – talking the democratic, bottom-up talk but walking a top-down walk – would never work. For PA to have staying power, it would need to embed itself organically in the diverse unique cultures of multiple localities. A few white, mostly middle-aged West London geezers (and Oldham-raised Frances Foley) couldn't do that, nor did they have the arrogance to believe they could. But finding the necessary change agents to pull PA into being across the country, in the face of institutionalised resistance from the major centre-left parties, was indeed searching for the proverbial needle in the haystack. And the asymmetry between the PA's human resources and the task facing them was almost comical. Stephen Clark, for example, a long-standing Labour activist and Compass member from Ealing, was handed the task of organising PA in London. All of it.

An obvious economy of scale that would not only maximise efficient organising effort but might deliver synergistic political outcomes was to identify 'clusters' of neighbouring seats where implementing PA could have knock-on effects from one to the next – potentially benefiting different parties in a virtuous chain. South-west London was one such cluster, home to hallowed Richmond Park, Twickenham and Kingston & Surbiton – all Lib Dem target seats where Labour's current small spoiling vote could make the difference between a progressive gain and a loss. To their immediate north, Brentford & Isleworth and Ealing Central & Acton were both Labour-held on puny majorities of less than 500 where an electorally irrelevant Lib Dem vote of around 3,000 could be equally vital. Another self-evident cluster, and as we'll see unique in several ways, comprised five seats in the greater Brighton area (Brighton Pavilion, Brighton Kemptown, Hove, Lewes and Eastbourne). In both of these clusters, Compass already had strong contacts and the sympathetic ear of least one sitting MP, and the prospects for PA seemed promising. Further along the south coast, with the help of former Lib Dem MP Andrew George, Roger Wilson and Steve Williams had started to make some progress in a 'Solent cluster' comprising the two Southampton seats (Test and Itchen, one Labour, one Tory, both marginals for Labour), two 2015 Conservative gains from the Lib Dems (Eastleigh and Portsmouth South), and the Isle of Wight. The latter was a bit of an oddity, a Green 'semi-target' where UKIP had placed second in 2015, polling over 14,00 votes, with the Greens best placed of the three other non-Tory parties, all polling on broadly level terms (between 5,000 and 8,000), but none within hailing distance of the Conservatives, sitting on a majority of nearly 14,000: stand-asides by the two other progressive parties at this election would at least enable the Greens to establish themselves as the principal centre-left challenger in the seat and by showing goodwill could facilitate further Green stand-asides elsewhere. (A further wrinkle was sitting Tory MP Andrew Turner's decision not to run again this time, having advised schoolchildren at a public event that homosexuality was 'a danger to society'.)

In other potential clusters, however fertile the terrain, the lack of an existing network of relationships made the PA's task of building an effective local campaign much harder. In suburban Merseyside, a trio of nearby seats – Wirral South, relatively safe for Labour; Wirral West, gained by Labour in 2015 with a majority of just 417; and across the Mersey Estuary placid Southport, a tight Lib Dem–Tory marginal where Labour's 8,500-odd votes in third place in 2015 was over six times the current Lib Dem majority – stood out. But, as the election campaign kicked off, Compass still had no pathfinder there. The same was true for other possible clusters in Wales – three Cardiff seats, the reasonably-safe-but-not-wholly-secure Labour-held West and South & Penarth, and North, a key Labour target if indeed it did start to make any inroads into the Tory majority; and in Cumbria – Carlisle (Tory-held with small Green and Lib Dem vote shares potentially holding the balance of power), Workington (Labour-held, vulnerable to the Tories' hoped-for surge in the North) and Copeland, February's Conservative by-election gain in a hugely ominous result for Labour and one that surely encouraged May's decision to call the general election.

That same Monday morning Foley pondered the map in the War Room, the metaphorical version of the challenge to get PA 'on the map' of this election was playing out on the *Today* programme, where Neal Lawson tried to persuade a sceptical Nick Robinson that, through the auspices of the Progressive Alliance, strategic stand-asides and tactical voting would make a measurable difference to the campaign. There was talk of a wave of tactical voting at every UK election campaign, said Robinson, but it never amounted to much in the end. Why should this time be any different? In the brief segment, Lawson had only a couple of minutes to correct the inaccurate question (as he pointed out, tactical voting – not only condoned but partly sponsored by the Labour and Lib Dem leaderships – had played a very significant role in the Tories' landslide 1997 defeat) before pointing out that whereas – certainly in 2015 – tactical voting had traditionally tended to be discussed only in the closing days of a campaign, this time it was on the agenda from the outset as across social media a variety of websites, discussion groups, and the like – Compass by no means the only one – were all actively helping voters find ways to make their votes count. The simple fact of the *Today* feature before the campaign had even officially begun testified that this time was different. The problem, if anything, was likely to be not a lack of interest in tactical voting but a profusion of different platforms offering people sometimes conflicting advice on how to vote.

Opposing Lawson was political scientist David Cowling of King's College, London. He didn't engage with Lawson's observations about what was actually going on, or even point out many of the challenging real-world hurdles PA would have to clear to make an impact on the election, but simply insisted that PA would fail because it was 'born not of strength but of despair and desperation'. Even if this was true, it didn't explain why desperation couldn't be a powerful motivator of voter behaviour: but Cowling's scepticism, if not the oddly moralising tenor of his argument, would be echoed pretty much to a man (and they were nearly all men) by the select number of academic UK political specialists whose brief moment in the spotlight came around at every election. The following weekend, Matthew Goodwin from the University of Kent would pooh-pooh PA on *Sunday Politics*; the following week it would be the turn of Rob Ford (University of Manchester); and so it went on. Uncharitably, one might wonder whether academic political scientists – who have been known to regard voter behaviour in a rather mechanical way – resented the idea of a bunch of enthusiasts appealing to voters on the basis of reason, commitment and shared values…

Academic scepticism was very far being from the PA's biggest worry, but it was in its smallish way a reminder of how many and how high were the bricks stacked in the wall they faced. The truth is, there was no real precedent or template in UK political history for what Compass was trying to achieve with the Progressive Alliance. It was neither a new party hoping to crack the closed shop of British politics, nor a single-issue pressure group using the election to advance and publicise its cause, but a campaigning force in its own right with a clear political orientation and set of values; one that, while it would not be standing any candidates of its own, nonetheless aspired to enlist and to endorse as many progressive candidates as were willing to work, through PA, with other progressives to help build a better society (or at least minimise the harm done to the one we already had).

In some ways – though its values and programme could hardly be more diametrically opposed to that of Compass – the closest albeit inexact parallel to what the PA hoped to achieve was UKIP. Although UKIP aped the forms and practices of a conventional political party for strategic purposes and briefly enjoyed a degree of success in that form (notably at the 2015 general election, and in some European, local and regional contests before and after), in reality it was a para-political entity – a campaign with one overriding end to which electoral politics were ultimately just one means (one reason why UKIP local councillors, once elected either as a means to signal support for the party's larger objectives, or as a sod-the-lot-of you protest vote, were generally so hopeless at conducting their duties satisfactorily). In promoting and ultimately realising that end – Britain's withdrawal from the EU – UKIP had been more successful than, probably, all but its most fanatical supporters could ever have predicted. Along the way, it had become, as protest parties always do, a screen onto which could be projected a variety of dissatisfactions connected only loosely, or not at all, to its core Euroscepticism: anti-immigrant sentiments, anti-multicultural sentiments, in fact whole barrowloads of anti-this and anti-that sentiments. But as Nigel Farage's serial failures in Westminster elections testified, few people, even perhaps including its own support base, were persuaded that UKIP could ever become a legitimate part of the governing and legislating process. So in the process of fulfilling its original ambitions, UKIP had also effectively removed the basis for its own existence. For the 2017 election, UKIP's leadership were attempting to relaunch themselves as a populist-nationalist, socially conservative, basically anti-immigrant party, but whether this would have the electoral traction of their previous incarnation – especially as the Tories busily moved their tanks onto UKIP's lawns, styling themselves the champions of the 'left behind' – remained very much to be seen. Regardless of UKIP's own fate, it had changed the trajectory not just of British politics but of British society, in profound ways and with lasting consequences.

What UKIP's rise and possible fall indicated was that it had never been a political party in the traditional sense. It engaged with party politics, actively and sometimes very effectively, in the interests of a vision, a dream it invited others to share. UKIP's dreams were antithetical to those of Compass: but if the PA could redraw the political map even half as successfully as UKIP had, the impact could be just as transformative.

Branding

Electoral politics relies on strong brands. To admit this isn't to reduce politics to a commodity or democracy to advertising – it's simply a recognition that the complex textures of political competition will inevitably be synthesised into simpler, more forceful and readily grasped forms, using the language of symbols, colours, slogans – i.e. brands. In 2017, Labour – under Jeremy Corbyn once more unashamedly red, no longer clad in the centrist pastels of the New Labour years – was 'For the Many, not the Few.' For the first fortnight of the campaign at least, until even her own press backers wearied of it, every Tory minister and MP, from Theresa May on down, parroted the party line of 'strong and stable government' (proof that whatever might be the case for Brexit, no slogan is certainly better than a bad slogan). The Lib Dems probably had a slogan too, if anyone could be bothered to find out what it was. So, if the Progressive Alliance was to compete effectively on this playing field, its own distinct brand identity would have to be quickly defined and secured.

To do this, Compass turned to SmallAxe, a small non-profit media and campaigning consultancy specialising in providing services to NGOs, charities, community organisations, the public sector and social businesses. Crucially for the PA's very pressing and specific needs, SmallAxe were a full-spectrum consultancy that combined creative, tech and political consultancy roles, and provided not just concepts but delivery – and, anticipating an early poll, had been on an election footing since the New Year. Just as important, they shared Compass' vision of the good society. The language on their website could have been taken from Compass' own, expressing SmallAxe's determination to take on entrenched special interests and, in their own words, 'create movements that are progressive, hopeful and powerful … To bring people together to act.'

Neal Lawson felt strongly that the PA had found the ideal partner both to put its vision before a wider public and to put it into practical political application. Frances Foley leaves no doubt that, from the two organisations' first contact in early April, the PA campaign became a genuine partnership throughout between Compass and SmallAxe. It was not only the standard client–agency relationship, but also picked up many of the more conventional demarcations of responsibilities (I do strategic vision, you do communications and daily tactics, say), giving way to a collective, participatory – yet, Foley says, remarkably cohesive and efficient – culture. Both partners shared the ideal of offering, to a public fatigued by endless sub-division and marketing to ever-smaller fragments, a unified story, enabling the kind of public conversation that had become all too rare.

PA and SmallAxe were gambling that the negative, small-minded Conservative campaign might turn out to be fatally out of tune with the public mood. Theresa May's endless warnings about the 'coalition of chaos' (fighting, as politicians so often do, the last election – aiming to repeat the Tories' successful SNP gambit in 2015) could misfire by offering only a binary, take-it-or-leave-it choice to an electorate that was, and knew itself to be, in two or many minds about a host of issues from Brexit on down. The PA, by contrast, might catch the temper of the times by creating a 'permissions structure' (SmallAxe were, after all, a consultancy and hence not immune to jargon) that allowed – indeed invited – people to take a broader perspective. It didn't ask people to swallow anybody's party line, hook and sinker, but told them it was OK to take a measured view of the bigger picture and work out where they saw themselves fitting into it.

The first issue to be resolved was the name of the campaign itself. Everybody felt the phrase 'progressive alliance' was a bit of a mouthful, so, in the weeks before the election was called, there was some unfocused discussion of a snappier, more Facebook-friendly brand identity. Somebody SF-minded proposed 'rebel alliance'; someone else countered with 'rabble alliance', and the idea expired quietly. Zoe Williams suggested 'coalition of losers', so understandably it remained Progressive Alliance for the time being. Then, like so much else, the question was effectively answered by the move to an election footing. A logo, website, flyers and so much else had to be designed and delivered, and no one could agree on an alternative, so Progressive Alliance it was, and has remained. As it turned out, with the proliferation of snappily but opaquely named competitors in the crowded 2017 field of tactical voting advice, 'Progressive Alliance' had the distinct advantage – unlike Best for Britain, Hope Not Hate, and the rest – of being and doing exactly what it said on the tin. As the idea of a 'progressive alliance' (without the capital letters) increasingly entered the national debate, the Progressive Alliance came to own not only the phrase, but also the concept.

The PA website was put together in a mad three-day rush and, of course, on a shoestring budget. NationBuilder ('Software for Leaders'), the hybrid content management/customer relationship system designed for political campaigns that powered the PA website, had been used by US presidential campaigns and had a price tag to match. Compass's coffers couldn't cough up anything like the money NationBuilder charged for the premium version, so the PA would have to limp through most of the campaign with analytics that left much to be desired. The SmallAxe team worked round the clock to produce the necessary architecture of a campaign website by the start of the first full week of campaigning. One of its key features was the 'VoteSmart' tool, supplying voting recommendations in key marginals based on Roger Wilson and Chuck Dreyer's analysis. In the rush to get the website functional, VoteSmart went live, along with everything else, somewhat prematurely and thus without a full sign-off of its initial recommendations from Lawson, meaning that some impolitic proposals (notably to vote Labour in Labour-held seats where the Greens had placed second in 2015 such as Bristol West) ruffled some feathers amongst PA staff and allies and had to be hastily adjusted.

Next up was the decidedly old-media question of posters. However twentieth (or indeed nineteenth) century the format, window bills and garden stakes remain one of the most readily visible and effective means of not only flaunting one's own convictions, but conveying a palpable sense of popular support to neighbours, activists and passers-by. Any canvasser will tell you that nothing so lifts (or alternately, depresses) the spirits after a long day of pounding the pavements and battling with recalcitrant letter boxes and yappy dogs behind them as turning the corner into a street liberally punctuated with bills in your (or your opponents') colours. The unmistakable colour-coding of the major parties – red, blue, orange, (in Scotland) yellow for the SNP, (in Wales) green for Plaid etc. – all make strong, simple and unmistakable visual statements to the world. They are surprisingly durable ones, too; though the Tories have tended to redesign their poster formats from one recent election to the next – perhaps reflecting a degree of uncertainty about the party's identity in modern Britain – Labour's and the Lib Dems' basic window bill design have remained essentially unchanged since the 1990s.

A PA window bill, however, was faced with the challenge of communicating a complex message in straightforward graphic terms. It was obviously possible for, say, a Labour supporter tactically voting Lib Dem simply to put up a Lib Dem poster;

but this was a crude statement of voting intention alone that furthermore would naturally be taken (not least by the party in question) as an endorsement of not just the local candidate but the party and its programme as a whole. How could the PA enable its supporters to signal that theirs was a provisional and considered vote under specific (local and national) circumstances, not necessarily or even significantly a buy-in to the party manifesto?

SmallAxe's first poster run, which established a pleasing and simple brand identity for the Progressive Alliance – red and green san-serif lettering on a plain white background – nonetheless struck many PA volunteers as unfit for their very pressing and specific purposes. With slogans such as 'Reset Politics: Vote Progressive', the posters risked confusing those voters (the vast majority) not already looped into the PA debate, implying they could expect a 'Progressive Alliance' party or candidate. At best, they were preaching to the choir. What really mattered – in fact, all that mattered for the coming seven weeks – was to find a way of indicating what PA meant in very practical terms: fundamentally, setting aside not party *affiliation* (which the 'Vote Progressive' message seemed to suggest) but, at least temporarily, tribal party *loyalty* for the greater good. So, Labour people voting Lib Dem; Lib Dems voting Labour; both voting Green (in Brighton) and so on. A clearer, indeed in-your-face, statement was needed to catch the eyes of the public, media and – not least – local political parties.

In the guerrilla spirit of the campaign, people started experimenting with their own versions. One of these freelance ideas, created for (perhaps inevitably) Richmond Park, was a tricolour design banded, top to bottom, yellow lettering on red (for Labour), black-on-orange (for the Lib Dems) and green-on-white (for the Progressive Alliance itself). Someone said it resembled the Ghanaian flag (minus the central star). The top two bands mimicked (without copying exactly – the copyright position on party fonts and logos wasn't clear, but no one felt like adding a lawsuit to the PA's workload) the respective corporate styles of the two parties to deliver the statement 'Labour … but voting Liberal Democrat in Richmond Park June 8th'; the bottom band presented the new PA logo, slogan ('Build a Progressive Majority') and URL. This prototype, which went up at A1-size in a front garden on a residential road in central Richmond much used by commuters, quickly indicated that something on these lines would indeed force PA into the conversation: in short order it caught the eye of Guido Fawkes, who featured it on his website with the erroneous (but flattering and helpful) caption that 'these boards are going up all over Richmond' under the headline 'Coalition of Rubbish'. Job done.

Still, the tricolour wasn't quite right: not sleek or direct or somehow modern enough, and failing to communicate the PA's larger vision beyond the 'instrumental' application of tactical voting. Suitably inspired, SmallAxe duly went back to their tablets and came up with a variation on the theme that captured exactly that:

'I ♥ Labour [or Lib Dem, Green etc.] … but voting Lib Dem [… etc. …] Here June 8th'.

The heart symbol encapsulated the values-driven politics that made the Progressive Alliance far more than just an anti-Tory 'coalition of losers' (or, indeed, rubbish). It was a palpable expression of non-confrontational politics, conveying the idea of pooling rather than side-lining one's own deeply held beliefs. It showed a desire to ally with others not as a least-worst option but in a spirit of generosity, commitment and even love: heart and head – and joined hands – not as opposites but as complementary, indeed conjoined, parts of the same body politic.

This feeling quality was key to the PA campaign. It was what would balance out the instrumental, technical aspects of a strategy necessarily focused on tactical voting. It ensured that PA statements would be about values, not policy (an approach which also conveniently enabled Compass to kick the hot potato of Brexit into the long grass for the duration of the campaign) and would underpin an upbeat, positive approach that counteracted the cynicism of tactical voting with an emphasis on the ends the tactics served. As Luke Walter of SmallAxe, another sci-fi fan, put it, it offered a *Star Trek* vision of the world – collaborative; peaceful; liberated from poverty, need and exploitation – against the Tories' *Matrix/Terminator* dystopia.

It had been a long time since progressives had seriously tried to offer an unequivocally optimistic prospectus unconstrained by timidity, piecemeal retail offers or machine politics. Could it work? Donald Trump had won the US presidency ranting about 'American carnage'. On the other hand, whatever one's views of Brexit, in the referendum it was the empowering (however mendacious) slogan of 'Take Back Control' that won out over 'Project Fear'. As they rolled out the tools of the campaign – videos and viral GIFs, the VoteSmart tactical voting recommendation tool (searchable by constituency name or postcode), Facebook pages and meetups for PA volunteers – Compass and SmallAxe were gambling on the fact that people had had enough bad news mornings and were ready to try changing the channel.

By the sea
If everywhere in the UK were like Brighton, the Progressive Alliance would have had a much easier job. The metropolitan

Brighton seats – Pavilion, Kemptown and Hove – made up three-fifths of a marine cluster including their immediate neighbour to the north and east, Lewes, and, next door to that along the coast, Eastbourne. Together they made up an intensely contested rainbow patchwork of political orientations unique in the entire country. Of the five, the only reasonably safe seat was Brighton Pavilion, the Greens' solitary parliamentary foothold where since 2010 Caroline Lucas had built up a majority of nearly 8,000. To either side of her, highly marginal Tory (Kemptown, 2015 majority 690) and Labour (Hove, majority 1,236) seats; eastwards was Lewes, narrowly regained in 2015 by the Tories after eighteen years as a safe Lib Dem seat (majority 1,083); and finally Eastbourne, another former Lib Dem seat cannibalised by their erstwhile coalition partners last time and another rice-paper majority of 733. In every one of these – not excluding Pavilion, where, throughout Lucas's tenure, Labour had continued to fight hard to unseat Britain's only Green MP, a stance that to anyone on the left apart from the most incorrigibly partisan seemed like the depths of blinkered fratricidal folly – the combined progressive vote handily outweighed the Conservatives (though this didn't take UKIP into account, a far from negligible presence even in this generally strong Remain area – polling between 3–6,000 votes in each constituency in the cluster, and crucially not standing in any of these seats this time around). But centre-left disunity had handed the Tories their narrow margins of victory in three of these seats. As Compass repeatedly pointed out, effective co-operation in this group of seats alone could reduce Theresa May's current majority by a quarter; even if no one expected the Tory victory this time to be as narrow as Cameron's in 2015, it was glaringly obvious that the battle to stem the size of May's majority, if that's what it was, could stand or fall by the left's performance across groups of seats such as these.

What made the 'Brighton cluster' so precious, however, was that here the culture of progressive unity arguably had deeper, self-sown roots – emerging quite independently of Compass – than anywhere else. Like much else in the 2017 election, these roots were sunk during the EU referendum campaign, though, in the view of Georgia Amson-Bradshaw, a Sussex University postgraduate student and Green Party member who would become a prime mover for PA locally, the idea of progressive collaboration had already been gestating in Brighton's lively and student-rich intellectual and political culture and the referendum effectively catalysed it into a more tangible shape. Unusually, the local Remain campaign was politically integrated. Indeed, whereas Labour kept David Cameron at arm's length during the EU referendum (mindful of the disastrous consequences for Labour north of the border in 2015 when Scottish voters seemed to punish the party for having co-operated so closely with the hated Tories in the previous year's independence referendum), in Brighton & Hove the progressive pro-Remain parties (Green, Labour and Lib Dem) produced joint campaign materials and campaigned as effectively a joint entity. In the aftermath of the vote to Leave, several of the younger Remain co-ordinators, including Amson-Bradshaw, Robbie Hirst (who would later briefly join Compass full-time as a paid staffer) and Sussex University Politics doctoral student Ian Lovering, determined both to keep up the fight to preserve Britain's ties to the EU and, more broadly, to sustain the goodwill and sense of common cause around the Remain campaign, set up Sussex Progressives (SP) as a grassroots umbrella organisation for Brighton and the surrounding area. Following an initial meeting that attracted some eighty people, a series of public meetings during the remainder of 2016 promoted ongoing campaigns around hot Brexit-related issues, such as EU nationals' right to remain in the UK following withdrawal from the EU.

As the year drew on, a certain tension emerged within SP (far from uncommon in nascent political organisations) around the right balance between, on the one hand, its debating/campaigning/protesting/consciousness-raising programme and, on the other, the prospect of more directed, outcome-oriented political activities, including becoming involved in electoral politics. For Amson-Bradshaw, who had attended Compass's 2016 summer conference at which progressive alliances were a major focus, SP had two parallel aims. The first was the simple action (though it wasn't always simple at all) of creating and holding the shared space in which activists from various political tribes and traditions could come together to make common cause on the issues that united them across their differences. From this perspective, maintaining the conversation was an outcome and an achievement in its own right. At the same time, however, given the structures within and only within which political change in Britain could be actualised, if SP wanted its values to prevail then at some point it was going to have to engage with those structures. So the second aim, as far as Amson-Bradshaw was concerned, was to become directly involved with electoral politics and political parties. In other words, SP was rehearsing in miniature the same debates that would take place within Compass as it morphed, at least temporarily, into the Progressive Alliance and put itself on an election footing. Having seen the momentum that could be generated by larger, higher-profile events – during the 2016 Liberal Democrat Annual Conference held in Brighton, SP sponsored a debate on electoral reform at which MPs including Labour's Stephen Kinnock and the Lib Dems' Tom Brake spoke alongside Klina Jordan of Make Votes Matter – Amson-Bradshaw became increasingly convinced that the idea of the progressive alliance offered a means both to concretise and to extend into the domain of 'actually existing politics' the co-operative, values-driven principles on which SP was based. Once the election was called, the prospect of a clearly defined, time-limited, real-world task concentrated minds and effort alike.

As a clearinghouse for progressives with no definitive policy positions other than its clear Remain stance (unlike Compass, SP didn't have to consider the implications for a nationwide campaign), and with informal membership and governance structures, Sussex Progressives lacked the institutional capacity to broker the discussions about PA in the area that kicked off as soon as the election was called. In a concerted write-in campaign, SP members actively encouraged their own parties, where appropriate, to consider standing down candidates. SP enjoyed cordial relations with local Green and Liberal Democrat parties, some of which disseminated news of SP meetings in their members' newsletters and invited SP speakers to address constituency meetings. Caroline Lucas's prominence in the Compass PA drive obviously helped, though as ever her party's ultra-democratic constitution and culture meant there was no 'official' party line even a few miles up the road from her constituency office next to Brighton Station. Labour, however, was a problem. In the first place, for much the second half of 2016, there was no functioning local Labour Party to talk to: as Labour descended into open civil war in the aftermath of the referendum, the NEC suspended the Brighton & Hove party – by this point, the largest in the country with over 6,000 members – following the usual accusations of far-left entryism and improper practice. Part of the eventual resolution of the crisis, which rumbled on to the end of the year, was to divide the city party – previously a unitary body covering all three Brighton seats – into separate CLPs. But from the SP/PA perspective, this move threw another spanner in the works, as Peter Kyle, the region's only Labour MP (in fact, the only Labour MP in the entire south-east), was a vocal opponent not only of Jeremy Corbyn but of alliances with other parties, too. In early May, *Observer* pundit and fellow Corbyn-hater Nick Cohen took a trip to Brighton and published a characteristically strident and abusive piece[16] under the headline 'A Progressive Alliance is Misbegotten and Doomed', which incorporated a hagiographic portrait of Kyle as a lone voice of sanity fighting the barbarians at Labour's gates (and claimed – quite erroneously – that Momentum activists were boycotting Hove in hopes of Kyle's defeat) while arguing that PA was doomed to failure for not, as he claimed, addressing what he called the 'foul sectarianism' of the far left (that is, the current Labour leadership). Having somewhat condescendingly praised the 'moral seriousness' of the Greens, in the next breath Cohen admiringly quoted Kyle's stated aim of converting Green votes in Hove to Labour – the logical extension of which, if successful, would be for the Greens to cease to exist as a distinct or significant political movement. Whether sectarianism was foul or fair apparently depended on which end of the telescope you were looking through. SP members, recalls Ian Lovering, were 'deeply disappointed' with

---

16 In March, Cohen had published a column in which he denounced Corbyn supporters (channelling the late Robert Conquest's description of Stalinist apologists during the Soviet purges) as 'fucking fools'. *The Observer*'s Readers' Editor subsequently printed an apology. https://www.theguardian.com/commentisfree/2017/mar/19/jeremy-corbyn-labour-threat-party-election-support

Kyle's rhetoric and – especially after the fraternal atmosphere of the united Remain campaign – the general Labour tone of defensive hostile tribalism.

In the end, Kyle's stance meant no agreement was possible in Hove, and both the Greens and Lib Dems stood against him. With UKIP's 3,265 votes of 2015 likely destined for the Tories, it was all too possible Hove could become the PA's poster child for the suicidal folly of progressives conspiring to defeat themselves. If so, the two neighbouring seats would offer a stark contrast: given Caroline Lucas's safe majority in Pavilion, the Lib Dems' stand-aside on her behalf could cynically be seen as easy-virtue-signalling (in a seat where the party had won less than 3 per cent of the vote in 2015: the Greens themselves were inclined to take this view), but it mattered all the same. Meanwhile the Greens' own stand-aside in Kemptown – their 3,000-odd 2015 votes helping offset the impact of UKIP's nearly 4,500 votes last time – could prove decisive.

Sussex Progressives threw themselves into the fight and were the PA's eyes, ears and arms on the ground, distributing Compass/PA materials almost daily at street stalls around the cluster (Eastbourne by the SP's own admission got rather neglected), running voter registration drives at the city's two large university campuses and hosting PA 'barnstorm' canvassing-recruitment events in both Brighton and Lewes.[17] As the campaign intensified, some within SP – acting as the hub of local PA activity – started to feel there was almost too much going on, and that its operations were not always carried out in a co-ordinated or focused way. As with the national picture, a proliferation of different campaigning groups with common or

---

17 On barnstorms, see Chapter Seven.

overlapping aims duplicating effort was one problem; another was the sheer difficulty of conducting a proactive campaign on the ground (i.e. canvassing) without the data and software infrastructure of the political parties. But the Progressive Alliance was never going to be – nor did it aim to be, nor would it be judged as – a slick streamlined machine. Its sometimes chaotic humanity was also part of its core identity. It's what kept it real and true to itself and to those it aimed to serve.

What was apparent was that, given the limitations of PA resources, nobody really knew what the impact of their efforts was going to be. SP's Ian Lovering nonetheless certainly felt that, just as Neal Lawson had told David Cowling on *Today*, the ubiquitous, highly focused and detailed discussions of tactical voting across social media platforms from the very outset of the campaign differentiated this election from all the others he could recall. But he, no more than anyone else, could say for sure whether the networked progressive hive-mind could work effectively in the right ways, in the right places, to make a difference. And, in any event, even in a best-case scenario metropolitan, bohemian, liberal Brighton was surely unlikely to be terribly representative of the country as a whole. Was it?

The Regressive Alliance

If anything awoke the PA team in a cold sweat in the dark reaches of the night, it was this: the fear that not only would their efforts fail, but in a mocking reflection, their own tactics would be used against them by their opponents – and used better.

From its long experience of defeat, the left had acquired a collective inferiority complex when it came to the right's ruthless aptitude for the manoeuvres, swerves, Machiavellian stratagems and downright dirty dealings of bare-knuckle electoral politics. Whether it was simply the access right-wing parties enjoyed to an essentially bottomless supply of corporate financial support, the top-dollar talent that money enabled them to hire and the massive national media campaigns it supported; or whether it was something in their ideological DNA that empowered conservatives to inflame divisive passions on race, class and nationalism to their own advantage, to manipulate, mislead and flat-out lie to the public with utter lack of scruple and apparent impunity: whatever the causes, many on the left felt deep down (even if they wouldn't admit it, perhaps even to themselves) that, when push came to shove, the other guys were simply better at this stuff. The blatant collusion between the Tories and the rabidly right-wing English tabloids, which had if anything intensified in recent elections, exacerbated the feeling of a far-from-level playing field. In defeat after repeated defeat, as (very) slender consolation, leftists and liberals clung to the belief that they, at least, had fought the good fight. If the other guy chose to grab your balls while you were boxing by Queensberry rules (and the referee either didn't notice or didn't care, or had been bought off before the fight even began) you won a moral victory even as they paraded the title belt around the ring while you sat slumped in your corner spitting blood and teeth into the bowl.

A cornerstone of New Labour's blueprint for power had been the conviction that this attitude was, fundamentally, bullshit. Epitomised by the carnivorous, take-no-prisoners, testosterone-fuelled approach of Tony Blair's spin doctor Alastair Campbell, New Labour's ground operation was fuelled by a determination that never again would the right get a free run; never again would the left give a single inch of ground to their opponents simply because, unlike them, they were unwilling to play dirty. And, for a while, it worked. But by the end of the Blair-Brown era, this confrontational stance had become bound up with the general wreck of the New Labour project and, under Ed Miliband, Labour once again found itself firmly on the back foot. The Tories' Australian campaign director Lynton Crosby, whose infamous 'dead cat' tactics had helped win Cameron's majority in 2015,[18] seemed to be the latest Mephistophelian incarnation of this apparently inexhaustible supply of right-wing campaign kingpins.

Being turned over by an unquestionably smart if unprincipled operator like Crosby was one thing. But to lose ground to a crew of far-right fools and nut-jobs would be quite another. If the Progressive Alliance found itself outmanoeuvred by UKIP and its supporters, it would pose some pretty fundamental questions about whether they were in the right business at all. Could it happen?

UKIP's thirteen historic months of heady success, from winning nearly 13 per cent of the UK-wide vote in 2015 (14 per cent in England and Wales) to the undreamed-of fulfilment of its overriding aim since the party's inception with Leave's narrow victory in the referendum, had been followed by its equally

---

18 In Crosby's own words: 'There is one thing that is absolutely certain about throwing a dead cat on the dining room table – and I don't mean that people will be outraged, alarmed, disgusted. That is true, but irrelevant. The key point is that everyone will shout, "Jeez, mate, there's a dead cat on the table!" In other words, they will be talking about the dead cat – the thing you want them to talk about – and they will not be talking about the issue that has been causing you so much grief.' During the 2015 election campaign, as Labour's proposed clampdown on tax loopholes appeared to be gaining traction, Crosby sent Defence Secretary Michael Fallon onto television to launch a baseless and highly personalised attack on Ed Miliband's defence policy, claiming that having 'stabbed his own brother in the back to become Labour leader' – a reference to Miliband's successful 2010 run against his older brother David for the Labour leadership – he would be 'willing to stab the United Kingdom in the back to become Prime Minister'. Sure enough, the ensuing 24-hour news cycle was dominated by discussion of Fallon's crude and slanderous outburst – and not by Labour's popular tax avoidance policies.

dramatic disintegration. Once Nigel Farage stepped down from
the party leadership (for the third time, but this time seemingly
for good) and reinvented himself as Donald Trump's fluffer-in-
chief, UKIP underwent a chaotic series of leadership contests
culminating in the election of the tweed-suited, chav-tastic
Scouser Paul Nuttall in November 2016. Nuttall's attempts –
following UKIP's surprising success in gaining former Labour
votes in northern English seats in the 2015 election – to relaunch
the party as a vehicle of white working-class anti-immigration
sentiment and social conservatism (as well as a guardian of the
flame of hard-as-nails Brexit) were undermined by his own
comically inept performance as UKIP's candidate in the February 2017 Stoke Central by-election, where Labour successfully
defended a seat with the highest proportion of Leave voters
in the entire country. As UKIP's sole (and semi-detached)
MP, Douglas Carswell abandoned the party in March to sit as
an independent in the Commons, having declared that, with
Britain's decision to quit the EU, 'the work is done', the party's
continuing purpose seemed unclear. In the May local elections,
UKIP would lose every single one of the 145 council seats it was
defending.

Yet even in its death throes, UKIP – or rather, the voters it
had briefly claimed to represent – posed a potential threat to the
progressive cause. In March, millionaire businessman Arron
Banks, the long-time party donor who was also the principal
sponsor of the 'unofficial' Leave.EU campaign in the referendum, fulfilled his longstanding threat to abandon the UKIP
'shambles', declaring his intention to set up a new populist
nationalist party, or 'movement'. He suggested the new entity
could model itself after Beppe Grillo's Five-Star Movement in
Italy, which had recently made major gains in parliamentary

elections there – or even 'a right-wing Momentum'. On the same day that the UK ambassador to the EU formally submitted notice of Britain's intention to quit, a website appeared announcing the launch of 'The Patriotic Alliance'. That month, the Huffington Post reported that Banks and David Cameron's former director of strategy, Steve Hilton, were discussing a plan to try to unseat up to 100 Remain-supporting MPs at the next election (at that point of course still not expected for another three years). Hilton's partner on his fundraising platform Crowdpac, Paul Hilder, declared that 'the new politics is coming', adding the ominous afterthought that 'democracy dies in darkness; and it has never been clearer that the status quo is failing.' As it happened, the ideologically unclassifiable Hilder would later play a significant part in helping the PA develop its own campaign tactics. Meanwhile, however, for Compass to hear its own language and thesis parroted in support of the populist right was a bizarre looking-glass moment that scarily called to mind Neal Lawson's tocsin, sounded the morning after Trump's election. Could a 'regressive alliance' generate sufficient momentum to confound their efforts? Notwithstanding a good deal of bad blood between UKIP and the Conservatives, there was some precedent for a pact: in 2010 UKIP stood aside in seven seats on behalf of Conservative candidates or MPs, four of whom won (and three of whom would later in that parliament defect to UKIP).[19]

In the end, cock-up, more than conspiracy, would drive the 'regressive alliance'. The early election seemed to take Arron Banks by surprise: at the time of writing, the Patriotic Alliance's most recent tweet remains the announcement on 4 April of

---

19   Douglas Carswell, Mark Reckless and Janice Atkinson.

the movement's launch 'in a month's time'. In keeping with the prevailing farcical air around late-period UKIP, Banks rejoined the party a month after leaving it in order to stand as its official candidate against renegade Douglas Carswell in Clacton (about which, he admitted on local radio, he knew 'nothing at all') – only to change his mind after Carswell himself chose not to run again. At UKIP headquarters, meanwhile, chaos reigned as Paul Nuttall barricaded himself in a room to avoid reporters' questions following a disastrous press conference. The party's repellent strategy – if it deserved to be called a strategy – of doubling down on anti-immigrant and anti-Muslim sentiment further narrowed the distance between UKIP and the openly fascist thuggery of the EDL. In a televised election debate late in the campaign, the SNP's Angus Robertson spoke for the majority when he told Nuttall to his face that the tenor of his anti-immigration tirades 'shames and demeans us all'.

But however dishevelled and disintegrating – a basket of deplorables if ever there was one – UKIP still had the capability to make a meaningful difference to the outcome of the election. As the filing deadline passed for the general election, it emerged that UKIP was fielding just 377 candidates nationwide – compared to over 600 in 2015. How much of this was down to a shortage of candidates or even simple incompetence wasn't clear (at 5 p.m. on 11 May, deadline day, UKIP were still unclear exactly how many candidates they would be standing as they suspected an unknown number had failed to file the papers on time), but Nuttall put the best possible construction on his party's diminished and diminishing presence, claiming that UKIP had chosen not to field candidates in a large number of seats where either a sitting Tory MP supported hard Brexit, or marginals where the Tories had a prospect of ousting prominent Remainers. So

Theresa Villiers in Chipping Barnet and Iain Duncan Smith in Chingford, for example, wouldn't have to worry about their right flanks, while the position of pro-European Labour MPs in northern Leave seats like Caroline Flint in Don Valley (2015 majority 8,885; UKIP vote 9,963) as well as those in London marginals like Tulip Siddiq in Hampstead & Kilburn (2015 majority 1,138; UKIP vote 1,532) suddenly became even more precarious than the polls were suggesting. BuzzFeed estimated that by not standing, UKIP could hand victory to the Tories in twenty-nine marginals (potentially adding fifty-eight to May's overall majority). Several of these seats looked set to be straight shoot-outs between the regressive and progressive alliances: none more so than Ealing Central & Acton, where the benefit to Rupa Huq's defence of her wafer-thin 274 majority of the Greens' stand-aside (1,841 votes in 2015) was effectively negated by the potential defection to the Tories of UKIP's 1,926 voters.

The PA had one major consolation as they nervously surveyed the prospect: Theresa May's campaign was doing an excellent job of demolishing the myth of the invincible Conservative campaign machine. With every robotic non-interview, every sterile campaign photo-op staged as far away from actual voters as she could get, every kneejerk repetition of the mantra 'strong and stable' government, a little more of the shine came off and she started to look a very ordinary politician indeed. If she was the best the professionals could come up with, surely the rank amateurs of UKIP couldn't do better? The Regressive Alliance might yet be its own worst enemy.

CHAPTER FOUR

HERE, THERE AND EVERYWHERE

(WITH RAKIB EHSAN)

If a progressive alliance is such a great idea, why hasn't anyone else done it?

A good question to which there are two short answers. The first is that the disproportionate and unrepresentative results delivered in the UK by first-past-the-post – an electoral system employed by no other EU or G20 member states bar the US, Canada and India, and today retained elsewhere mostly in former British dependencies and colonies – combined with the fragmentation of the centre-left vote faced with (prior to the rise of UKIP at least) a united Right, make attempts to 'game the system' almost inevitable.

The second, even shorter, answer is that others have, often, and continue to do so, in a wide and varying range of national political cultures. The eleven examples briefly surveyed in this chapter, which are in no way exhaustive, have been deliberately selected from a diverse global set of political ecologies to illustrate the different motives, forms, methods of implementation and outcomes that electoral alliances and pacts have taken and continue to take. Some – the pre-Second World War French Front Populaire and 1970s Programme Commun – are drawn from political history. Others, including the Broad Front in Uruguay, the Chilean New Majority, the Portuguese left coalition and the Labour–Green compact in New Zealand, are ongoing at the time of writing. Some are pre-electoral pacts such as the Progressive Alliance sought to fashion in the 2017 general election in the UK; others are coalitions arising from electoral outcomes that in some cases fulfilled, in others confounded pre-poll assumptions. One – the Programme Commun – is not an electoral pact at all, but a formal agreement amongst parties of the left on basic economic and social priorities that formed the basis over a decade for both an electoral alliance and (at the subsequent election) separate campaigns, but with a common understanding of coalition government in the event of electoral success. In every case, I have tried to draw out those factors that have made cross-party alliances more or less likely to be sustainable and durable.

There is no one lesson to be derived from such a diversity of examples – which, as I say, could easily be extended – except perhaps this: at one time or another, almost every leading party of the left or centre-left in every country has found virtue in co-operating with parties further to its left and/or closer to the political centre. As we shall see in Chapter Six, such arrangements are not entirely unknown in the UK either.

And perhaps one other lesson, most important of all: if progressives fail to make common cause, sooner or later their opponents will – possibly with calamitous consequences that go far beyond electoral defeat. For that reason, the chapter concludes with a reminder of the failure of the parties of the German left during the early 1930s to recognise that their most terrible enemies lay elsewhere – with consequences that haunt us still.

The brief utopia of the Popular Front (France 1936–1938)

The most famous example of the parties of the left making common cause, the Popular Front (Front Populaire), arose in France during the years immediately preceding the Second World War. The alliance, which included the French Communist Party (PCF), the French Section of the Workers' International (SFIO) and the Radical and Socialist Party, brought together centre-left social democrats and more radical left-wing political forces in an unprecedented, if short-lived, alliance in the face of the European political and economic crises of the 1930s.

Anti-parliamentary street demonstrations organised by a collective of far-right leagues culminated in riots on the Place de la Concorde (near the seat of the National Assembly) on 6 February 1934. For alarmed social democrats and socialists alike, this was seen as an orchestrated effort by the far right to stage a coup d'état against the Third Republic. Meanwhile, the rise of fascist and nationalist authoritarian regimes across Europe – above all, the Nazi seizure and consolidation of power in Germany and the ruthless evisceration of the workers' movement that ensued – prompted the Communist International (Comintern) to reassess its evidently failed policy directives to European workers' parties. Witnessing how the absence of SPD–KPD co-operation in Germany (see below) had contributed to the rise of Nazism, Stalin directed European communist parties to abandon their 'social-fascist' stance[20] and adopt instead a pragmatic anti-fascist position which entertained co-operation with social

---

20 Until the Soviet party line changed with the shift to the Popular Front strategy, European communist parties maintained the grotesque fiction that their social-democratic opponents – as supposed defenders of monopoly capitalism – were functionally indistinguishable from the parties and movements of the far right: hence 'social fascists.'

democrats. Combatting fascism was now the main imperative. The relations between communists and social democrats were somewhat less poisonous in mid-1930s France than elsewhere, and in short order the Popular Front came into being. A few months after its Spanish sister-alliance Frente Popular emerged victorious in Spain, the Popular Front won a comprehensive victory in the May 1936 legislative elections (with Socialists outnumbering the more centrist Radicals in their common bloc for the first time). The government formed was spearheaded by SFIO leader Léon Blum, and entirely composed of Radical Socialist and SFIO ministers (the PCF supported the Popular Front from outside the Cabinet).

In government, the Popular Front introduced new labour laws through the 1936 Matignon Accords. This created the right to strike and to collective bargaining, increased the pay of the lowest-paid workers by 15 per cent, limited the standard working week to forty hours and prohibited overtime. Domestic economic reforms included the democratisation of the Bank of France, bringing the arms industry under public ownership, and introducing measures to prevent illicit price hikes. To face down the threat of the far right, Blum decided to enforce the dissolution of the country's fascist leagues. However, the Popular Front continued to be actively fought by far-right movements, with the fascist group Cagoule staging multiple bombings to disrupt the government.

The Popular Front's eventual demise was rooted in economic mismanagement and an incoherent foreign policy agenda. Wage rises were neutralised by high levels of inflation and French business increasingly transferred capital overseas. The outbreak of the Spanish Civil War meanwhile created deep divisions in French politics. While the left supported the Spanish republican government in Madrid, the conservative Catholic right were on the side of the nationalist insurgents. Blum's cabinet was itself divided on the matter – the outcome being that the government felt it had no option but to pursue a policy of non-intervention, a decision that was widely seen as a betrayal on the French (and international) left.

By 1938, the mounting European crisis had exacerbated the ever-present strains between the right and left wings of the Popular Front coalition, which themselves were pulling further towards their respective extremes. The Radicals (despite their name, essentially a social-liberal party) excluded their socialist partners altogether from the Cabinet; that autumn, the PCF withdrew altogether from the Popular Front in protest at the government's role in the Munich Agreement.

The Popular Front never faced the voters again: by the outbreak of the war, the coalition had disintegrated and the Third Republic itself was dissolved in the aftermath of defeat and occupation and the establishment of Marshal Pétain's authoritarian-right Vichy regime. The Popular Front's inception and collapse alike testify to the difficulty, especially in established democracies, of forming broad electoral coalitions of widely divergent parties (in this case, social liberals, social democrats and the revolutionary left) outside of situations of exceptional gravity or crisis, and the comparable difficulty of sustaining such coalitions beyond the medium term. The memory and myth of the Popular Front, however, endures – not least because of the outpouring of cultural production in its early phase, and the association with its heroic, tragic counterpart in Republican Spain – and the phrase has become a byword amongst progressives debating, or longing for, realignments and alliances on the left.

The Common Programme: a platform for left unity (France 1972–1982)

The Common Programme (Programme Commun) was not an electoral pact but a radical reform programme co-signed on 27 June 1972 by the French Socialist Party, the PCF and the Radical Movement of the Left (not genealogically connected to the pre-war Radicals but again, its name notwithstanding, a liberal party ideologically to the right of the Socialists). The move reflected the French left's desperation to remedy its repeated and punishing electoral defeats throughout the Fifth Republic (established 1958) at the hands of the apparently immovable Gaullists; it can also be seen as a belated aftershock of the events of May 1968 when the Paris student insurgency briefly threatened to transform into a general workers' uprising and, arguably, disunity and paralysis on the parliamentary left contributed to de Gaulle's ability to recover his authority. Following de Gaulle's death in 1970, and with Cold War tensions in Europe easing (making partnership with the PCF easier), the left parties saw an opportunity to present a united front against de Gaulle's less charismatic successors.

The Common Programme called for the economic, political and military transformation of the French Republic. The socialist reformation of the French economy would entail a reduction in working hours to forty hours a week, higher wages, an expansion in social security and a substantial increase in public housing. It would also include the 'compensated nationalisation' of major industrial companies in key strategic sectors, bringing numerous banks and financial institutions under state ownership, increased market regulation and stronger worker participation in company decisions. Transforming France's existing system of governance would involve the decentralisation

and democratisation of government institutions, the safeguarding of individual civil liberties and stronger restrictions
on police custody. A 'politics of peace' would guide the Republic. This would include abolishing France's nuclear deterrent,
reducing compulsory military service to six months and supporting the dissolution of NATO and the Warsaw Pact.

The policy platform of the Common Programme paved the
way for the Socialist Party's François Mitterrand to stand as a
united left candidate in the 1974 presidential elections, which he
eventually lost by a narrow margin (less than 2 per cent) to the
Gaullist Valéry Giscard d'Estaing. Following setbacks for the
left in the 1977 legislative elections (in which the Socialists outpolled the Communists for the first time since 1936), PCF leader
Georges Marchais stood against Mitterrand in the first round of
the 1981 presidential elections. In the second round, however,
he endorsed him and Mitterrand narrowly emerged victorious
as the Fifth Republic's first left-wing leader. Following the Socialists' victory in the ensuing parliamentary elections, Socialist
Prime Minister Pierre Mauroy formed a left-unity government
including four PCF ministers.

Mitterrand's presidential manifesto '110 Propositions pour
la France' clearly bore the imprint of the 1972 Common Programme, and after a quarter of a century in opposition he fully
aimed to put into practice a radical agenda of economic and
social reforms that would signal a clean break from market
capitalism. Mitterand's programme centred on an extensive
series of nationalisations in the industrial and financial sectors,
the creation of 150,000 public-sector jobs, substantial rises in
welfare provision and the minimum wage, and comprehensive
state loans and subsidies to industry. However, the Common
Programme – largely unrevised since 1972, notwithstanding the

damaging impact of the 1973 oil crisis on the French economy, with unemployment tripling under d'Estaing's presidency – was ill-prepared for the difficult and worsening situation the new President inherited. The deepening global economic crisis in the aftermath of the second oil shock of 1979 had coincided with the rise to power of the New Right – notably Margaret Thatcher's victory in the UK and Ronald Reagan's election to the US presidency the following year. Perhaps most important of all to France, the year following Mitterrand's election saw the Socialists' sister party the SPD defeated in France's closest European ally, Germany, in favour of the fiscally and socially conservative Christian Democrat Helmut Kohl. This international politico-economic environment meant that the French Socialists came to power on an economic policy agenda whose isolation risked rendering it obsolete. Mitterrand aimed to implement a neo-Keynesian policy of reflation in France at a time where other Western countries such as the US, the UK and West Germany were committed to deflationary austerity – effectively inaugurating the era of neoliberalism.

Mitterrand's contrasting expansionist policies inevitably left France with an enormous deficit – only partially offset by increased taxes on employers and the introduction of a 'solidarity tax' on private wealth. Faced with resistance from the financial market and an uncongenial macro-economic climate, and lacking international allies (not least in the European Community, as it then was), in 1983 Mitterrand performed a stark U-turn and renounced France's socialist experiment, accepting the private market economy and pursuing policies of fiscal and monetary restraint for the remainder of his two terms as president. This 'austerity turn' helped France to gradually rebuild its economy and shrug off the effects of recession and, thanks to the economic recovery, in 1988 Mitterrand defeated conservative Jacques Chirac by a full 8 percentage points on the second round. But it also fractured the 'Union of the Left', which had originally carried him to power: the Communist ministers resigned following Mitterrand's abandonment of the Common Programme and Mitterrand governed from the centre (his successor as Socialist leader, Michel Rocard, in the early 1990s proposed an unrealised concordat with the parties of the centre-right).

The Common Programme is a unique example of an attempt by the parties of the left in a major European nation to formulate common policy ahead of, and essentially independently of, deciding electoral arrangements. It enabled both co-operation and competition in successive elections without fundamentally undermining the shared political concordat. Its failure owed much to the parties' reluctance to make the policy-drafting process an ongoing or rolling one, with the result that by the time the left took power, fully nine years after the Common Programme was drafted, its prescriptions were badly at odds with the changed economic situation.

One Israel under Barak? (Israel 1999–2000)

The diametrical opposite of the UK's first-past-the-post, Israel's ultra-proportional electoral system has always delivered a highly fragmented Knesset (the country's unicameral legislature), and has made coalition governments an absolute norm, as well as encouraging pre-election alliances to give structure to the inevitable post-election negotiations. As the shape of Israeli politics has changed and diversified over the last three decades with several major realignments, these tendencies have intensified.

In May 1999, incumbent Benjamin Netanyahu called early general elections (Israeli governments rarely run to full term) for the position of Prime Minister and for the Knesset (confusingly and, as we shall see, problematically, despite being head of government rather than state and as such relying on members of the Knesset for his legislative capability, from 1992–2001 the Prime Minister received his own mandate by a separate ballot). Netanyahu, leader of the right-wing populist party Likud, ran for re-election. His principal challenger was Labour Party leader Ehud Barak, who led a 'One Israel' alliance including Labour, Meimed – a social-democratic political party which strongly supported a two-state solution – and Gesher, a centre-right breakaway party from Likud. Gesher's inclusion, and the non-involvement of the leftist secular party Meretz, tilted the alliance towards the centre. This was no accident, as Barak aimed to transform the traditionally statist, union-dominated Labour Party into a more centrist polit-ical force, modelling this on Tony Blair's sensationally successful New Labour 'project'. The pre-election agreement between the three parties included a pre-distribution of cabinet positions: in the event of a One Israel victory, Gesher leader David Levy would be appointed Deputy PM and Minister of Foreign Affairs, while Meimad's Michael Melchior would be made Minister of Social and Diaspora Affairs.

Promising to engage in constructive peace talks with Palestine and to withdraw Israeli forces from Lebanon, Barak comfortably defeated Netanyahu in the Prime Minister election (56.1 to 43.9 per cent). However, Barak's personal popularity did not translate to the One Israel alliance as a whole, which won only twenty-six out of 100 seats. As a consequence, One Israel had to form a convoluted coalition with a host of mostly sectional parties – precisely the outcome the alliance had been formed to prevent. The additional members of the coalition that eventually arose were Meretz, the socially conservative Shas, the centre-right

Yisrael BaAliyah (formed by former Soviet refusenik Natan Sharansky to represent the views of Russian Jewish immigrants), the Centre Party, the right-wing settler-interest National Religious Party and the religiously conservative United Torah Judaism. (By lamentable convention, Israeli governments do not include or seek support from Israeli–Arab parties, notwithstanding the potential support the seven Arab Knesset members might have offered Barak's foreign policy agenda.)

The parties of this mosaic (or mishmash) coalition were not only ideologically disparate – indeed, in some respects diametrically opposed – but also ideologically committed. Inevitably, disputes arose quickly and repeatedly. In particular, the religiously conservative elements – a perennially distorting and destabilising influence in Israeli governments since the foundation of the Zionist state – proved the source of much intra-coalition disunity with their more secular partners. United Torah Judaism left the coalition just two months after the government was formed over a perceived breach of the Sabbath. Gesher withdrew in April 2000 over disagreements with Barak's policy on Palestine and Lebanon. Meretz left in June, and the National Religious Party, Shas, and Yisrael BaAliyah only two weeks later. One Israel itself was investigated for party-funding irregularities in what became known as the 'Barak Organisation Affair'. Following the outbreak of the Second Intifada later that year, Barak resigned and what remained of his precarious government collapsed. Despite hoping for a more authoritative mandate, Barak was soundly beaten by Likud's Ariel Sharon – and subsequently retired from politics.

The failure of One Israel and Barak's short-lived tenure as Israeli Prime Minister demonstrated the difficulties a progressive party can encounter when governing with minor parties with particularised interests. Israel has not had a Labour Party prime minister since Barak's brief but tumultuous leadership. While Israeli politics has a uniquely religious and prominently geopolitical complexion, the experience of One Israel shows not only the importance of constructing cohesive progressive alliances, but also the need to take careful political consideration over who to include in coalition governments and where to seek external parliamentary support.

You say one thing, they say another: die neue mitte and the 2009 Hesse debacle (Germany 2008–2009)

The 'red–green' Social Democrat–Green Party coalition (1998–2005) re-defined Germany's social market economy and welfare state under the chancellorship of Gerhard Schröder. Emulating the 'Third Way' pioneered by Bill Clinton and Tony Blair, under the Agenda 2010 and the Hartz IV reforms, Schröder's Neue Mitte (New Centre) spearheaded a centrist economic agenda which sought to deliver job-seeking incentives through the tightening of welfare provision, increased labour market flexibility, and employment laws reformed in favour of business owners.

As in other developed-world social-democratic parties, Schröder's pivot to the centre – intended to restore SPD fortunes after a long period dominated by the conservative CDU – provoked intra-party dissent even as it delivered electoral success. Unlike in the UK, however, the conventionality of coalition governments under Germany's proportional electoral system (mixed-member proportional representation, with Bundestag members elected in equal numbers for single-seat constituencies through first-past-the-post and from party lists to achieve a proportional distribution) means that choosing potential coalition partners becomes an important focus of such internal debates.

Within the SPD, the transformation of Germany's social market economy and streamlining of its welfare state under Schröder's chancellorship drove a wedge between the Keynesian traditionalists on the party's left, who became an increasingly dissenting force, and the Seeheimer Kreis liberal modernisers on the right, who gave staunch support for Schröder's reforms. The traditionalist left-wingers demanded the party secure the restoration of its social-democratic identity eroded by the Neue Mitte, while the Seeheimer Kreis modernisers insisted that the fundamental recasting of the SPD's economic programme was and remained a sheer necessity, given the transformations brought about by globalisation.

The party's traditional leftists have started to acknowledge their common ground with the anti-privatisation and re-regulation economic policies of Die Linke ('the left') – a successor party to the SED (the East German Communist Party) and owing to these associations with the Stalinist past something of a pariah party in German politics since reunification in 1990. Proposals from the SPD's left wing that Die Linke should be regarded as suitable coalition partners in a future federal coalition are thus highly inflammatory to the party's economic liberals, who vehemently maintain that coalitions with Die Linke – such as that currently in place at state level in Brandenburg – are electoral poison to moderate-minded German voters and will prevent the SPD regaining the essential centre ground of German politics.

Such intra-party factionalism and ideological division surrounding the potential coalition partners has threatened the SPD's political credibility, as illustrated by the 2008–2009 Hessen Landtag political deadlock. In the aftermath of the 2008 Hessian state elections, neither SPD–Greens nor Christian

Democrat–Free Democratic (CDU–FDP) coalitions could command a majority in the Landtag, leaving a fifth party in the role of kingmaker – Die Linke. While the SPD's left wing were more than willing govern in a 'parties of the left' coalition with the Greens and Die Linke, the 'Neue Mitte' moderniser faction of the Hesse SPD was bitterly opposed to the prospect of power-sharing with a party they viewed as unrepentant neo-communists. The ensuing irreconcilable disputes within the SPD led to the resignation of Hesse party leader Andrea Ypsilanti and the subsequent dissolution of the Landtag, with another state election duly scheduled for January 2009. Seen by voters as unstable and disunited, the SPD was unsurprisingly punished and suffered a 13 per cent point drop from a year earlier – enabling a centre-right CDU–FDP majority coalition to take power. The entire saga was a political debacle, with the SPD's evident strategic uncertainty fatally undermining the party's credibility.

The 2009 federal election saw the CDU, its Bavarian sister party the Christian Social Union (CSU) and the FDP form a new centre-right coalition with Angela Merkel as Chancellor. Die Linke gained twenty-two seats from the previous election. In 2013, Die Linke replaced the free-market-oriented FDP as Germany's third party (the latter failing to reach the 5 per cent vote threshold for representation in the Bundestag). A CDU–SPD 'Grand Coalition' led by Merkel was established in the name of national stability. Notwithstanding the prominence of former SDP Finance Minister Oskar Lafontaine in Die Linke, a hypothetical SDP–Greens–Die Linke coalition was never seriously considered by the SDP leadership. Interestingly, it would have commanded 320 seats – nine more than the CDU/CSU total of 311 seats.

The Neue Mitte agenda pursued under Schröder contributed

to deepening ideological divisions within the SPD. This has inevitably created obstacles impeding the establishment of effective progressive alliances which could challenge centre-right dominance in the Merkel era at both state and federal level.

Frente Amplio: the Uruguayan progressive coalition (2004–)

Frente Amplio (the Broad Front) is a Uruguayan multi-party coalition of progressive centre-left and left-wing socialist political parties. The governing force in Uruguay since 2004, the coalition has produced the country's last two presidents: José Mujica (2010–2015) and Tabaré Vásquez (2005–2010; 2015–), and having demonstrated both durability and stability notwithstanding considerable ideological diversity, can fairly claim to be the most successful global example of a progressive alliance. Beyond its parliamentary caucus, the Broad Front has particularly close relations with the trade union Plenario Intersindical de Trabajadores – Convención Nacional de Trabajadores (PIT–CNT) and the country's co-operative housing movement.

The Broad Front originally came into being in 1971 as a coalition of over a dozen fractured leftist parties which all faced increasing government repression and shared a common – and as events would show entirely justified – concern at growing authoritarianism in the country as elsewhere in Latin America during this period. In the 1971 election, the Broad Front won a credible 13.8 per cent of the vote – including an impressive 30 per cent share of the vote in the capital Montevideo. But these were the last elections before a decade of repressive right-wing military-dominated dictatorial rule from 1973–1984. Following the restoration of democracy the Broad Front coalition was resurrected and in the free elections of 1984 its vote share increased to 21 per cent.

Having steadily built up its support in Uruguay's restored democracy, Frente Amplio candidate Tabaré Vásquez emerged victorious in the 2004 presidential election. With Uruguay, in common with other South American economies, suffering a severe banking crisis in 2002, in the ensuing recession (with unemployment reaching 21 per cent, and the percentage of Uruguayans in poverty rising to over 30 per cent), Vásquez undertook to revitalise a stagnant economy, gave a strong commitment to social justice, and promised to address the lingering legacy of human rights violations under the 1973–1985 military dictatorship. The new administration developed an innovative national strategy based on six complementary pillars: 'enhancing productivity, fostering social development, encouraging innovation, strengthening democracy, improving regional and global integration and promoting policies that consolidate and promote Uruguayan culture'.

Vásquez's victory signalled an increased willingness among the urban middle-class to support progressive left-of-centre politics. Indeed, his victory reflected a broader regional trend of left-wing political success in Brazil, Argentina, Chile and Venezuela. At the same time, the evident stability of the Frente Amplio and the broad-based nature of its coalition has also made it appealing to traditionally conservative middle-class voters. The progressive alliance currently commands a majority in both the Senate of Uruguay and the Chamber of Representatives (both elected on a PR system). The Broad Front has historically comprised not only centre-left, left-wing socialist and communist parties but also Christian democrats. The current coalition includes the social-democratic Uruguay Assembly, the Socialist Party of Uruguay, the Communist Party of Uruguay and the Christian Democratic Party of Uruguay. In power, the Broad Front has tended to be in favour of a market economy and comprehensive social programmes.

Despite its being considered a progressive coalition, constituent parties of the Broad Front such as the Uruguay Assembly and Christian Democratic Party are essentially centrist and traditionally adopt more fiscally as well as socially conservative positions. However, the coalition parties have proved able to co-operate on a shared support for the fostering of social development, internationalism and democratic reform. The Broad Front continues to serve the important purpose of opposing right-wing conservative nationalist politics – primarily in the form of the National Party of Uruguay. Like other Latin American alliances (see, for example, the Chilean New Majority below), the Broad Front is sustained by its connections to extra-parliamentary social movements and institutions.

Bangladesh's Grand Alliance: a story of dominance (2008–)

Bangladesh has inherited from its former imperial overlord, Britain, both first-past-the-post elections and a two-party system. As always with FPTP, this has led to lopsided victories that fail to reflect the distribution of the popular vote: most notably in 2001, where despite winning a 40 per cent vote share, the centre-left secular Awami League won just sixty-two of 300 parliamentary seats, with the religious-conservative Bangladesh National Party (BNP) and its allies winning a two-thirds majority on 46 per cent of the vote. By the time of the next election in 2008, the Awami League had taken decisive action to forestall another such debacle, forming the Grand Alliance with the more economically liberal Jatiya Party led by General Hussain Ershad as its chief partner alongside smaller parties such as the socialist Jatiyo Samajtantrik Dal and communist

Workers Party. This was a full-blown electoral alliance, including a pre-election pact under which the Awami League conceded forty-six out of 300 parliamentary constituencies to Jatiya.

The 2008 elections were notable for pitting the progressive Grand Alliance against a rival conservative alliance, the Four-Star Alliance, led by the BNP and including Islamist political party Jamaat-e-Islami, given a free run by the BNP in thirty-four constituencies, with three smaller allied parties also conceded two seats each: Bangladesh Jatiya Party (BJP), Islami Oikya Jote and Jamiat-e-Olama-e-Islam.

Led by Sheikh Hasina Wazed, the Grand Alliance 'gamed' Bangladesh's FPTP system to tremendous effect and, in the 2008 elections, won 57 per cent of the popular vote and 263 (almost 90 per cent) of the 300 elected parliamentary seats in the Jatiya Sangshad[21] – dwarfing the Four-Star Alliance's total of thirty-three. The Grand Alliance broadly operates in accordance with three core principles: Bangladeshi nationalism, social democracy and, perhaps most importantly, secularism. The crucial difference between the Grand Alliance and its rival alliances, past and present, is its commitment to Bangladesh as a secular state where the rights of the country's religious minorities – including its sizeable Hindu minority – are upheld and protected. Despite the involvement of the economically liberal Jatiya Party in the alliance, it generally adopts a social-democratic (interventionist, Keynesian) economic approach. By contrast, its primary rival the BNP has an extensive history of leading alliances including Islamist political parties which desire a Bangladeshi nation governed under a strict

---

21 Three hundred seats are directly elected through single-seat constituencies, with an additional fifty reserved for women selected by the ruling party or coalition.

interpretation of the Sharia. This would effectively entail the curtailing of the rights of the country's Hindu, Shia, Buddhist, Christian and Sikh religious minorities. Therefore, the Grand Alliance's constituent parties are bound by a firm belief in a 'Bangladeshi secular patriotism' which incorporates all law-abiding citizens, irrespective of religious affiliation.

Electoral pacts under FPTP are always liable to fall victim to disputes over seat allocation, and the Grand Alliance is no exception. In 2012 the Alliance experienced the defection of the centrist Liberal Democratic Party (LDP) over exactly this issue: the LDP is now a senior partner and part of the new BNP-led Eighteen Party Alliance.

The 2014 parliamentary elections saw the Grand Alliance consolidate its overwhelming dominance – ending with the Alliance winning 280 out of the 300 seats in the Jatiya Sangshad – but were held under deeply controversial circumstances. Major opposition parties boycotted the election citing government oppression, leaving 154 out of 300 constituencies uncontested. During the campaign, BNP leader Khaleda Zia was placed under house arrest. Tensions intensified following the execution of senior Jamaat-e-Islami figure Abdul Quader Mollah for crimes committed during the 1971 Liberation War. The lead-up to the election was marred by widespread arrests of opposition political figures, destruction of private property, violence towards Bangladesh's religious minorities and state-sponsored extra-judicial killings.

While political violence and corruption are longstanding problems in Bangladesh, the Grand Alliance's apparent tilt towards authoritarianism also poses larger questions around the sustainability of fundamental progressive values in a coalition which 'games' first-past-the-post as effectively as the Grand

Alliance did in 2008, and the corrupting effects of untrammelled power.

National coalition v. local interests: the United Progressive Alliance in India (2004–2008)

Like its smaller neighbour Bangladesh, India retains FPTP for elections to the 545-member national parliament the Lok Sabha (House of the People). India boasts a vibrant and, indeed, to the outsider bewilderingly diverse multi-party democracy, traditionally dominated by the secular/social-democratic Indian National Congress (INC) and the Hindu-chauvinist, socially conservative Bharatiya Janata Party (BJP), but with as many as forty regional parties finding parliamentary representation, the two larger parties have long fashioned electoral alliances to achieve governing majorities. The size and diversity of India, as well as governmental traditions, mean there is also a powerful and long-established tier of regional government unlike anything in the UK. As we will see, this has recently created ultimately insuperable difficulties for the long-term maintenance of stable coalitions/alliances.

The United Progressive Alliance (UPA), a coalition of left-of-centre political parties in India, came into being in the aftermath of the 2004 Indian general election. With neither the existing INC-led progressive coalition nor the BJP-led National Democratic Alliance (NDA) able to command a parliamentary majority in the Lok Sabha, the Left Front (itself in fact an alliance of Marxist parties in West Bengal), Samajwadi Party and Bahujan Samaj Party opted to offer 'external support' to the UPA. These leftist parties, despite having ideological differences with INC, supported the Alliance in order to ensure a secular government for India. The BJP has often been accused by secular political parties of pursuing an aggressive Hindu supremacist agenda. Along with other minor parties such as Janata Dal (secular), the Left parties collectively promised to support a UPA government if it faced a vote of no confidence. This was in effect a 'confidence and supply' arrangement familiar to observers of Westminster-style politics, though unusual in being a multi- (rather than two-) party agreement with moreover an overriding ideological objective.

However, the UPA quickly began to encounter difficulties, largely due to intra-coalition disputes at state level. Marumalarchi Dravida Munnetra Kazhagam (MDMK) began to drift away from the alliance after co-operating with the UPA-rival All-India Anna Dravida Munnetra Kazhagam in the Tamil Nadu state elections and officially exited the coalition in March 2007. The Bahujan Samaj Party (BSP) withdrew its support from the UPA after Congress began opposing the Uttar Pradesh state government – where the BSP were the ruling party. Finally, the People's Democratic Party (PDP) decided to withdraw from the UPA following Congress's decision to support a National Conference government in Jammu and Kashmir State. When the government decided to go ahead with the US–Indian nuclear deal, the Left Front withdrew support from the UPA.

The withdrawals of MDMK, BSP and PDP demonstrated the difficulties of maintaining a progressive multi-party coalition at national level when having to contend with complex state-level political dynamics. While India's unique constitutional arrangements make any UK parallels very inexact, it is easy to see that a progressive alliance or coalition at Westminster that included the SNP in particular could fall foul of developments in the Scottish Parliament.

The New Majority in Chile: from optimism to factionalism (2013–)

The New Majority (Nueva Mayoría) is a Chilean progressive electoral coalition established in 2013 to support the presidential candidacy of Michelle Bachelet. The New Majority consists of the four main parties of the Concert of Parties of Democracy: the Socialist Party of Chile, the Christian Democratic Party, the Party of Democracy and the Social Democrat Radical Party. In addition to these parties, the New Majority alliance includes the Communist Party of Chile, the Citizen Left, the Broad Social Movement and a group of centre-left independent politicians. In March 2014, the regionalist Northern Force Party joined the New Majority to merge with the Broad Social Movement to form MAS Region. As the above summary indicates, the New Majority is notable for its broad spectrum of political opinion, from the centrist social-market-oriented Christian Democrats to the Communist Party. This breadth gives the New Majority a strong social base, but also presents problems in terms of potential ideological and policy disputes between its constituent members.

Following her successful campaign to be the newly formed New Majority's sole presidential candidate, Bachelet stated the coalition's central objective would be establishing a system of universal and free access to higher education within a six-year timeframe. Bachelet's principal opponent in the 2013 presidential election was Evelyn Matthei – candidate for the right-wing, conservative alliance Alianza. Matthei's party, the Independent Democratic Union (UDI), was founded by Jaime Guzman – a former civilian collaborator of military dictator Augusto Pinochet.

The 2013 elections were a resounding success for the New Majority. Following a second-round run-off, Bachelet won

62.16 per cent of the vote, soundly defeating Matthei. In the parliamentary elections, New Majority gained control of both chambers of Congress – holding twenty-one out of thirty-eight seats in the Senate and sixty-seven out of 120 seats in the Chamber of Deputies.

However, New Majority has encountered difficulties under Bachelet's presidency, and at the time of writing faces complex challenges as the November 2017 elections draw near. A sluggish economy, mismanagement of key reforms and a spate of political scandals have done serious damage to the progressive alliance's electoral credibility. Intra-coalition tensions between constituent parties have given rise to questions over the New Majority's cohesiveness and ability to provide stable government. Disputes between the right (Christian Democrat) and left (Communist) factions of the alliance on issues such as taxation and higher education have exposed fundamental incompatibilities within the coalition.

To make matters worse, there has also been the rejuvenation of Chilean conservative politics, with a host of centre-right parties rallying as a bloc around former President Sebastian Pinera. This new 'Let's Go Chile' (Chile Vamos) alliance was created in January 2015 from four constituent parties – UDI, National Renewal, Independent Regionalist Party and Political Evolution. As elsewhere, one sees that progressive alliances – if successful – almost inevitably generate corresponding alliances on the Right.

Perhaps the most worrying political development for the New Majority has been the creation of the Broad Front (not to be confused with the Uruguayan alliance of the same name) in early 2017. Composed of left-wing parties such as Democratic Revolution, the Humanist Party and Power, the Broad Front intends to contest the November 2017 elections and threatens to appeal to leftist New Majority supporters who have become disillusioned under Bachelet's presidency. With a splintered left vote and the resurgence of centre-right conservative politics, the New Majority's tumultuous period in power is in danger of being brought to a halt in the coming elections.

Portugal: European poster child of the Progressive Alliance (2015–)

Current Portuguese Prime Minister Antonio Costa established a left-wing coalition following the 2015 legislative election. The incumbent centre-right Portugal Ahead coalition, composed of the liberal-conservative Social Democratic Party (PSD) and Christian-democratic People's Party (CDS), won the largest share of the vote (38.6 per cent) and secured 46 per cent of the seats in the 230-member unicameral Portuguese Assembly.[22] Costa's Socialist Party (PS) won 32.3 per cent of the vote and 37 per cent of seats. Although the parliamentary arithmetic enabled the PS and other left-wing parties to fashion a progressive coalition with a parliamentary majority, Costa was initially reluctant to establish what he labelled at the time a 'negative coalition'.

However, after rejecting a 'national unity' coalition with Portugal Ahead, the PS, the Left Bloc, the Portuguese Communist Party and the Greens commenced negotiations to form a left-wing majority coalition. Whether, given the significant policy differences between the left parties, these discussions would have borne fruit had not Portuguese President Aníbal Cavaco Silva controversially nominated Portugal Ahead to form a new

---

22 Portugal's proportional electoral system allocates seats from central party lists across domestic and overseas multi-member constituencies using the d'Hondt formula.

government, is unknowable. In the event, Portugal Ahead's programme was rejected in parliament by 127 votes to 103, and following an agreement between the PS, Left Bloc, the Communists and the Greens, a minority government led by Costa, with 'external support' from the other left-wing parties, was formed in November 2015.

This surprise alliance of left parties was initially unthinkable. The moderate centre-left Socialist Party includes politicians sympathetic to Blair's 'Third Way' and Schröder's 'Neue Mitte' neoliberal economic agendas. In contrast, the radical Left Bloc has close ties with Greece's far-left anti-austerity Syriza. The long-established Portuguese Communist Party, which holds to a traditional Marxist–Leninist stance, campaigned on policy pledges such as the nationalisation of Portugal's banking sector and energy industries. Both the Communist Party and Left Bloc have extra-parliamentary wings and encouraged mass disobedience in opposition to austerity, as well as sharing a desire for Portugal to exit NATO.

The eventual agreement between the moderate PS and the coalition parties further to its left entailed a moderating of the latter's more hard-line positions, with the PS insisting on abiding by the EU's budget deficit rules and the Eurozone's financial rules. Costa's broader economic agenda placed importance on reassuring investors and fellow EU member states that Portugal would continue to respect its existing international commitments. What ultimately enabled this unprecedented left alliance to coalesce was a shared desire to oust the fiscally conservative Portugal Ahead alliance and ease its socially ruinous austerity policies. The constituent parties in the alliance could agree relatively easily on domestic economic measures such as the reversal of salary and pension cuts for state employees, the restoration of four public holidays scrapped by Portugal Ahead, and the raising of Portugal's national minimum wage.

Predictably, the 'moderate' wing of the PS expressed reservations over the agreement, with politicians such as Francisco Assis arguing the PS would have been wiser to remain in opposition and shape the agenda of a minority Portugal Ahead government as opposed to being 'held to ransom' by the radical left. However, and despite the Eurozone's ongoing difficulties at the start of his administration, Costa's minority government, externally supported by parties to his left, has presided over a period of rising wages along with the delivery of relatively low budget deficits. A March 2017 poll placed the governing Socialist Party on 42 per cent – a 10-percentage-point increase from its vote share in the 2015 election.

Beyond coalition: the Labour–Green Memorandum of Understanding (New Zealand 2017–)

In June 2016, New Zealand's Labour and Green parties signed a historic agreement – a Memorandum of Understanding (MoU) – to fight the conservative National Party government in the run-up to the next election (to be held before November 2017). It is the first such agreement between the two parties. The agreement – which lasts only until the election and does not commit the parties to a formal coalition – states the two parties will 'work together in good faith and mutual trust' in order to defeat the conservative National party in 2017. It also lays out the possibility of a joint policy announcement or campaign.

The background to the MoU lies in a lengthy and largely unsatisfactory period of Labour-led coalition government under Helen Clarke from 1999 to 2008, after the 1999, 2002 and 2005 general elections all produced hung parliaments.

In 1999, a coalition of Labour – a moderate centre-left party – and the democratic socialist Alliance – which had actively positioned itself as a left-wing alternative to Labour – replaced the National Party, receiving parliamentary support on a 'confidence and supply' basis from the Greens. However, by the end of Clarke's first term as prime minister, divisions between the Alliance parliamentary party and the mass membership threatened to split the party. While the parliamentary party was relatively willing to support the Labour government, Alliance activists were less willing to do so, viewing the Alliance's participation in the government as a betrayal of its democratic socialist principles. This spilled over into a bitter personal dispute between leading Alliance politician Jim Anderton and party president Matt McCarten – with Anderton eventually leaving the party and forming a new party of his own: the Progressive Party. In the ensuing 2001 general election, the Alliance failed to win a single seat, while Anderton's Progressive Party won two. The election was also marked by growing tensions between the Labour Party and the Greens, particularly on the issue of agricultural genetic modification, which Labour supported while the Greens were strongly opposed – leading to Clarke labelling the Greens 'goths and anarcho-feminists'. In the wake of these events, in both 2001 and 2005, Labour formed coalitions with Anderton's Progressive Party and gained 'confidence and supply' support from the centrist, socially liberal United Future and (in 2005) another centrist party, NZ First, while the Greens supported the government on selected issues only.

Clarke and Labour were finally defeated in 2008 by the National Party, which has now had three consecutive terms in power. Since Clarke's departure, Labour has failed to find a leader who can match National Party PM John Key's charisma and widespread popularity. The Labour–Green MoU has opened up the possibility of a new era of (in Labour leader Andrew Little's words) 'stable, credible and progressive alternative government' in New Zealand, established on a more durable basis than the ad hoc coalitions of 1999–2008. The MoU included a 'no surprises' policy, meaning each party will inform the other of upcoming major speeches or policy announcements; it proposed co-operation in the 2016 local elections; and established monthly meetings between the two parties. Little declared the MoU to be 'a fresh start and a sign of newfound strength in our relationship and our mutual commitment to changing the Government.' Green Party co-leader Metiria Turei said the two parties were stronger together than apart. 'We are separate parties with our own policies and ideas, but with more than enough in common to work together.'

Although the pact does not include NZ First, whose support is widely seen as crucial, Labour and the Greens have kept the door open to forging agreements with other parties. 'We are both agreed this is not a monogamous relationship,' Little has said. 'We are determined to work together, to achieve a change of government, and a government that offers a genuinely progressive programme and we welcome any other party who will join us for those two objectives.'

On the day the Memorandum of Agreement was signed, each party tweeted a heart symbol to the other on its official feed.

•   •   •

The Labour–Green Memorandum of Understanding is only the most recent – but in some ways the most mature and potentially sustainable – of many examples of pre- and post-electoral pacts and coalitions, some of which have been discussed here. The New Zealand MoU, unlike many such arrangements, opens up the possibility of policy co-ordination and debates (well short of a joint platform) and a variety of trust-building collaborative arrangements – such as co-operation in local elections – that could enable the two parties to present voters with a stable and coherent partnership by the time of the general election. It styles itself explicitly as a progressive alliance and may offer a model for the kind of arrangements available in the UK's comparable political culture.

This selective account of progressive alliances and coalitions, past and future, makes one thing plain: how difficult fashioning and sustaining such arrangements invariably is, regardless of different electoral systems and social or political contexts. But progressive parties worldwide continue to make the effort: not solely to gain power for power's sake, but because centre-left movements and political parties periodically recognise that they can achieve more working together than in competition with one another – and that after all in collaborating they are doing no more than fulfil their own common ethos. The various successes, failures and fates of the individual alliances discussed here are of course inextricably bound up with their immediate political contexts and cultures. In that sense, general lessons are hard to draw. But one universal truth can be readily acknowledged: all of these often stressful and contentious attempts to bridge differences amongst centre-left parties succeeded, if in some cases only for a short period, in bringing to power progressive governments that would otherwise never have seen the light of day, and forestalled the often reactionary right-wing administrations that would have taken their place.

So as difficult and frustrating as this process can be, the

struggle is worth it – as a final cautionary historical example amply shows.

The SPD and KPD non-pact: the collapse of Weimar democracy and the rise of the Nazis (1919–1933)

The German Social Democrats (SPD) have a long, rich and often proud history, but their calamitous defence of the Weimar Republic and failure to forge a fraternal compact with the Communist Party have been pinpointed as fatal factors in the Nazis' eventual seizure of power in Germany.

The SPD was arguably the one major political party which truly identified with the democratic German Republic promulgated in Weimar following Germany's military collapse in the First World War – wishing to defend the republic from attacks by both the radical right and the left. The prime movers of the democratic Weimar constitution arising from the 1918 November Revolution – brought about by not only the trauma of defeat itself but also the extreme economic hardships suffered by Germans in the final months of the war and the crisis of legitimacy of the governing Imperial aristocratic–military elite – the SPD proved willing to sponsor brutal crackdowns on the radical (Communist) left in the revolution's aftermath. The SPD essentially allied itself with traditional economic and military elites against Bolshevism in the process of establishing a democratic parliamentary republic which preserved capitalist property relations – most infamously, in the crushing of the Spartacist uprising of January 1919, culminating in the murder of the German Communist leaders Rosa Luxemburg and Karl Liebknecht by ultra-right paramilitaries. The legacy of these decisions taken in the frantic and chaotic early months of the Weimar Republic was an enduring poisonous hostility between the SPD and the reconstituted German Communist Party (KPD) to its left.

Having thus broken decisively with its nineteenth-century origins in revolutionary Marxism, the SPD as the pre-eminent 'party of Weimar' staked its authority and reputation on the parliamentary republic and on market capitalism's ability to deliver broad-based prosperity. However, the party's thorough-going identification with the Weimar Republic meant that as the Republic lurched from one crisis to another – most damagingly, the Great Inflation of 1923 which intensified Germany's already pronounced social stratification and irre-trievably alienated large sections of the politically moderate middle class, whose savings were rendered worthless – meant that almost inevitably it came to be seen on both left and right as the symbol of a failing system. As the original SPD-led 'Weimar coalition' faltered, the SPD found itself first sharing power (from 1928 to 1930) with conservative–nationalist and bourgeois parties, and then excluded from office altogether as Germany was governed from 1930 by a succession of right-wing, increasingly authoritarian governments. In the depths of the Great Depression, Chancellor Heinrich Brüning of the Catholic Centre Party imposed policies of savage austerity and deflation, leaving Germany with a ravaged welfare state, depressed wages, high indirect taxes and calamitous unemployment.

As Weimar Germany entered its terminal crisis, support for the hitherto politically marginal Nazi Party surged. At the same time, a growing section of the SPD's working-class base turned to the revolutionary solutions offered by the KPD. Although Hitler regarded the parties of the democratic and revolutionary left with undifferentiated hostility and contempt, the SPD and KPD saw one another as treacherous political foes. The SPD's mechanical defence of the Weimar Republic from radical forces meant that it essentially viewed communism and Nazism as 'equal dangers' to German parliamentary republican democracy. For its part the KPD, keeping the memory of the SPD's involvement in crushing the 1919 insurgency still fresh and wholly unforgiven, treated the Social Democrats ('social fascists') rather than the Nazis as their chief enemy, a pro-capitalist organisation which had duped and ultimately betrayed the German working classes through its pseudo-socialist rhetoric. Despite the manifest and spiralling threat of Nazism, throughout the early 1930s, the leaderships of the SPD and KPD (whose policy in any event was ultimately dictated by Stalin) were never able to reach any agreement on how the common and universal danger of Nazism might be addressed and challenged.

As a tragic-ironic coda, in the last free and fair all-German election in November 1932, no single party won the 293 seats required to command a parliamentary majority in the Reichstag. The Nazis won 196 seats; a hypothetical SPD–KPD anti-Nazi bloc would have held 221. Though the collapse of popular support for the Weimar Republic would in any case have left the parties of the left short of potential allies for any coalition that might have prevented a Hitler government, their internecine hostility ensured that the subsequent manoeuvres that eventually led to the Nazis taking power in January 1933 took place entirely within the circles of the authoritarian nationalist right. The left was excluded from the death throes of the Weimar Republic, and within months it, and millions more, would be silenced altogether.

CHAPTER FIVE

THE CAMPAIGN PART II: 6–27 MAY

At a Richmond public meeting on 7 May Vince Cable remarked that, were he resident in Ealing Central & Acton, as a Liberal Democrat he would 'find it difficult to vote against' Labour's Rupa Huq. His comments, secretly taped by a Tory mole, were splashed across the right-wing press the following morning beneath hysterical headlines declaiming dirty dealing by Corbynite fellow travellers. But from Compass's perspective, if the blackshirts at the *Mail* were sufficiently rattled to shriek about 'an extraordinary endorsement of Jeremy Corbyn's "coalition of chaos"' the PA must have been doing something right. Its enemies' alarm testified that the idea of the Progressive Alliance was starting to gain political traction. A month out from polling day, the job was to make sure all the *Mail*'s nightmares came true.

Instrumentality

A spectre stalked the cookie-strewn offices of the Progressive Alliance: the spectre of instrumentality. The term originally surfaced in an internal position paper – one of many attempts at a succinct, forceful, rigorous and user-friendly account of PA. It pointed out that in its novel focus on the mechanisms of electoral politics, gaming the broken system of FPTP to achieve progressive ends, the PA campaign could end up a prisoner of the mentality it sought to end. In particular, how the PA approached the progressive voters it aimed to enlist, and the organisations and institutions of the progressive political parties themselves – especially Labour, with its tradition of bureaucratic direction from the top and suspicion of alternate political cultures. Under-discussed in press accounts of Labour's internecine strife under Corbyn, given the readymade 'Trots v. social democrats' narrative a lazy and under-resourced political press corps found far easier to comprehend and promote, was the cultural divide separating the professionalised politics of the PLP, the unions and the Labour bureaucracy they jointly controlled from the stubbornly utopian, determinedly unprofessional style of the voluntary party of which Corbyn was exemplar and tribune.

The problem was briefly summarised. Should the Progressive Alliance ever be actualised, the Tory press would instantly denounce it as an anti-democratic 'stitch-up' (an ironic charge given May's explicitly stated aim when calling the election of delegitimising parliamentary opposition, if not eliminating it outright). The PA team feared PA could indeed become a stitch-up: *if* it became a means of preserving politics as usual rather than transforming it. If the PA argument did ever find a receptive ear in Labour in particular (the most thoroughly wedded to the old politics, from its persistence with FPTP to its sclerotic, hierarchical internal structures), it would be Compass's essential task to ensure that any agreement didn't seek to 'instrumentalise' centre-left voters – that is, to treat them as a homogeneous bloc, deliverable on an agreement signed and sealed in the proverbial smoke-filled (these days, vapour-filled) room. Everyone involved agreed that this was the exact opposite of the PA campaign's aims. In fact, as far as Neal Lawson was concerned, if PA was approached or even achieved in a spirit of politics as usual it would not only be bound to fail – it would deserve to. That had never been Compass's approach to politics – hence the decision to broaden its base and open up to members of all parties, and none – and it couldn't, shouldn't and, if Lawson had anything to say about it, wouldn't be the approach the PA took either.

So, for example, when Mike Freedman suggested – following Len McCluskey's public statement that a 'good' outcome for Labour (translated: an outcome that could preserve Jeremy Corbyn's leadership) would be returning 200 MPs – that the PA present itself to Unite as the best means to improve such a dismal scenario, an alarmed Lawson quickly hit the pause button. From his time working under Gordon Brown, Lawson had more first-hand experience of union bosses than most in the PA team and laboured under no illusions that they played by very different rules than Compass. 'These people are the worst instrumental players on the pitch' he warned in an email: 'they will eat us for breakfast.' Since McCluskey quickly rowed back on his defeatist comments, the issue became moot. But the point had been made: *how* PA worked mattered as much as *what* it achieved.

From then on, 'instrumentality' became the PA benchmark for what '60s US radicals used to call a 'gut check' – the instinctive sense of whether your actions remain true to the core values you intend them to serve. For Compass, not only could the end (a Tory defeat/a progressive majority) never in itself justify the means: in a profound sense, the means was the end.

Compass had no interest in securing top-down PA by leaders' diktat, even if that were achievable. Rather, ongoing open and democratic debate within and between centre-left parties at every level would make the PA campaign a genuinely democratic, participatory exercise for all progressives. Not only would this be more likely to forge alliances that were durable, grounded and ultimately effective (in persuading a strong majority of progressives of all stripes to support a candidate from a single mutually agreed party), but it would itself exemplify the principles of collaboration, open conversation, curiosity and pluralism that alone, in Compass's view, could deliver meaningful change for the better once electoral success was secured: PA, mindfully undertaken, would be the change it wanted to see.

The gut check was a regular necessity because, in committing itself to electioneering, Compass was already entering foreign territory, the preserve of party machines, databases, voter ID, get-out-the-vote and all the other necessary, but reductive, techniques that had so debased the coinage of contemporary electoral democracy. Never mind that in modern campaigning, viral Facebook memes and Snapchat had supplanted party election broadcasts and public meetings (though the latter, at least, were to make a surprising comeback in the 2017 election), the mind-set was the same. On everyone's mind were Ed Miliband's infamous '4 million conversations' he hoped would win him the 2015 election. In reality, 4 million exercises in voter identification – 'Hello, are you going to support Labour in this year's general election? Thank you very much' – fell far short of what any normal person would consider a conversation. The PA campaign was grounded in a conviction that a genuinely transformative progressive politics required real, not simulated or scripted conversations: conversations that didn't simply aim to draw voters' attention to a given party's retail offer on energy prices or pensions, but allowed people to express their hopes, their dreams and their desires for a better world.

Like others in the PA team, Frances Foley felt passionately that there was a genuine hunger for an authentic political conversation – a hunger that not only went unassuaged but was actually intensified by the way politics as usual was conducted. Her previous work for Unlock Democracy, which included organising political discussions with serving prisoners on the nature and unequal distribution of power, had persuaded her that the measurable decline in mass political engagement since the mid-twentieth century – what the punditocracy were quick to dismiss as feckless apathy – was in truth often people's considered abstention from a system that had ceased to speak to them. Even the kneejerk throwaway that 'they're all the same' – so often heard on broadcast *vox pops* and so infuriating to the professional political classes, well aware of their often profound differences with their political opponents – lazy and ill-informed as it might be, bespoke a desire for a politics beyond the Gadarene rush towards the sliver of the 'centre ground' on which British elections were traditionally fought.

So, as the campaign drew to its midpoint, while keeping a firm grasp of the electoral wheel the PA also started to raise its eyes to the post-election horizon. When (as everyone was still firmly anticipating) progressive voters awoke on 9 June to find Theresa May celebrating her significantly increased majority, it would be important that the PA campaign had not been so narrowly focused that electoral success became the sole benchmark of its achievements. Rather than take the inevitably frustrating result as outright failure, the PA hoped that the values and possibilities and relationships its campaign had opened up would enable disappointment to be channelled effectively and quickly into ongoing organising and activism for the future.

How to enable such conversations in the midst of an election campaign that still needed to manage the brute politics of motivating progressive voters to the polls in sufficient numbers, and with sufficient clarity of understanding about the electoral process, was the million-dollar question. It was hard enough for Lawson and other PA spokespersons to make the point in media appearances that Compass's approach to PA was about more than just tactical voting. But the PA were convinced that people of all political convictions harboured a genuine appetite for the chance to speak their minds, to be listened to, to engage authentically with those who they agreed with and those they didn't and not to be endlessly 'managed' by campaign strategies that insulted not only their intelligence but also their hearts and the integrity of their hopes and dreams. The Bernie Sanders insurgency in the 2016 US Democratic Party primary campaign had demonstrated it. In a perverse and self-defeating way, Donald Trump's campaign had demonstrated it, too. And, in short order, Jeremy Corbyn would prove this wasn't simply an American phenomenon. But for now, the PA – inheriting in this regard the mantle of the 1960s counterculture – had to take the risk of committing to a radical authenticity in what it did and how it worked as well as what it believed, in the genuine conviction that, ultimately, there was no other way.

The Greens: stick or twist?

Approaching 11 May, the filing deadline for the election – the latest date on which candidates could be placed on (or withdrawn from) the ballot paper – the leadership of the Green Party found themselves on the horns of a painful dilemma.

Since the start of the campaign, the Greens had taken concrete steps towards PA in over two dozen constituencies, standing down candidates in favour of Labour or the Liberal Democrats. But little about the process had gone quite how Caroline Lucas and her co-leader Jonathan Bartley had intended or hoped, and the party was now facing a near-crisis. Every day seemed to bring news of another Green stand-aside. And the larger centre-left parties – while generally (in Labour's case, flatly) refusing to enter into any reciprocal arrangements themselves – now seemed to be operating almost with the expectation that Green candidates would step down wherever it suited their (Labour and the Lib Dems') interests. Local Green parties who had not yet stood down their candidates were reporting tremendous pressure on them to do so, particularly on social media, where it amounted at times to virtual bullying. The party's national vote was set to decline dramatically, which in itself would have significant consequences in terms of its entitlement to Short money (public money supporting opposition parties, which is calculated largely on the basis of national vote share). All this confronted the Greens' leadership with an agonising choice. For the past month, the party had flown the rainbow flag of a centre-left electoral alliance, but by the end of that month, they still seemed to be the only ones gathered round the standard. Should they stand by the mast – even if it meant going down with the ship? Or was it time to chart a different course, even at this late hour?

The problem went back to the motion authorising local Green parties to explore alliances, which had been overwhelmingly passed at the Greens' spring conference just six weeks earlier (a bare fortnight before May called the election). Carefully worded, the motion referred to electoral alliances rather than progressive ones – reflecting that many Greens disputed the Lib Dems' (or indeed Labour's) 'progressive' qualifications given their commitment to ongoing economic growth, as well as the leadership's view (chiming with that of Compass) that a 'progressive alliance' proper entailed far more than simply gaming the electoral system. The motion also stressed that the immediate goal was, above all, to achieve electoral reform, the only means by which the Greens could realistically hope to break through at national level from their current solitary beachhead in Brighton Pavilion. So it seemed Green parties should actively seek, at the very least, public commitments from other parties' candidates to proportional representation before agreeing to stand aside in their favour.

Three clauses in this motion would have far-reaching and largely unintended consequences. First, in keeping with the Greens' decentralised, ultra-democratic party rules, the motion stressed that the initiative for forming alliances rested solely with local parties. The national party would advise, but not instruct. Anticipating opposition to the motion from local Green parties who had been assiduously working their seats, the leadership had intended this clause to signal that local parties would not be forced to step aside against their will. In fact, as foreshadowed by the size of the majority (over 90 per cent) in favour of the alliance proposal, if anything it was received rather as a green light for parties throughout the country actively to set about exploring the prospects for alliances and Green stand-asides. Two friendly amendments were also included in the final motion: one removed the assumption that alliances would be negotiated only in a minority of constituencies; the other committed the national party to actively promote electoral alliances when local parties had voted in favour of one. The first of these raised the prospect of Green step-asides becoming a nationwide norm; the second ensured that the Green Party nationally – which for media purposes meant Caroline Lucas – would be very strongly associated in the public eye with the cause of electoral (or, notwithstanding the motion's squeamishness on the term, progressive) alliances.

Even if the potential implications of all of these elements were not fully gathered in April, the leadership anticipated having plenty of time to address them before the issue went live at the next general election. While Lucas's office expected May would call an election well before 2020, by early April they had come to believe that, before making a decision, she would wait (like Thatcher in 1983) for the local elections in May to confirm her position in the opinion polls, in which case September/October would be the earliest plausible general election date – thereby giving the Green leadership the summer to equip local parties at the very least with the necessary negotiating skills to ensure Green electoral sacrifices wouldn't go entirely unrecompensed by other parties. So May's 18 April announcement caught the Greens slightly off-guard and ensured that, given the radically collapsed timeframe and the party's tiny resources, there was no chance to undertake this vital groundwork.

As soon as the election was called, Caroline Lucas wrote an open letter to Tim Farron and Jeremy Corbyn inviting them to discuss an anti-Tory alliance. She was gambling there were senior staffers in both parties – especially the Liberal Democrats – who were sympathetic to the idea, but she had few illusions about her prospects of instant acceptance.[23] Still, she thought that – not least in light of the other parties' desperate

---

23 Some YouGov polling and anecdotal evidence also suggested that there were Labour members who were enthusiastic about working with other parties.

positions in the polls – there might have been some indication of openness, even if this first move took the form of a painless sacrifice in some utterly unwinnable seat somewhere. Instead, as far as Labour in particular were concerned, her proposal slammed head-first into adamantine rejection – founded as far as it was possible to tell in the Corbynites' deep-seated conviction that, given the fuller and fairer airing for the party's platform that they hoped and expected from an election campaign, Labour (and only Labour) would be propelled upwards in the polls by a kind of popular uprising. For the Liberal Democrats, however, it was the opposite problem: still convinced that Corbyn was 'electorally toxic', they were deeply reluctant to take any steps that could see them accused of working towards a Corbyn premiership.

So, if an alliance were to materialise, very evidently the Greens were going to have to make the first move – and equally clearly, given the reserve or outright hostility of national leaderships, progress would require good personal relations at local level. The first such arrangement of the campaign was reached within days of the election being called in Ealing Central & Acton, where Labour's Rupa Huq was desperate to defend her tiny majority of 274. Huq committed to support PR, fight for tougher action on climate change, oppose a hard Brexit and continue to consult regularly with local Greens if re-elected. The arrangement was taken independently of the Greens' national leadership, but from their point of view, in the absence of reliable dance partners fully signed up to an electoral alliance (entailing reciprocal stand-asides on behalf of Green candidates elsewhere), Ealing offered a model of good practice. Unfortunately, the model was never consistently adopted elsewhere.

As the campaign got going in earnest, local Green parties

almost seemed to be in competition with one another in their haste to stand down their candidates. The leadership believe that, without question, the extremity of the national political situation – desperate times calling for desperate measures – contributed to a situation where many Greens saw the formation of an anti-Conservative front as an overriding imperative well beyond party loyalty, and not only accepted but welcomed their sacrifice in order to be part of such a movement. Unfortunately, the other parties didn't seem to share the sentiment. As the number of Green stand-asides steadily mounted, approaching forty by the start of the week of the filing deadline, Neal Lawson and the PA were quick to publicly applaud each 'courageous and unselfish step'. But, while Lucas, Bartley and their colleagues shared the desire to limit the Tories' hold on power, they were also committed to growing the Greens' presence in British politics, and they suspected that some in the Labour Party especially regarded that presence as irrelevant or even illegitimate. Put bluntly, some Labourites just didn't take the Greens that seriously and held the view that, if you were really serious about changing the country, you should join the Labour Party. It also quickly became clear that in many seats Greens were standing aside (or indeed failing to select candidates in the first place – contrary to explicit advice from the leaders' office, conscious that if parties failed even to go through the motions of standing they would derive themselves of crucial bargaining power) without obtaining the most minimal gestures or even acknowledgment by the (mostly Labour) beneficiaries of their actions.

To some extent, Caroline Lucas was a victim of her own success in advocating for a collaborative left politics. Many local Greens saw her widely reported support for PA over many months as effectively a premature endorsement of moves to stand candidates aside. Although the national leadership had never anticipated stand-asides in more than a minority of exclusively marginal seats, ideally always linked explicitly to support for PR, the clauses in the conference motion that granted local parties almost total autonomy over their decision to run or not – and that allowed for alliances and stand-asides in effectively unlimited numbers of seats – weakened inhibitions in local parties about the larger consequences of a flood of Green candidate withdrawals. By early May, there was a growing backlash from party members who – whatever their views on electoral alliances in principle – feared an unregulated tsunami of stand-asides that could see the Greens reduced to the fringe status they had endured (as the Ecology Party) in the 1970s. There was also a widespread feeling that other parties, insofar as they were playing at all, weren't playing by the same rules. For example, Lib Dem demands that Lewes Greens stand down their candidate in return for the Lib Dems' relatively stress-free withdrawal in neighbouring Brighton Pavilion were described by local Greens as 'emotional blackmail'.

Lucas and Bartley shared these concerns. They also increasingly felt that the whole notion of progressive/electoral alliance had become confused with, if not simply folded into, the much narrower issue of tactical voting – which the Greens had never endorsed. The Greens resisted tactical voting as a generalised tactic for reasons both principled – the problem, so familiar to Compass, of an overly mechanistic, 'instrumental' approach to politics – and very practical. As the likeliest party to see its vote squeezed by tactical voting in 571 of 573 seats in England and Wales (all bar Brighton Pavilion and – possibly – Isle of Wight: see below), the Greens simply couldn't afford to be seen urging tactical voting in general if they hoped to survive as a national party. In the crucible of the election campaign, the Greens' visionary wood of a transformed politics through a progressive alliance threatened to become lost amidst the trees of electoral calculus – in fact, they risked ending up with neither wood nor trees. The Progressive Alliance's vote recommendation (through the VoteSmart tool on the PA website) of 'any progressive party' rather the Greens in Bristol West – the only seat in the country where the Greens had finished second in 2015, with the Conservatives a feeble fourth 5,500 votes behind, double that behind Labour, and out of the running – though consistent with the PA's governing algorithm for non-marginals, for many Greens rubbed salt into the wound.[24] The party confronted a performative contradiction: one which seemingly required it to annihilate itself in the cause of a more plural politics that wouldn't, apparently, include any Greens.

In these circumstances, as the filing deadline neared, the national leadership felt they had no choice but to try to draw a line in the sand. Just forty-eight hours before the deadline, Caroline Lucas and Jonathan Bartley put out a statement that, with an unmistakable undertone of bitterness, accused the other parties 'betraying the people they represent' by failing to respond to the Greens' example. 'The time has now come,' she declared, 'for the Greens to focus entirely on winning votes up and down the country.' The Greens' highly devolved structures meant this Churchillian 'stand your ground' edict lacked any real constitutional purchase beyond the leaders' (especially

---

24 Labour's eventual majority increased almost sevenfold, from 5,673 in 2015 to an extraordinary 37,336. The Green vote almost halved, and the party finished narrowly third behind the Tories. The PA took the view that its policy was consistent, refraining from making specific recommendations in non-marginals. The real problem was with heavily-trafficked sites such as www.tactical2017.com, *The Guardian* website, and others that indiscriminately recommended Labour votes in non-marginals like Bristol West and Holborn & St Pancras.

Lucas's) personal authority: fortunately, from their perspective, this was considerable. The party in the country responded and the stand-asides stopped.

For Neal Lawson and the Progressive Alliance, this move was a last-minute change of heart that risked confusing and undermining the principle on which until then the Greens had so creditably stood. While sympathetic to Lucas's position and her party's plight, he saw it as betraying a fundamental naivety that the Greens seemed to have been so unprepared for an eventuality – that Labour and the Lib Dems wouldn't show up at the party – that, after all, had always been possible if not probable. It may have been a snap election, but it was always going to be a long game. In Lawson's view, having raised the standard of the progressive alliance, the Greens should have played their string to the end. They had stuck when they should have twisted. But, then, some Greens (unfairly) even regarded Lawson himself – notwithstanding his self-description at the fateful spring conference as a 'green liberal socialist' – with suspicion for his long history with Labour. As the PA campaign proved again and again, relationships and trust weren't easy to build, manage or sustain. For her own part, Caroline Lucas didn't and couldn't regard heroic martyrdom as a sustainable basis for her party's long-term prospects. Her office had no doubt that, without the national leadership's intervention, fifty or more additional Green candidates would have stepped down by the Thursday deadline, with damaging and potentially hard-to-retrieve consequences.

What nobody knew – and until votes were actually cast, couldn't know – was whether, notwithstanding the leadership's last-minute move, Green voters would interpret the party's now very public identification with the campaign for a progressive alliance as an invitation to vote tactically in constituencies where Greens were fielding a candidate – and, if so, what impact this might have on the outcome of the election a whole.

Tribes

Why was it proving so hard to get Labour and the Lib Dems even to talk seriously about PA, let alone to participate? What part of 'we're all in this together', wondered Neal Lawson, didn't they get?

If the Progressive Alliance had one over-arching concept, it was the principle of anti-tribalism. The entire PA programme was founded on the unshakeable conviction that the zero-sum-game of conventional party politics – in which each faction claims a monopoly not only on wisdom but on moral rectitude, in which every gain for anyone not fighting under the same colours as me is experienced as a loss, and in which anyone not with me is against me – was a busted flush. In fact, to most involved with the PA campaign, it seemed plain silly. Zoe Williams said she found it laughable. In a society where social identities and groupings – like family arrangements, gender and sexuality, working patterns, right down to one's choice of energy and internet providers – were growing ever more provisional and flexible, to insist on lifelong, unquestioning fealty to the pontifical authority of the Labour Party or any other such body seemed ridiculous, out of step with the times and doomed to failure. Compass's controversial 2011 decision to open itself up to members of political parties beyond Labour – a move that undoubtedly exacted a cost in terms of the organisation's influence on Labour policymaking during the Miliband regime, when Compass might have anticipated a much more receptive hearing than in the Blair years – reflected this bottom-line commitment to pluralism as a fundamental governing principle.

Having converted itself, at least for the duration of the 2017 campaign, into an electioneering organisation, Compass was confronted squarely with a chicken/egg question: was eroding the tribal ramparts the prerequisite of forging a progressive alliance? Or was PA as a practical political tactic – a least-worst solution in a world of extremely limited options for the left – itself a means whereby tribalism could be overcome?

Even though 'tribalism' was a dirty word for the PA, that didn't mean most in Compass couldn't understand well enough why tribes persist. It isn't simply despite the mutable, mobile and networked world that had come into being in the last two decades, but in important measure because of it. Human nature aside – with its apparent hard-wired drive to belong and gather – the rapid and apparently ceaseless pace of social, economic and cultural change naturally encouraged people to hold on all the tighter to the shrinking number of institutions that seemed to offer continuity and stability – political parties amongst them. 'All that is solid melts into air,' as Marx and Engels famously described the economic and social transformations of the industrial revolution. Then, it was the great challenge of the emergent social-democratic and socialist parties to stay abreast of the new social formations brought into being by urbanisation and industrialisation. Today, many voters looked to their political representatives to arrest or mitigate the pace of the new wave of change in the globalised information age. Because the parties were ill-placed to do so – because, in fact, it couldn't be done – and because in their own eagerness to stay relevant, the old social-democratic parties in particular had in fact embraced many of the changes their core constituencies most feared, they over-compensated by shoring up the most superficial if comforting aspects of their shared group identities: us against them, my way or the highway, the only game in town. The familiar phrase 'the narcissism of small differences' aptly characterised a political world in which, precisely *because* many of the ideological divergences that formerly set clear blue water between right and left, conservatives and progressives, had been eroded by the technocratic managerialism of the neoliberal consensus, parties needed to reassure their traditional voters by emphasising above all that – still, whatever it looked like from the outside – they weren't the other guy. Political tribalism was another of Gramsci's morbid symptoms: a consequence of anxiety and ideological frailty, not of dynamism, relevance and self-confidence. Those entering the game late on and from the outside were consistently struck by the oddity of this whole setup: during the Richmond Park by-election, the Greens' Andrée Frieze noted with surprise how readily party members retreated into tribal silos and the level of sheer dislike between Labour and the Lib Dems. In her view, 'the only way to change this is through communication. Members of different parties need to work together on common aims to build up trust and understanding. It's the bunkers we put ourselves into that cause the problems.'

While understanding the problem may have helped take the edge off Compass's irritation in dealing with the resistance they met from the bastions of the old politics, it didn't mitigate the frustration one iota. Following the announcement of the election, Compass members in unwinnable Labour seats trying to move emergency motions at CLP meetings that the local party stand down its candidate in favour of (typically) an electable Liberal Democrat found themselves ruled out of order – just as Mike Freedman had been in Richmond the previous autumn – unable even to have the democratic debate they sought. Clause One of the Party rulebook was invoked as an *ex cathedra* ordinance that Labour must always field candidates[25] (though these ironclad rules seem to be malleable enough on the rare occasions when it's suited the party leadership – most famously in Tatton in 1997).[26] Change, if it was to happen, would require a major cultural shift within the party.

On 30 April, *The Guardian* published a pro-PA open letter to Labour's leadership. Stressing the gravity of the threat from a huge Tory majority, the letter applauded the Green stand-aside in Ealing Central and the Lib Dems' decision to do likewise in Brighton Pavilion and urged reciprocity from Labour in Pavilion and the Isle of Wight as a 'moral' action as well as a means to unlock precious Green votes to Labour's benefit in a swath of other seats. It was signed by Neal Lawson and Mike Freedman alongside a number of public figures including Helena Kennedy, Billy Bragg and what seemed like the entire commentariat of *The Guardian* along with three Labour MPs: not only, as expected, Clive Lewis but also London MPs Jon Cruddas and Tulip Siddiq. Their intervention marked the first time – since Lisa Nandy and Jonathan Reynolds joined him in appealing for Labour not to run a candidate in Richmond Park – that Labour MPs other than Lewis had been willing to speak out for PA.

The answering silence from the Labour leadership was deafening.

---

25 The relevant wording reads: 'The Party shall … promote the election of Labour Party representatives at all levels of the democratic process.' The fiercely limiting interpretation placed on this highly general statement by Labour Party administrators – i.e. that honouring the clause requires the Party to field candidates in all elections – is blatantly tendentious. A key argument of Labour members supporters agitating for political alliances is that by not fielding candidates in one or more unwinnable parliamentary seats (Richmond Park, say), the party will in fact far more effectively 'promote the election of Labour Party representatives' by inviting reciprocal gestures from other parties, at parliamentary or local level as it may be. In other words, not standing candidates can help fulfil the party's constitution, not confound it.

26 For a fuller account of Tatton, see 'Martyrs' below.

Everyone knew that Labour's problems with PA weren't simply a matter of a sclerotic institutional culture. As the only plausible alternative party of government – whether as a majority or minority or at the head of a coalition in which Labour would be massively the largest component – Labour inevitably received a degree of public scrutiny far more intense than that directed at any other opposition party. It was genuinely a national party, seeking to win seats in almost every region (bar the home counties) in ways that no other did or could, certainly not the diminished Liberal Democrats who at this election were a credible force in (generously) thirty seats nationwide. So, for Labour to concede there were any 'no-go' areas for the party – however blindingly obvious it was that this was so – was a much bigger deal than for the others. (The Conservatives evidently faced the same issue in swathes of immovably Labour seats: unlike Labour, however, the Tories had no alternative right-wing party to stand aside for.)

In some ways, the Liberal Democrats' reluctance to get round the PA table was even more infuriating than Labour's. Unlike Labour, the Lib Dems were committed to proportional representation – a system that all but ensured coalition governments, and thus cross-party alliances before and/or after elections. As a party, they had no culturally predisposed hostility to working with others – quite the reverse, in fact. And their traumatic experience of coalition with the Conservatives (and the electoral fallout) had made it very clear that the party's public support preferred it to hold a centre-left, not a centre-right line.[27] Yet Tim Farron's continuing quixotic

---

27 The British Election Survey in 2014 suggested that some 45 per cent of Liberal Democrat voters placed themselves on the political left, and a further 30 per cent in the centre – only 25 per cent regarded themselves as right-of-centre.

insistence on 'replacing' Labour as the principal opposition party (following on from Nick Clegg's strident denunciations of Labour during the Coalition, which had made him something of a hate figure in Labour circles and made his Sheffield Hallam seat a top Labour target) ensured that relations between the parties remained in the deep freeze. Speaking on the Andrew Marr show on 30 April, Farron declared a Conservative majority after the election was not in question, with May heading for a 'colossal coronation' – a situation that in his view rendered any discussion of either pre- or post-election party pacts with Labour 'meaningless'.

As the candidate filing deadline approached, all of these calculations and variables coalesced, improbably enough, around the Isle of Wight. This was a notional Green target seat – in truth, a very unlikely one, but a seat where Green and Labour enjoyed roughly equal vote shares and a Lib Dem/Labour stand-aside and endorsement would put the Greens in a clear second place behind the Tories. However remote the chances of a Green gain, stand-asides here by the other parties would not only have bolstered the chances of progressive gains in the 'Solent cluster' but would have been totemic: the crucial goodwill gesture that in turn would have prompted more Green stand-asides (and potentially forestalled the Greens' 'stand firm' directive), more Green activists campaigning for other parties, and more tactical voting. Throughout the febrile first week of May, an agreement hovered tantalisingly just over the horizon of political possibility. Shortly after the election was called, Roger Wilson and Steve Williams secured a trilateral meeting, brokered by the former Lib Dem MP for St Ives, Andrew George, with Lib Dem Isle of Wight council leader Daniel James and a senior local Labour figure. At this meeting all found themselves agreed in principle to back a local progressive alliance. Other local influencers including former Portsmouth council leader (and 2017 Lib Dem candidate in Portsmouth South) Gerald Vernon-Jackson came on board. But when the proposed pact – kept impressively confidential, with no leaks to the media – was passed back to the local party organisations, things went awry. The compressed timescale of the snap election may simply not have given negotiations sufficient time to mature; as it was, Labour's national leadership remained aloof, while the local Lib Dems were equally unresponsive. A local Lib Dem party meeting that Vernon-Jackson was slated to address got rescheduled at the last minute. Roger Wilson believes that the national spotlight thrown on Labour and the Lib Dems in the Isle of Wight may even have hardened local resistance to outside pressure. In the event, there would be just two Lib Dem stand-asides in this election, both in favour of the Greens – the easy feel-good win of Brighton Pavilion (few from any party on the left genuinely wanted to see Caroline Lucas defeated), and Skipton & Ripon, enabling the reciprocal Green stand-aside in nearby Harrogate & Knaresborough (where the Lib Dems were best placed but miles behind the Tories) were as far as the PA was concerned barely more than a start.

In any case, ultimately it was Labour's willingness to play ball that would determine whether the Progressive Alliance could achieve the kind of game-changing move it was aiming for. And time was running out fast now. Over the first weekend of May, Neal Lawson drafted a private letter to Jeremy Corbyn's office to press further the arguments in the open letter the previous week. He spelled out yet again the concrete gains Labour stood to make if it was prepared to stand down a single candidate in favour of the Greens in the unwinnable Isle of Wight. Lawson calculated that Labour could at a stroke shift up to a dozen Tory-held marginals into likely Labour gains by the further Green stand-asides such a gesture would encourage. The letter went to Labour HQ on the Sunday afternoon before the 11 May filing deadline. Lawson was assured that it was 'with the leader's office' and awaited Corbyn's reply. Although by this point he waited more in hope than expectation, he had also become aware that some senior Labour figures – responding to Labour MPs in vulnerable heartland seats desperate to secure the benefit of Green stand-asides – were now actively trying persuade the leadership seriously to entertain the offer. So there seemed at least a slight chance that this last roll of the dice could pay off.

It didn't. Lawson never got a reply. Or even the courtesy of an acknowledgment. But an answer in a different, even brutal, form wasn't long coming...

Martyrs

If Steve Williams was a stick of rock, he would have 'The Labour Party' imprinted all the way through him from head to toe. A softly spoken Liverpudlian long resident in the south-east, since joining the party in 1971 he has been consistently active in its cause, fighting mostly steep uphill battles in profoundly Tory parts of the country allergic to socialism in all its forms: as a parliamentary candidate in South West Surrey in 1983 where he still lives today; multiple terms as a CLP officer, even winning the (very) occasional election as a borough and town councillor; literally thousands of letterboxes leafleted, doorbells rung and miles of pavement pounded in his party's cause. But what's truly remarkable about Steve is precisely that he isn't remarkable. He typifies the lifelong immersion in and service to Labour's core values, through lean years and fat (there always seem to be more of the former), you'll encounter in constituencies the length and breadth of the country. If, despite all the crises, car crashes, divisions and disappointments over many decades, Labour can today still lay claim to be the party that best expresses the democratic, humane, inclusive and fundamentally fair spirit of ordinary Britain, it's because of the selfless commitment of people like Steve. They are Labour's lifeblood.

But, as of 4 p.m. on 8 May 2017, Steve Williams is no longer a member of the Labour Party. Neither are his SW Surrey CLP colleagues Robert Park (who first joined Labour in 1964) and Kate Townsend (Secretary of the constituency party until 8 May). They didn't resign. They were expelled, upon receipt of an email from the party's 'head of disputes', just hours before a constituency party meeting to discuss local strategy for the impending general election campaign – which, as the expulsion letter took pains to point out, they were no longer entitled to attend. Their crime? To have dared to expressed publicly their support for Louise Irvine, the Lewisham GP standing in SW Surrey as the candidate of the National Health Action Party in a direct challenge to local Conservative MP Jeremy Hunt, scourge of nurses and junior doctors, supervisor of an unprecedented crisis in NHS finances and patient care and, in a crowded field, one of the most detested politicians in the country. Steve Williams and his comrades had been recorded by BBC radio endorsing Irvine and urging Labour to stand aside its centrally imposed candidate and ally instead with others behind an indisputably progressive candidate who, with a united front behind her, might conceivably even pull off a memorable win in this otherwise rock-solid Tory seat.

Every political movement needs its martyrs. Williams, Park and Townsend were the Progressive Alliance's.

Once again, the PA's revolution was being fomented in the unlikeliest of settings. A town of half-timbered houses, ancient pubs hung with horse brasses, and detached houses down leafy lanes behind high walls and wrought-iron gates, Godalming was even more improbably radical terrain than Richmond.

Then again, Tolpuddle doesn't often vote Labour either.[28]

The Godalming Three's unintended Calvary started in 2015 and, as elsewhere, its roots lay in their reaction to that year's election results. No, not those results: Jeremy Hunt's re-election with a nearly doubled majority (almost entirely at the expense of the defenestrated Liberal Democrats) was predictable, if dispiriting. Rather, what would become the SW Surrey Progressive Alliance was called into being by the outcome of that year's local elections – further proof if any were needed of Tip O'Neill's[29] old nostrum about all politics being local. In 2015, in one of the not-uncommon near-whitewashes delivered by FPTP in local elections (and far more visibly, also that year at national level in Scotland) the Conservatives took fifty-three of the fifty-seven available seats (the other four going to independent residents' representatives), despite the three progressive parties between them polling nearly a third of the popular vote (the Tories won just over 50 per cent). The frustration at the perpetual impasse faced by the opposition parties, who demonstrated at election after election that even in such eternally Tory country they enjoyed far from negligible support individually and collectively which, however, they could never translate into more than the

---

28 Three times in the past 132 years, to be exact. Jim Knight held the seat from 2001–2010; the only previous occasion was a by-election gain in 1962, when – interestingly in light of developments nationwide a half-century later – the Tories shed some 5,000 votes to an anti-Common Market candidate.

29 A long-serving (1987–1997) Boston Democrat and Speaker of the US House of Representatives.

occasional isolated against-the-odds seat, played a major role in setting up a local chapter of Compass, chaired by Labour's Steve Williams, as a forum to enable cross-party discussion on local issues. The group – which drew over seventy people, Labour, Lib Dems, Greens and unaffiliated, to its inaugural and subsequent meetings – wasn't originally conceived as a vehicle to explore electoral pacts. In fact, it began with the explicit aim of fulfilling a felt need for substantive, detailed political discussion and debate that the local parties themselves – preoccupied as local parties tend to be with highly functional questions of electioneering, fundraising and the like – weren't truly addressing. But importantly, it also sought to define an identity for itself beyond simply 'not [or anti-] Tory', by developing a policy agenda that could put forward positive answers to pressing questions for the local community: housing, education, transport, the environment and so on. In so doing, the individuals hailing from different parties quickly discovered, and in a very concrete and practical context, that what separated them – typically different specific policy responses to problems upon whose diagnosis they agreed – was very much less important than the common values they largely shared, and which separated all of them from the Tories. As relationships and trust rapidly deepened, they found it surprisingly easy to build on their ample common ground and park their remaining – real, but not defining – differences.

By the time of the 2016 EU referendum, a culture of exchange was well established in Surrey. In part, because of this, as in Brighton and elsewhere, the local Remain campaign was a good deal more integrated across the progressive parties than the national one. The ensuing common experience of shattering defeat and sense of national crisis concentrated minds even further and a determination to try to reverse the disasters of Tory misrule – starting small and close to home – set in. A public meeting in October attracted over 250 people to a Godalming hall to hear Vince Cable, Caroline Lucas and Howard Kaye, the previous year's Labour candidate for the seat, preach the case for a progressive alliance. The local Compass chapter numbered many of the most active members of the various centre-left constituency parties and this helped ensure that, in autumn 2016, identically-worded motions supporting the principle of a progressive alliance for the following year's County Council elections, and authorising party officers to start exploring the practicalities of such a move, were passed at Labour, Liberal Democrat and Green constituency party meetings.

If 'ferment' didn't seem so out of keeping with Godalming's general air of hedge-trimmed propriety, one might have said there was a growing ferment locally around the idea of PA. And it wasn't just an idea. By the time of the next public meeting, 'Progressive Politics: Moving Forward' – prearranged, as luck would have it, for 19 April – PA was doing just that. Another large audience heard Jonathan Bartley for the Greens, Kate Parminter (Lib Dem deputy leader in the Lords) and Neal Lawson (standing in for the advertised Clive Lewis) speaking to a cause that took on acute relevance the day the Commons voted under the Fixed-Term Parliaments Act to sanction the snap election. At the meeting there was a clear enthusiasm – Robert Park calls it a 'passion' – for the idea of a single agreed progressive candidate. But locally, PA didn't have to wait till 8 June: a dress rehearsal was pending already, in the form of the 4 May County Council elections.

Off the back of the Compass-generated activity, discussions had been ongoing amongst the local parties since early in the

New Year. The positions each ultimately adopted presaged their actions in the ensuing national election campaign. The Greens expressed a readiness to participate early and consistently. Disappointingly, given the support expressed for PA by prominent (but, crucially, at the time non-elected) Lib Dems like Cable and Parminter, the Lib Dems were unable, now or later, to agree amongst themselves to commit to an electoral alliance. And as for Labour…

It's far from unusual for any of the parties, in areas where they stand little or no chance of victory, to be unable to run a full slate of candidates, particularly in local elections. So had Labour got left off the ballot paper in Surrey through ineptitude or lack of interest, no one at regional office would have turned a hair. There are, after all, more urgent battlefields for Labour than Godalming. But, when SW Surrey CLP unanimously voted not to select a candidate and endorse the Liberal Democrat's Penny Rivers in the Godalming North ward (this despite the Lib Dems' failure to reciprocate – reflecting a particularly warm and close relationship between Rivers and Labour stalwarts like Steve Williams, fostered through their common involvement with Compass), this decision for principled abstention provoked an urgent and coercive reaction. Regional officers arrived in town with instructions that candidates were to be selected – and, if necessary, imposed – upon the local party.

It wasn't only the most vocal disciples of PA who considered it stupefying for their party to be wasting time and precious resources – not to mention goodwill, with which Labour at this point was scarcely oversupplied – on pressganging candidates into unwinnable contests; not least when Labour's solitary sitting Surrey County Councillor, former MEP Robert Evans, would need all the help he could get to hold on in his Stanwell

Moor ward alongside Heathrow Airport. The local party adopted a policy of non-co-operation with the regional office's efforts. Bizarrely, however, when the music stopped, no candidate
had after all been found to run in Godalming North, though
one was successfully imposed next door in Godalming South
– thereby inadvertently creating a perfectly designed controlled
experiment in the viability of PA.

The outcome spoke for itself. In South it was business as usual:
in the absence of a progressive alliance, the Tories romped to
their expected victory. But in North, it was a different story.
Penny Rivers (whose election address quoted the murdered
Labour MP Jo Cox) was elected – the first non-Tory councillor
there in over thirty years – and left no doubt about the reasons
why: 'It just goes to show the progressive alliance can work because here I am – living proof.' PA could work, and in the most
hostile political conditions. To Williams and other members of
the local Compass chapter, Rivers's party affiliation was an irrelevance: thanks, and only thanks, to PA, their deeply blue patch
of Surrey now had an unequivocally progressive voice speaking
up on the County Council. Flushed with victory, PA supporters
immediately turned their eyes to the general election campaign
which had effectively been on hold locally during the local
elections. Just two days later, on 6 Saturday May, what would
prove to be a fateful 'Progressive Forum' public meeting was
convened with the stated aim of identifying a single progressive
candidate in SW Surrey whom all the non-Conservative parties
could support.

By this point, it had become obvious who that candidate
should be. In 2015 Louise Irvine, a Lewisham GP and BMA
Council member who had organised a successful legal challenge against the coalition government's reduction of services

at a local hospital, had run in SW Surrey against Hunt on behalf of the National Health Action Party (NHA). Having indicated her willingness to do so again, she was in attendance at that night's Progressive Forum. Also present were Susan Ryland, the Green candidate – who had already expressed her willingness to stand aside – and the Lib Dems' Ollie Purkiss. Labour's centrally imposed candidate David Black[30] refused even to attend – and prophetically warned Williams that he and others faced expulsion from the party if they persisted in their plans.

To coin a phrase: they were warned; nevertheless, they persisted.

Notwithstanding that Williams and his colleagues surely knew by now the party's hard line on alliances and stand-asides (by this point, three weeks into the national campaign, Labour's rejection of Caroline Lucas's overtures was also a matter of record), it wasn't recklessness, still less a desire for martyrdom, that prompted them to take the steps they now did. Williams harboured a slim hope, based on recent history, that here at least if not elsewhere an alliance might prevail. He was thinking of Tatton in the 1997 general election, when Labour and the Lib Dems agreed not to stand candidates to allow the white-suited former BBC foreign correspondent Martin Bell to run as a crusading independent: a clear run at the despised former Tory minister Neil Hamilton, deeply implicated in the 'cash-for-questions' scandal. Famously, Bell won, overturning Hamilton's majority of nearly 16,000. While it was becomingly ever more apparent that the battlements of deep-seated party tribalism weren't going to fall overnight, standing aside as in Tatton for an independent (an indisputably progressive one, whose positions

---

30 Labour took the decision that all seats which had yet to select a candidate at the time the election was called would be assigned one via a centrally run selection process.

on many issues echoed those of the Labour leadership) seemed eminently achievable. This in essence was the sentiment Williams, Park, and Townsend shared with BBC radio reporter Ross Hawkins after a straw poll at the Progressive Forum voted 9:1 in favour of Louise Irvine as their preferred candidate.[31]

They weren't the only ones to talk to the BBC, but they were the only ones whose views were excerpted and broadcast on the *Today* programme the following morning. Undoubtedly, it was this publicity that sealed their fate. Their expulsion followed the next business day, shortly before the scheduled CLP's campaign meeting – meaning that most members arrived at the back room in The Star pub where the meeting was to be held entirely unaware of the fate of their Secretary and two other leading members. When the news broke, there was 'bedlam', says Williams – who, now barred from attending the meeting itself, was poignantly if farcically seated with Park and Townsend at a table just outside the glass-walled room where the meeting was unfolding. Within, the CLP voted against authorising any funds whatsoever to support the local campaign, directing their support instead to the nearest key Labour marginal some thirty miles northwards in Brentford. And while Labour busily cut off its nose to spite its face, around them the Progressive Alliance became a reality. Penny Rivers not only endorsed Louise Irvine but invited her to use her house as her campaign headquarters. In return (and despite the Lib Dems voting to run a candidate in SW Surrey – at least they debated the matter) the small NHA

---

31 There was no question of the Progressive Forum, which lacked any democratic legitimacy, mandating candidates to stand aside: however, the clearly expressed sentiment, which of course included many members of political parties, could reasonably have been taken as a justification for debating the proposal within those parties. The NEC's swift action may have been intended partly to forestall this, in light of the upcoming CLP meeting.

party stood down its candidate in Oxford West & Abingdon, a tight Lib Dem–Tory marginal where the Green candidate (Larry Sanders, brother of Bernie) had already migrated to the safe Labour seat next door. On 8 June, Louise Irvine finished second to Jeremy Hunt. The 13,500 votes polled by Labour and the Lib Dems wouldn't nearly have overhauled Hunt's 21,590 majority – but then the combined Labour–Lib Dem share in Tatton in 1992 had also fallen some 7,000 votes short of Neil Hamilton. Who knows?

As for the Godalming Three, if Labour's hitmen thought that would be the end of the matter, they were wrong. The national media quickly picked up on the story – Steve Williams suspects Neal Lawson may have had a hand – and, for a few surreal days, Williams's phone was buzzing with interview requests, culminating in an appearance on the BBC's *Sunday Politics*. Far from taking the opportunity, as he could easily have done, to lambast the Labour Party, Williams calmly explained to interviewer Jo Coburn that he remained as staunch a supporter of Labour as ever. In favouring a potentially electable progressive candidate who would support a Labour government at Westminster over a futile and doomed Labour candidacy, he said, he had one overriding motive: 'to see Jeremy Corbyn in Downing Street.' Calm and polite as always, Williams was too generous to make the obvious point: that it was a shame a party not short of enemies wasn't able to distinguish its true friends or, for that matter, its own best interests.

Polls

An obsessive focus on opinion polls was absolutely not the Compass way. The minute monitoring of incremental shifts in public opinion, as measured by the reductive – and in the UK, as US polling savant Nate Silver liked to point out, notoriously unreliable – dipstick of supposedly 'representative' 1,000-strong random samples of the population, all boiled down to the crude metric of voting choices, ran counter to Compass's core principles of listening, engaging, thinking through problems and accepting that if you asked difficult and complex questions you were likely to come up with difficult and complex answers that wouldn't fit on the back of a postcard, let alone a professional pollster's tablet. It wasn't that the PA team, in some ethereal way, felt themselves to be 'above' the banalities of polling numbers: it was simply that those numbers, even if you could trust them, could never adequately represent the hopes and ambitions for a better society to which Compass had always sought to give voice.

At the same time, there was no getting way from the truth that Compass, having chosen to fling themselves into the grubby, frenetic business of electioneering, polls mattered. They mattered for a variety of reasons. In the first place, they would inevitably shape the unfolding narrative of the campaign as a whole, the arc of progress or retreat for one party or another. As everyone was aware, polls didn't simply passively reflect an independently existing reality of voter opinion – they profoundly coloured voters' understanding of the choices facing them. In 2015, the polls' – quite inaccurate – prediction that Ed Miliband's Labour was set to form either a minority or a coalition government encouraged the media to make the SNP's inevitably important role in such a scenario the dominant issue of the campaign's latter stages: English voters' worries about the Scots Nats tail wagging the Labour dog, and the implications for the Union as a whole, played a decisive part in Labour's failure to make its expected advances south of the border. Had the polls been accurate, debate might have focused instead on the prospects of continuing austerity under single-party Tory rule.

The PA campaign, though not wedded to any one party and seeking to challenge the whole universe of politics-as-usual, couldn't take place in a vacuum. Just as the identification of PA clusters and target seats drew on former Lib Dem MP Andrew George's Twenty-Twenty seat analysis augmented by Roger Wilson, Chuck Dreyer and others' careful statistical analysis of constituencies where the 2015 results provided grounds for promoting alliances in the reasonable expectation of success, so the innovative options Compass sought to put before voters would be framed in the context of what, according to the polls, appeared to be the likeliest outcome of the election. In fact, the entire PA argument at the level of practical politics – as distinct from the underlying Compass premise of urgently needed social and cultural transformation – relied on a degree of statistical credibility to which, before any real votes were cast, only public polling could lend weight. Put simply, if the PA's stated aim was to join centre-left forces 'to achieve a change of government' – less euphemistically, to get rid of the Tories – it would help if the polls suggested that was even a plausible, never mind a probable, eventuality.

So, given what the polls were saying in the campaign's first weeks, it was hard to get a hearing. For example, an article in *The Observer* in early May gave considerable play to a claim from psephologist Martin Baxter, who ran the Electoral Calculus website (one of several such number-crunching poll-aggregator sites), that the Conservatives were heading for such an enormous majority – 174 seats! that even the most implausibly wholesale and watertight progressive alliance, with every single 2015 voter for all centre-left parties (including the Lib

Dems) lining up dutifully behind a single progressive candidate, would only succeed in reducing that majority to a still-bullet-proof sixty-four. The basis for Baxter's prediction? The polls, of course, which at that point continued to show the Tories holding an average lead over Labour of between fourteen and twenty points. As Baxter pointed out, figures such as these would make the Green stand-asides all but irrelevant to the outcome of the election. The Progressive Alliance risked becoming a worthy sideshow. Against such a backdrop, Compass was thrown onto the defensive. Responding to Baxter's forecast, Neal Lawson acknowledged the obvious fact that for PA to work, 'this requires a Labour Party that is doing creditably well, and clearly we haven't got that.' But, he insisted, 'that does not invalidate the principle for progressives to campaign, work and vote together, because that is going to reduce the Conservative landslide.' And he added, returning to one of Compass's central themes – and because a campaign purely to reduce a catastrophe to a mishap, however worthy, was as any adman would tell you a tough sell – 'we never thought about this as just deal-making politics. For us, it is about a better political mix.'

The polls undoubtedly also affected the judgment calls made by the parties themselves. Labour's structures and culture may have made their participation in PA all but impossible from the outset: but the party's flat-lining polls and the apparent near-certainty of electoral catastrophe – though logically making a very obvious and urgent case for desperate remedies such as PA in this most apparently desperate of circumstances – also probably deprived the party leadership of the leverage it needed to push through such a radical change of policy had it ever been inclined to do so. Standing down candidates would have been seen – and would have undoubtedly been portrayed by Tory publicity and the Tory press, to say nothing of Corbyn's vocal opponents in the Parliamentary Labour Party – as effectively an admission of defeat and an acknowledgement that only a 'stitch-up' could preserve even an adequate remnant to provide effective opposition. Given his own continuing isolation in the party's upper echelons, and the lack of any senior voices (bar Clive Lewis) speaking out in support of PA or even of preliminary discussions to explore whether and how Labour might co-operate with other parties, Jeremy Corbyn could, in all likelihood, never have got Labour's involvement with the Progressive Alliance past the NEC or his own shadow Cabinet.

But, in any case, there's absolutely no indication the idea was ever seriously considered by Corbyn or any of his close associates – not even John McDonnell, who, in his long years alongside Corbyn in the political Siberia of the Campaign Group, had frequently spoken (though in rather general and abstract terms) of the need for Left unity and electoral reform, and was, by comparison with most Labour frontbenchers of the past, less sectarian in his general outlook. (Some felt McDonnell was more open to the idea of an alliance with the Socialist Workers' Party than with the Greens, let alone the Lib Dems.) Perhaps, reasonably enough, Labour's leaders felt they had enough to do without igniting a new source of fratricidal strife. Perhaps they felt that having finally got their hands on the levers of Labour power after thirty years on the outside, they had no intention of entering into discussions with other parties the inevitable outcome of which – whether before or after an election – would be the dilution of the red-blooded socialist prospectus they wanted to put before the British people. Or perhaps, as the Greens surmised, they were convinced that a Labour surge was around the corner and they simply wouldn't need anyone else's help.

It wasn't just Labour, however. Tim Farron's reading of the polls decried Corbyn, as he colourfully put it in a *Guardian* interview, as 'electorally toxic'. He remained firmly convinced that had Labour given way to internal and external pressures to stand down in the Richmond Park by-election, whatever the maths said a 'Red–Orange' alliance would have repelled Richmond's affluent, privileged electorate in ways that an 'Orange–Green' alliance hadn't. And looking at the small number of seats where the Lib Dems could realistically hope to challenge in the forthcoming contest – Richmond's suburban neighbours Twickenham and Kingston & Surbiton, and a scattering of similarly affluent, highly educated seats such as Bath and Oxford West & Abingdon – he made the same diagnosis: the Lib Dems had nothing to gain and everything to lose by appearing to be part of a plot to hoodwink the voters and smuggle Jeremy Corbyn into Number 10. The counter-argument, of course, was that the remoteness – if the polls were at all accurate – of such an outcome would effectively neutralise this argument as nobody seriously imagined Corbyn was within a country mile of Downing Street. But Farron still didn't fancy the optics. And, convinced as he was of the virtues of his '48 per cent strategy' and that Brexit was a game-changer that would redraw the British political map, he clung to his repeatedly stated ambition of 'replacing' a politically bankrupt and directionless Labour Party as the principal opposition to the Tories.

Then again, the polls in truth made no happier reading for the Lib Dems than for Labour. If PA relied, as Lawson said, on a 'creditable' showing from Labour, a respectable showing from the third (UK-wide) party was equally vital. And the polls obstinately refused to show any uptick whatsoever for the Lib Dems from the 7–9 per cent range they had inhabited throughout much of the Coalition and since. Labour's poll numbers under Corbyn were little worse than Gordon Brown's final showing in 2010 (though considerably worse than the levels Ed Miliband had achieved from 2011–2014). But in 2010 the Lib Dems had won 23 per cent of the national popular vote (remember Clegg-mania?), contributing to a 56 per cent majority of the vote for the 'progressive parties' (factoring in the SNP in Scotland and the SDLP, but not Sinn Féin, in Northern Ireland).

Given all this, from the outset the PA's tacit aim became the preservation, rather than the expansion, of as many progressive voices as possible in a House of Commons destined, everyone believed, to be overwhelmingly dominated by the Conserva-tives. Beyond that, success in PA seats in the context of general calamity – if achievable and demonstrable – would make the case for electoral alliances going forward as the only practical way to scale the mountain of a massive Tory majority: this was, in effect, the 'I told you so' strategy.

If Labour's leaders really did know something about the polls nobody else did, the local elections falling, unusually, midway through the general election campaign on 4 May would offer the only concrete proof before the nation went to the polls a month later. But the results delivered almost unmitigated woe for Labour, which lost over 300 seats to the Tories, including in such eternally Labour areas as Tees and Glasgow, while the Tories capitalised on the extermination of UKIP to gain over 500 – unprecedented for a governing party. The only small consolation – or, from the Tories' perspective, point of minor concern – was that as some analysts pointed out the results in the locals scaled up to the equivalent of an eleven-point lead over Labour nationally: impressive, but significantly below their average seventeen-point lead in the polls at that stage (and only four points improved on David Cameron's lead in 2015, which delivered a majority of just twelve). Were the polls to tighten markedly, the race might start to seem less of a foregone conclusion.

And then, gradually and erratically but unmistakably, they started to do just that.

The *Guardian*/ICM poll of Monday 15 May was the last to show the Tories with a twenty-point lead. Not coincidentally, as it proved, the fieldwork for this poll was mostly conducted before the weekend-long dissection of Labour's manifesto, leaked to the press the previous week in what pundits derided as yet another example of the party's hopeless dysfunction under Corbyn – but which instead supplied a four-day platform for public discussion of strikingly expansionist policies, many of which seemed to strike a chord with an austerity-weary public. The following week, the Tories unveiled their own manifesto. Almost everyone, regardless of political leaning, immediately concurred in finding it a vacuous and flimsy document whose only eye-catching policies (such as the abolition of free school lunches) seemed callous and mean-spirited. And then there was the shambles of the Tories' headline policy on social care, raising the means-tested threshold for state-supported care in old age to £100,000 but crucially including people's property in the calculation of resources for the first time. The 'dementia tax,' as the policy was instantly dubbed by Labour, received such a drubbing – not least in the Tory press, who regarded it as an Exocet targeted at homeowners in London and the south-east – that four days later Theresa May performed a dramatic reversal and insisted that the policy 'absolutely' incorporated a cap on costs (in direct contradiction to her own ministers' previous statements). This U-turn – combined with her insistence that it was no such thing, which struck many as frankly an insult to voters' intelligence – arguably dealt May's personal authority (already eroded by the remote, robotic tenor of her public appearances) a blow from which it never recovered. By the following weekend, two polls showed the Tory lead sinking below 10 per cent for the first time in the campaign. From then on, although the Tory lead never vanished entirely and varied widely from one survey and pollster to another (from as high as 14 per cent to as low as 1 per cent), the general trend line was an ever-narrowing (and strikingly, very much a two-party) race.

Nobody in the PA team, any more than anyone else in the country, knew quite what to make of these figures. On the one hand, they gave everyone renewed hope (or hope for the first time) that the outcome might not be as predetermined as they'd imagined. A Conservative victory of some kind still seemed a near-certainty – even as Labour closed, the Tories' own support never dropped below 40 per cent (levels not seen since John Major's shock victory in 1992). But the all-important swing from Labour was reducing to levels where Tory gains might be far smaller than originally anticipated – *if* the polls were right. In such a situation, a Labour marginal preserved from Tory gain might not simply be an island in the expected flood – if the Tory majority was much smaller than expected, every single MP became proportionally more important in the overall political calculus.

If the polls were right, that is. Nobody around PA really believed they were. The steady uptick in the Labour vote was greeted with general scepticism. Everyone knew that Labour under Corbyn and post-Brexit was in trouble with its core white working-class vote; press reports indicated that Labour's traditionally rock-solid support amongst Black and ethnic minority voters had started to fray; the party's schizophrenic and lukewarm position on Brexit (having voted to trigger Article 50 and, seemingly, in favour of exiting the single market and perhaps the customs union too, it wasn't clear what besides tone really separated Labour from the Tories) imperilled its support in metropolitan Remain areas. Anecdotally, Labour MPs reported horrendous canvassing returns and doorstep hostility to Corbyn while television *vox pops* seemed always to be full of life-long Labour voters opting for May's 'strong and stable', Brexit-trustworthy brand. So, if the additional votes the polls were recording were real, where on earth were they coming from?

Still. As time went on, it became apparent that the pollsters – anxious to remedy their errors of 2015 which led to a systematic over-estimation of the Labour vote – were making some eye-catching assumptions about their raw data. In particular, it emerged that a major difference between the polling companies that showed the Tories streets ahead of Labour and those that showed the gap closing to (in some cases) within the margin of statistical error was that the former simply didn't believe a particular category of their respondents – young voters. Voters under thirty were telling pollsters both that they were determined to vote, and that when they did they would be voting overwhelmingly for Labour. But a majority of polls systematically discounted these responses from younger voters on the grounds that, come polling day, young people had for decades shown themselves to be less organised, less motivated and less reliable than senior citizens in particular, who voted in very large numbers (and now voted predominantly Conservative). As a consequence, as both academic and amateur psephologists poring over pollsters' original tables pointed out, sometimes negligibly small Tory leads in the raw sample data became far larger in the (adjusted) published polls. For example, an ICM poll on the very eve of the election which, as published in *The Guardian*, showed a twelve-point Conservative lead, before ICM's turnout adjustment filter was applied had the Tories ahead by just a single point. Come election night, a number of assumptions about voter behaviour were going to be put to the sternest of tests.

Most extraordinarily of all, just a week out from the election, a YouGov poll in *The Times* (based on a seat-by-seat projection extrapolated from respondent profiles rather than a standard nationwide sample) predicted a hung parliament with the Conservatives on just 310 seats – down twenty-one from David Cameron's 2015 result. This wild outlier was greeted with derision by Conservatives: Jim Messina, Barack Obama's former campaign manager now working for the Conservatives, tweeted that he had 'spent the day laughing' at the 'stupid' poll. Though Messina's frictionless transition from 'Hope and Change' to 'Strong and Stable' typified the kind of value-free instrumental political hackery that was anathema to the PA volunteers, in their hearts many of them expected he would be proven all too right come election night.

If you were on the left, it was always better to dampen expectations and defer to the immortal wisdom of Michael Frayn in *Clockwise*: it wasn't the despair. You could take the despair. It was the hope you couldn't stand.

CHAPTER SIX

'THOSE WHO DO NOT REMEMBER THE PAST...'

Given the exigencies of FPTP, it should come as no surprise that electoral pacts in the United Kingdom, though a rarity, are historically far from unknown. The first progressive alliance, and undoubtedly the most significant of all in historical terms, was the 1903 Gladstone–MacDonald act between the Liberal Party and the Labour Representation Committee (LRC) – the precursor of the modern Labour Party. In order to avoid splitting the anti-Conservative vote, the Liberals agreed to stand aside in thirty-two seats (the policy was not universal: in a further eighteen constituencies LRC candidates were opposed by Liberals). In the 1906 election, twenty-four of the twenty-nine LRC MPs elected were in seats where the Liberals did not stand – the great majority of Labour's inaugural parliamentary caucus and the initial steps on the path to the first Labour government in 1924. By contrast, the 'regressive alliance' of 1951 and 1955 was a historical footnote at best: the Conservatives stood down in five Liberal-held constituencies to allow the Liberals a clear run at Labour, as a result of locally initiated agreements subsequently ratified by the national party (the Liberals won all five seats, contributing five-sixths of their MPs in both parliaments).

Within much more recent memory, two late-twentieth-century examples of electoral pacts/alliances on the centre-left of British politics offer precedents as well as warnings for contemporary efforts to manage (or, depending on your views, manipulate) an electoral system that has historically most often worked against centre-left voters.

The SDP–Liberal Alliance, 1982–1988

Many, perhaps most, Labour supporters would strongly contest the idea that the avowedly centrist 1980s Alliance between the newly formed Social Democratic Party (SDP) and the Liberal Party was a 'progressive' alliance at all: not least as the publicly stated original aim of the SDP, formed in 1981 as a breakaway from the increasingly left-leaning and disunited Labour Party, was to replace Labour as the principal UK party of the centre-left. The party's apparent shift to the right under David Owen's leadership (1983–1988), when it seemed better disposed to Mrs Thatcher's Conservatives than to Neil Kinnock's Labour, further qualifies its claim on a 'progressive' identity as the term has been used in this book, and as it was understood by the Progressive Alliance in 2017. In their own time, however, both the SDP and the Liberals under the leadership of David Steel (who consistently regarded himself and his party as somewhat to the left of centre) self-identified as 'progressive' parties that consciously sought to break with the self-defeating traditional structures and ideologies of UK politics and offer a new prospectus for modern Britain. That many of their policies, though moderate (and intentionally so) in the context of the period – which saw Labour and Conservatives more ideologically polarised than at any point since before the First World War – seem, by today's standards, strikingly progressive speaks volumes about the subsequent direction of travel of post-Thatcher, post-New Labour Britain. These included large-scale capital investment by the government in both industry and national infrastructure, an unstinting pro-Europeanism, the cancellation of Trident (at that stage not yet commissioned as a replacement for the former Polaris nuclear weapons system) and a wide range of constitutional reforms, foremost amongst them electoral reform. (In fact, a number of commentators – including *Guardian* columnist and former SDP candidate Polly Toynbee – drew comparisons between Labour's 'left-wing' 2017 manifesto, rightly regarded as marking a dramatic shift leftwards from the New Labour era, and the SDP's 'centrist' programme of the 1980s.) The Alliance itself – as an example of a mature, co-operative relationship between different parties – was intended to model a different, progressive way of working from the mud-slinging tribalism of the old politics. Finally, and perhaps most importantly for our purposes, the Alliance marked the most thoroughgoing attempt in British political history to overcome the obstacles of FPTP by conjoining two separate political parties into a single entity for campaigning (and, had it ever come to that, governing) purposes and presenting a united prospectus to voters. Its ultimate failure in electoral terms suggested that those obstacles were even more daunting than the creators of the Alliance had originally believed.

The SDP was formed in March 1981 by the former Labour cabinet ministers Roy Jenkins, David Owen, Shirley Williams and Bill Rodgers – instantly dubbed the 'Gang of Four' by the media – who, having failed to arrest their party's shift to the left since losing the 1979 general election (Labour adopted policies such as unilateral nuclear disarmament, withdrawal from the EEC, a command economy and mandatory reselection of MPs), had become convinced that only a new party could represent the moderate majority of centre-left voters whom Labour had in their view abandoned. Determined to 'break the mould' of British politics, the Gang of Four were eventually joined by twenty-eight formerly Labour MPs and one Tory (and, in short order, saw their parliamentary ranks further boosted through sensational by-election victories for Jenkins and Williams). In its early days the party became a media sensation and, during 1981–82, soared ahead of both Thatcher's unpopular government and the equally unappealing and still divided Labour Party, at one point hitting an unheard-of 50 per cent in the opinion polls.

From the moment the new party was launched, the question was raised of its relation to the Liberal Party, which by the early 1980s had recovered from its post-war nadir to a reliable national vote share around 12–14 per cent, though under FPTP this had only delivered eleven MPs in 1979. Though the Liberal Party in the country, which had some affinities with the New Left of the 1960s, was culturally quite distinct from, if not at odds with, the SDP's self-styled professionalism and somewhat managerial style, the policy differences between the parties seemed wholly negotiable and it would have been obviously ruinous to split the centrist vote. David Steel, for his part, immediately, wholeheartedly and very publicly embraced the prospect of a deal that could transform his party's standing and prospects, famously telling activists at a triumphalist Liberal party congress in autumn 1981, as polls showed the then-still-notional combined SDP–Liberal force sweeping the country, to 'go back to your constituencies and prepare for government'.

The formal deal constituting the Alliance presented British voters with an unprecedented package: two separate parties running on a joint manifesto, with a dual leadership (Jenkins as 'prime-minister designate' and Steel as leader of the Alliance campaign in the country) and candidacies in seats throughout the country allocated to either party in roughly equal proportion. To get to this point, the parties had set up numerous joint policy commissions and working groups and undergone a protracted negotiating process to allocate seats. It is worth noting that, even for two parties with so little meaningful ideological division and – given that the SDP was a brand-new party – no baggage of previous electoral animosity, the seat-allocation process was protracted, difficult and often contentious. Local Liberal parties in particular were reluctant to surrender the chance to run in seats which they had been carefully husbanding for years to the parvenus of the SDP at the very moment when, completely unlooked for, electoral success seemed a real prospect. For their part, the SDP tended to regard Liberals as amateurs, political dabblers and minnows who were lucky to have the chance to ride to victory (as it seemed in 1981–82) on the SDP's coattails. Although the negotiations were completed to both sides' relative satisfaction (or equal dissatisfaction)[32] well before the 1983 general election, the protracted semi-public quarrels over seat allocation did some damage to the Alliance's claim to represent a 'new politics' and opened up a line of media questioning around the coherence of the Alliance's joint structures that never entirely went away.

The Alliance failed to make the breakthrough it sought. By the time of the 1983 election, Thatcher's government had recovered

---

32 Three unreconciled local Liberal parties ended up running rebel Liberal candidates against the official SDP–Liberal Alliance in the 1983 election.

following the Falklands War and the start of the 1980s boom, and the Alliance's popularity had sunk from its heady peak of 1981–82. In the election itself, the Alliance parties conducted their joint campaign, at both national and local level, enthusiastically and with relatively few divisions, and won over 25 per cent of the popular vote (just 2 per cent behind Labour), the best performance by a third party since the 1920s. But FPTP utterly defeated the Alliance: support from one voter in four was rewarded by just twenty-three seats in total (only five of them for the SDP) – that is, less than 4 per cent of Commons seats. Between then and the next election in 1987, although some policy differences opened up between the two parties after Owen took over from Jenkins as SDP leader (notably on nuclear disarmament, on which Owen was a good deal more hawkish than most Liberals), the structures of the Alliance largely held and were, in some respects, streamlined. Once again – and this time with far fewer disputes – the two parties agreed a joint manifesto, divided seats between themselves, co-ordinated campaign strategy and tactics and in all respects presented a public face of effective partnership. But the outcome in 1987, despite some promising by-election results in the run-up to the election, was a virtual replay of 1983: despite securing 23 per cent of the popular vote, just twenty-two Alliance MPs (seventeen Liberal, five SDP) were returned to Westminster.

The Alliance did not long outlive this second defeat. The possibility of a merger between the two parties had been publicly mooted at least since the 1983 election and, with the SDP's particularly glaring failure at two elections, the arguments for preserving two separate party organisations now seemed less persuasive than ever. The Alliance's very success – in terms of two political teams cojoined at the hip working towards a common end – seemed to argue against maintaining it in the same dual-monarchy form. In fact, there was evidence that it was precisely the dual, rather than the integrated, aspects of the arrangement that deterred voters – notably the joint leadership, which some believed was simply too alien and confusing a concept given the UK's tradition of strong single-party govern-ments. Since taking over as SDP leader, David Owen had been a consistently implacable opponent of a merger, but he was now side-lined by his own party and, under his successor, the two parties combined in 1989 to form the Liberal Democrats.[33]

The failure of the Alliance in the first instance once again proves just how high are the barriers posed by FPTP to new parties without a strong sectoral or geographical base. From that perspective, the Alliance was simply too narrow for its electoral pact to make a decisive impact (in terms of MPs – its near-doubling in 1983 of the Liberal-only vote in 1979 was a striking achievement). The Alliance would have needed an agreement with Labour to deliver on the seat numbers its sup-port in the country deserved – which of course was an impossi-bility, given the ideological gulf between them, enduring bitter-ness over the Gang of Four's 'betrayal' of their former comrades and above all the SDP's original stated aim of replacing Labour altogether. In truth, the possibility of any such agreement would have obviated the need for the SDP to exist in the first place, as it would have implied a party with policies moderate enough to have prevented a split ever happening. Which, in a sense, is what happened, only the other way around: Neil Kinnock's main aim

---

33 Owen briefly preserved a rump three-member SDP in the Commons but, following a series of humiliating by-election results that culminated in finishing behind the Monster Raving Loony Party in Bootle in 1990, formally wound up the party. Its members served out their terms as independent MPs.

– privately held – in the 1987 election was not to win outright but to re-establish Labour rather than the Alliance as clearly the principal opposition to the Tories. Having achieved this, he set about abandoning most of Labour's left-wing policies before the 1992 election. David Owen himself partly blamed Labour's recolonisation of the centre-ground under Kinnock for extinguishing the SDP's raison d'être.

All of this leaves an ambiguous legacy for the Progressive Alliance in 2017 and beyond. The failure of the Alliance's relatively narrowly based partnership to gain sufficient electoral traction to break through strongly suggests that Compass's project of building as broad a coalition as possible – had it been successful – was the right approach. In fact, by consolidating the centrist share of the vote alone, the Alliance's contribution may have been a negative one, although the evidence is ambiguous (the Alliance attracted weak Conservative as well as Labour voters). But, as early as 1983, the then Labour leader Michael Foot was blaming the Alliance for splitting the anti-Tory vote and allowing Thatcher her landslide. Such, certainly, is the folk memory of the Alliance within Labour. The circumstances that made a larger centre-left partnership impossible in 1983 or 1987 have resonance today: as long as Tim Farron insisted that Labour under Jeremy Corbyn was 'electorally toxic' – or even fantasised that, armed with the votes of the 48 per cent Remain bloc, the Liberal Democrats could supplant Labour as the main party of opposition – the prospects of a workable pact in 2017 were moribund. While there is a Labour–Liberal Democrat understanding that Conservative-led austerity ought to be eased, there are big disagreements over how the UK's market economy should be managed. Labour under Corbyn is committed to not only the renationalisation of the railways, but also bringing the country's energy and water industries under public ownership. This could perhaps be a bridge too far for the next Liberal Democrat leader – especially if he or she was closely associated with the 'Orange Book' liberal economic revolution under Nick Clegg's leadership. Corbyn's vision of a mixed economy may not be compatible with the Liberal Democrats' broad support of a market liberal economy. Large-scale spending commitments for the abolition of university tuition fees and renationalisation projects are potential sources of disagreement.

In itself, the Alliance remains the most thorough example of a genuinely unified electoral partnership – fully accepted and endorsed (with whatever reservations) on both sides by national leadership and mass membership alike, with joint candidates representing either party (in a minority of cases, jointly selected) agreed by negotiation in every seat, running on a unitary platform – that British politics has ever known. Therein, too, however, lies a note of caution: the process of arriving at this point, especially candidate selection/seat allocation, was far from easy even under these most congenial of circumstances. How much more difficult to achieve such an outcome with parties lacking a common culture, with distinctively different ideological positions, and histories of bitter electoral competition?[34] As we shall see, one legacy of the Alliance was a decided reluctance to go through anything like this process again by

---

34 The speed with which tribal barriers to co-operation arise between ostensible ideological bedfellows was illustrated from the opposite end of the political spectrum by the reaction to Tory-supporting journalist Toby Young's attempt in spring 2014 to establish an online forum where members of UKIP and the Conservatives could find common ground, as a stepping-stone to a notional pact in the 2015 general election. On the contrary, the online exchanges revealed deep animosity and suspicion: 'they regard each other not as estranged members of the same family but as bitter enemies' lamented Young in the *Spectator*. It seems that the lessons that activists typically draw from electoral competition in similar voting pools is not the need for collaboration but that democracy is a Darwinian struggle for survival.

those who remembered it first time out. The Progressive Alliance may have to crack this nut if it is to go beyond its 2017 achievements in future elections.

The 1997 Blair–Ashdown compact

TABLE 1: CONSERVATIVE V. LABOUR–LIBERAL DEMOCRAT VOTE IN GENERAL ELECTIONS SINCE 1979

General election	Conservative vote	Lab–Lib combined vote
1979	13,697,923	15,846,022
1983	13,012,316	16,237,883
1987	13,760,935	17,370,921
1992	14,093,007	17,560,090
1997	9,600,943	18,761,114
2001	8,357,615	15,539,274
2005	8,784,915	15,357,890
2010	10,703,754	15,443,352
2015	11,299,959	11,763,166
2017	13,636,690	15,249,730

Labour and the Liberal Democrats are by far the two most important 'progressive' voting blocs in the UK. Any 'progressive alliance' that fails to embrace both (let alone, as in 2017, either) of these parties is likely to have only a marginal impact on outcome, whatever its other civic virtues (such as demonstrating the practicability of cross-party co-operation generally). Table 1 shows that in every general election since Margaret Thatcher's landmark victory in 1979, the Labour–Liberal Democrat[35] combined vote has exceeded that of the Conservative Party. (Indeed, there has only been one occasion since 1945 where the Conservative vote exceeded that of the combined Labour–Liberal Democrat vote: Anthony Eden's victory in 1955). It has become a cliché of political commentary that if the twentieth

---

35 In 1979: Liberal; in 1983 and 1987: SDP–Liberal Alliance.

century was one largely dominated by the Conservatives, this was in large part because of splitting of the 'progressive vote'. In the late 1990s, perhaps uniquely, both Labour and the Liberal Democrats were led by men who subscribed to this reading of British political history. This would lead to a unique experiment in cross-party progressive co-operation which might have transformed British politics – had it not been perversely checkmated by its own success in 'gaming' the FPTP system.

The 1992 general election marked a watershed moment in British politics. Despite numerous pre-election polls showing that Labour and the Conservatives were effectively neck and neck, John Major's Conservatives won an outright parliamentary majority of twenty-one. This was Labour's fourth straight defeat at the national polls. The election was also a disappointment of sorts for the Liberal Democrats, fighting their first election since the 1989 merger with the SDP. Under Paddy Ashdown's leadership, the party lost almost 5 per cent of the Alliance's highly creditable, if ultimately futile, 23 per cent vote in 1987 and was reduced to twenty MPs (in an enlarged House of Commons).

The result of the 1992 election led some observers to ask seriously whether Conservative political hegemony was interminable, and prompted a major rethink on the progressive side of British politics. Discussion inevitably focused on possible Labour–Liberal Democrat co-operation. In 1992, as in the previous (and following) elections, the combined 'Lab–Lib' vote comfortably exceeded that of the Conservatives. Beyond the numbers, various contingent factors made this a more plausible prospect than at previous elections and, chastened by its run of defeats, Labour was more receptive to overtures from any source that might finally help it back to power. With the SDP (and, above all, David Owen) consigned to political history and both Labour and Lib Dems under new leadership, much of the poison had been drawn from the wounds of the 1980s. Labour's own painful 'policy review' process under Neil Kinnock, which had jettisoned most of the left-wing platform on which the party had suffered crushing defeats in the 1980s, had seen the party move in a centrist direction that was more ideologically congenial to the Lib Dems.

Paddy Ashdown was initially the driving force pressing for greater Labour–Liberal co-operation. In so doing, he was merely renovating a common theme for his Liberal Party predecessors. In the 1960s, Jo Grimond had called for a 'realignment of the left'. From 1976–1978, the Lib–Lab Pact struck by Labour PM James Callaghan and David Steel preserved the minority Labour government's precarious hold on office. Insofar as the SDP originally conceived of itself as a 'replacement' for Labour (Bill Rodgers envisaged the new party eventually claiming nine-tenths of Labour's support), the Alliance could be interpreted as the Liberals partnering with a new, 'improved' Labour by another name. In the immediate aftermath of the 1992 election, Ashdown spied (yet) another opportunity to realign the left. A month later, he delivered a speech to party activists in his Somerset constituency in which he argued for the importance of progressive parties working together to construct a non-socialist alternative to the Conservatives. Ashdown specifically encouraged Labour to support constitutional reform, embrace the market economy, and further loosen its ties to the trade unions. The speech was received favourably by some leading Labour figures such as Robin Cook and Peter Mandelson, but newly elected Labour leader John Smith, keen to maintain his political independence, was reluctant to co-operate. Smith was firmly of the opinion that Labour were on the cusp of winning a parliamentary majority on their own, and opposed Ashdown's insistence on weakening the union link. However, Smith's unexpected death in 1994 changed the picture. Labour's new leader Tony Blair took a clear view that Labour's path to power lay through the 'centre ground' of British politics – and his own ambitions to transform the party included embracing the UK's market economy, softening Labour's relationship with the unions and developing stronger ties with the business community.

Thus Labour and the Liberal Democrats – or rather, Blair and Ashdown – shared a great deal of common ground on policy matters. As Major's administration deteriorated, Ashdown abandoned his party's sometime stance of 'equidistance' between Conservative and Labour and unambiguously staked out a position on the (increasingly crowded) centre-left. If deliverable, Labour–Lib Dem co-operation held the prospect of far greater returns than the Alliance since, even as Blair set about repurposing his party into 'New Labour', it still retained swathes of heartland seats in parts of the country where the Liberal Democrats were an irrelevance. But the nature of this closer co-operation between the two parties was very much open to debate. The most dramatic option would have been an electoral pact where the two parties would field common candidates. Blair was quite keen for such an arrangement in the south-west of England – historically a Liberal heartland where Labour was positioned behind both the Liberal Democrats and Conservatives in many constituencies. Ashdown, however, having already experienced the time-consuming, draining and divisive process of seat allocation within the Alliance, dismissed the idea, convinced that such an arrangement would be unworkable and would be received unfavourably by the rank and file of both parties. The Alliance had also convinced Ashdown that the more public a pact, the more the media would focus on the internal distribution of power (for instance, who would get which jobs in a coalition government) and constantly seek out splits, real or perceived.

So the co-operation which started to take shape was more subtle and nuanced. Blair and Ashdown agreed it would be wiser to pinpoint a select number of policy areas where the two parties agreed and make it clear that there would be co-operation on these issues during the next parliament. The purpose of this strategy was to ensure that the parties maintained their own identities by holding different views in certain areas of public policy but to ultimately create an atmosphere of co-operation which would encourage progressive anti-Tory tactical voting in the next general election. The respective chief whips, Labour's Donald Dewar and the Liberal Democrats' Archy Kirkwood, began co-ordinating Lab–Lib 'joint attacks' at PMQs to weaken Major's standing and reinforce the idea of the Conservatives as a spent political force which stood in the way of a 'Progressive Britain' jointly represented by Labour and the Lib Dems. This co-ordination reached the very top, with Blair and Ashdown conducting a 'progressive pincer movement' against the increasingly beleaguered Major.

Growing co-operation between the two parties lead to the Cook–Maclennan proposals, a policy document jointly drafted by Robin Cook of Labour and Robert Maclennan of the Liberal Democrats (perhaps ironically, an ex-Labour SDP founder member and its final leader before merger with the Liberals). This essentially focused on how Labour–Liberal Democrat co-operation could drive an ambitious agenda for constitutional reform. Its core proposals were the incorporation of the

European Convention on Human Rights into British law; Scottish and Welsh devolution (with proportional representation being used to elect representatives to the devolved parliaments); an elected authority for London; proportional representation for European elections; and a referendum on voting reform for Westminster elections. The Cook–Mclennan proposals were made public – strengthening the image of an anti-Tory progressive partnership – and in their turn inspired Ashdown's 'Partnership for Britain's Future'. This articulated Labour–Liberal Democrat co-operation in a number of key policy areas, including reforms of the welfare system, greater investment in education, and independence for the Bank of England and adherence to the criteria for entry into the proposed European Single Currency. Many of these proposals also found their way into Labour's 1997 manifesto: Labour in return offered the crucial concession of a Royal Commission on proportional representation for Westminster elections.

The discussions between the two parties advanced to a stage where Blair and Ashdown entertained the possibility of Liberal Democrat MPs holding cabinet posts in a Labour government. It has been claimed by Peter Mandelson that this would have involved the inclusion of two Liberal Democrat MPs – Alan Beith and Menzies Campbell – in Blair's first cabinet. However, years of Labour–Liberal Democrat discussion, strategic planning and publication of jointly authored documents were effectively side-lined by the result of the 1997 general election. As Blair and Ashdown hoped, the Conservatives were unceremoniously dumped out of government, having suffered a net loss of 178 seats. There was very clear evidence of anti-Tory tactical voting nationwide on a large scale, helping the Liberal Democrats to win forty-six seats – the most for any third party since 1929. The problem was a very unfamiliar one for progressive parties of an excess of success. The election saw a Labour landslide of historic proportions, with the party winning a parliamentary majority of 179. Following the election, leading Labour figures such as Chancellor Gordon Brown and Deputy Prime Minister John Prescott expressed their opposition to any Liberal Democrat involvement in government. In reality, the size of Labour's majority had destroyed any argument for it. The nail in the Blair–Ashdown coffin was Labour quietly burying its commitment to hold a referendum on electoral reform, following the Roy Jenkins Commission's recommendation to adopt the 'Alternative Vote Plus' system for Westminster elections. This abandonment of what, for the Lib Dems, had been a central plank of the compact was felt by Ashdown as a disillusioning betrayal.

Conclusion

The Blair–Ashdown compact identified a number of policy areas where Labour–Liberal Democrat co-operation could be established. Importantly, Blair and Ashdown were policy bedfellows who favoured a market economy with a 'social conscience', an ambitious devolution programme, a Labour Party which weakened its ties with the trade unions and Britain as a more willing and constructive participant in the EU. However, the Blair–Ashdown compact never became reality due the sheer scale of Labour's victory in the 1997 general election.

In 2017, Britain has entered an era of coalition governments and party co-operation. Two of the last three general elections have resulted in hung parliaments. It is very conceivable that after the next election a rejuvenated Labour Party and the Liberal Democrats under a more likeable, high-profile leader (such as former Glasgow Labour Party councillor Vince Cable) will together command a parliamentary majority in a hung parliament. While there is plenty of room for co-operation in policy areas such as constitutional reform, there are also potential stumbling blocks in the form of economic management, electoral reform and Brexit.

Tony Blair's vision of a 'progressive century' dominated by a reunited centre-left may have become discredited along with its author; and Blairite progressivism certainly did not include the more radical politics towards which Labour has moved under Jeremy Corbyn. But some believe that the 'Overton window' – the prevailing understanding of what is politically possible at a given point in time – may be moving to the left in the wake of growing inequality, perpetual austerity and the other manifest and manifold failures of neoliberalism. If so, the centre-left has not only the opportunity but arguably the duty to seize that moment and work in all possible combinations to usher in, perhaps, the next progressive century.

CHAPTER SEVEN

THE CAMPAIGN PART III: 28 MAY – 7 JUNE

Re-grouping: a party and PA 2.0

Neal Lawson wanted to hold a party. From the very outset, when everyone still anticipated the Progressive Alliance campaign would be a three-year marathon rather than a seven-week sprint, he'd harboured the idea of a public event where the idea of PA could announce itself in capital letters to the world: something much more than a press conference, more like a US-style campaign rally – a celebration, light on policy and loaded with the feel-good factor to fire up supporters and catch the eyes of a jaded media. Secretly, he wanted balloons – red, white and green balloons released from catwalks as a band blasted out the PA campaign song and the new politics burst into vibrant three-dimensional life.

It wasn't quite like that in the end. Lawson never did get his balloons (no catwalks in the event venue – a former Whitbread brewery close to the Barbican, in the heart of London's City). But the PA did stage a bloody good night out for hundreds of people. And Lawson chose the date wisely – the Monday after the filing deadline – to tell the world that PA was still very much alive and fighting despite the major centre-left parties' refusal to get involved and, not least, give the PA team a needed pick-me-up after a difficult and disappointing week. Now that they knew the full extent and the limits of formal party alliances, the Progressive Alliance was going to have to shift gears and work flat-out for the duration of the campaign on the politics of the practically possible rather than the utopian. That was going to require different methods, a good deal of hard-headed and probably thick-skinned (because some people weren't going to like the results) data-crunching and as much presence on the ground as could be mustered from Compass's growing list of supporters and volunteers.

But not tonight. Tonight was an opportunity for the team to remind one another of how much they had already achieved – even if they hadn't yet persuaded the political world to transform itself the way it needed to – and to spread the good news as exuberantly as possible to the outside world. If Labour and the Lib Dems wouldn't come to the PA party, more fool them. One way or another, the party was going ahead. The appetite was palpable: tickets (not free) for the 1,000-seat venue were snapped up within days of going on sale. Working the phones, Lawson assembled a long (in retrospect, probably too long – brevity has never been the left's strong point) and varied roster of speakers and performers. The PA's tried and trusted stalwarts were there, of course: Zoe Williams, the Greens' Jonathan Bartley and Siân Berry (Caroline Lucas was preparing for a televised leaders' debate) and Paul Mason. Less familiar faces, too, were on the list, such as Naomi Smith from the Lib Dems' Social Liberal Forum, US volunteer organiser Claire Sandberg (of whom more later) and video messages from the charismatic Yanis Varoufakis in Greece (raising a clenched fist in a salute of solidarity) and rather less charismatic but warm and sincere Uffe Elbæk, leader of the Alternative Party in Denmark. The audience saluted PA trailblazers like Andrée Frieze from Richmond and Sophie Walker of the Women's Equality Party, and rose as one in outraged sympathy and appreciation for Steve Williams, representing the Godalming Three onstage alongside Penny Rivers and Louise Irvine. There was splenetic performance poetry from Luke Wright, uproariously funny protest songs from Christian Reilly and a scatological turn from 'Tory MP for Buckland & Ruttington' Sir Ian Bowler (the comic Nathaniel Tapley). In the very front row, a Hawaiian-shirted, white-haired, bearded freak, many years out of Woodstock, periodically jumped from his seat and turned to pump skinny arms and clenched fists victoriously at the audience. Once or twice he needed gently shooing away when it looked as if he was about to rush the stage. Nobody knew who he was; but all that mattered was that he was, as Lawson observed, 'our freak'.

The star turn, undoubtedly, introduced by Lawson as 'the best MP in the country', was Clive Lewis, Labour MP for Norwich South. Of the handful of Labour MPs who had spoken out in recent months on behalf of the principle of PA – others included Lisa Nandy and Jonathan Reynolds ahead of the Richmond Park by-election, and more recently Jon Cruddas and Hampstead & Kilburn MP (and PA beneficiary) Tulip Siddiq, co-signatories to the previous week's *Guardian* letter – Lewis was by far the most consistent and outspoken, and had become a fixture at Compass meetings on the topic. Firmly on Labour's left and an early and consistent supporter of Jeremy Corbyn (though a dispute over Labour's line on Trident had seen him reassigned from the defence to business briefs the previous year, and in February he had resigned from the shadow Cabinet

following Corbyn's imposition of a three-line whip on triggering Article 50), his unusual biography for a Labour MP (not
only a former TV journalist but also an officer in the Territo-
rials, serving a tour of duty in Afghanistan) ensured he was
frequently spoken of as a possible successor to Corbyn. All this
made Lewis an important ally for Compass. It also meant that,
certain of having his comments reported by a media keen to
foment splits in Labour's fragile fabric, he always had to measure his words carefully. Tonight was no exception. Speaking in
generalities rather than specifics, Lewis spoke up for electoral
reform and praised the idea of a collaborative, broad-based
progressive front while saying nothing that could be construed
as criticism of Labour's current benighted attitudes towards PA
– no name-check for the Godalming Three, and Lewis was out
of the room by the time they took the stage. If this ultimately
made his speech more unexceptionable than inspirational, PA
weren't complaining: Lewis had rock-star quality – in short
supply in politics generally, and especially on the left – and
he was an undisputed ally. By keeping his powder dry, Lewis
could protect his flank and the possibility that someday soon he
might acquire decisive power to shape Labour policy on PR and
even PA. So be it. The art of professional politics, after all, is not
only to seize but also to choose your moments.

This is a lesson the PA team now also had to take on board. The
morning after the night before, the War (and Peace) Room set
about launching, effectively, PA 2.0. They now knew the full tally
of formal alliances: altogether there were thirty-nine seats where
at least one party had stood aside to allow the best-placed progressive party to stop the Tories, and a further three where one
party had stood aside in favour of a less-well-placed progressive

party.[36] All but two of these involved Green stand-downs (with the Lib Dems reciprocating in Brighton Pavilion and Skipton and Ripon, and the NHA and/or WEP also standing aside or endorsing other parties in some seats). There were odd other instances where individual candidates had taken it upon themselves to break with their own party's obduracy – for example, ultra-marginal Bury North (Tory majority over Labour just 378), where the Lib Dems' (Somerset-domiciled) candidate Richard Baum sensibly urged his supporters to vote Labour – and, of course, numerous others where unsupported and effectively under-resourced paper candidates largely allowed other parties a free run at the Conservatives while local activists poured into the nearest winnable or defensible marginal seat.

Compass now similarly had to become more highly goal-oriented than ever before. Instrumentality, perforce, would prevail between now and 8 June. From here on under, PA 2.0 as a campaign had two basic strands. The first was to encourage tactical voting by progressives wherever it could make a difference: to this end, the VoteSmart tool on the PA website went live, recommending a tactical vote in 211 constituencies. For the most part, the recommendation was based on the 2015 results, which had almost eliminated three-way marginals (in England; in Wales and of course much more in Scotland, the picture was more complicated)[37] of the kind that formerly were quite common; but there were a few tricky calls, for example, in former Lib Dem seats where the party had lost so badly in 2015 it either had surrendered second place to Labour, or risked doing so. Whether Labour was genuinely the strongest

---

36 For a full list of progressive alliances in the 2017 general election, see Appendix A.
37 See below, 'Other Counties'.

progressive challenger in these seats – some of them never hitherto Labour-held – or whether the Lib Dems could be expected
to recover their previous strength, was one of the PA's most
difficult calls: the final results would prove just how difficult.
Elsewhere, VoteSmart recommendations created some bruised
feelings. The anger provoked in some Greens by the website's
failure to recommend a Green vote in Bristol West has already
been mentioned. But to do so, given the numbers, would
have been to allow an ethical response and a wish (that the
Greens be rewarded, in an increased vote if nothing else, for
their efforts) to prevail over common sense; and if the system
was to be gamed, one had to play the game. So in Bristol West
and all the other seats where the Greens had shown strongly
– but not strongly enough, and in most cases crucially in Labour-held seats – in 2015, the recommendation was either for
Labour (if the seat seemed safe from the Tories, as in Bristol
West) or for 'any progressive party'. It was a rough justice in
a way, but at least consistent. And the PA took pride in not
adopting the same line as votetactical2017.com and other resources who were urging 'tactical' Labour votes in even the
safest Labour seats: a stance that stored up significant problems
for the future of democratic politics under FPTP. (On the door-
steps of Holborn and St Pancras, a safe Labour seat, voters told
Sian Berry, who had achieved excellent results in making the
Green Party the third largest party in London in the mayoral
elections of 2016, that despite their admiration they dared not
vote Green this time in case the apocalyptic polls were correct.)
The Greens perhaps took some consolation from the VoteSmart
recommendation of a Green vote in the Isle of Wight, at least.

The second plank of PA 2.0 was to support progressive candidates in a select number of seats, as resources allowed. This

entailed, in the first place, undertaking a kind of triage on the list of PA seats, eliminating both those non-marginals where stand-asides seemed unlikely to affect the result (e.g., Brighton Pavilion, safe for Caroline Lucas, or relatively safe Labour seats such as York Central and Eltham) and those seats where Compass lacked sufficient local contacts to be able to make an impact: PA seats in this category included Gower, both Bury seats, Hyndburn and others. (Westmorland & Lonsdale was an interesting outlier: although Compass did put resources into nearby Carlisle, enthusiasm for helping Tim Farron save his seat proved to be in short supply amongst local, mostly Labour and Green, volunteers, and it was quietly dropped from the target list.) In their place were added a number of seats where alliances hadn't been achieved but a strong-on-the-ground Compass presence enabled both physical canvassing and, crucially, the flow of information to make virtual targeting by Facebook ads etc. possible. The great majority of these, naturally, were key marginals (and in some cases, for reasons that weren't entirely clear, adjacent non-marginals, such as Cardiff North and its safe Labour neighbour Cardiff West). There were one or two punts, like SW Surrey for obvious reasons; and also the odd 'instrumental' choice, most notably Clive Lewis's seat, Norwich South, which, though never seriously at risk despite Lewis's anxiety at the start of the campaign (which local Greens regarded as silly, and consequently refused to stand down their candidate: they were amply justified by the result, which saw Lewis' majority soar to over 15,500 while Labour failed to gain neighbouring Norwich North by just 500 votes – some of Compass's resources could usefully have been diverted there), it was obviously politic of Compass to be seen supporting. In all, there were ultimately thirty-one 'official' PA target seats, of which only nine had local alliances.

Targeting

Central to the way major British political parties approach a modern election campaign is the idea of targeting. It's called that for a reason: imagine a campaign as a series of concentric circles that also mark progress over time, with the campaign focus steadily moving through the outer rings with the broadest radius at or before the start of the election campaign proper to the innermost, smallest and most tightly defined zone on Election Day itself.

The outermost, most straightforward and most generally understood ring involves the targeting of campaign resources – which, in Britain's tightly financially regulated campaign environment, means above all human resources, that is party volunteers – to those seats where they will be most valuable. None of the parties spends more than the bare minimum of time and effort campaigning in those seats they regard as unwinnable, based on past performance (sometimes they will quite literally field paper candidates whose campaign amounts to little more than the state-guaranteed postal delivery of an election address to every household in the constituency: this is particularly the case for the Liberal Democrats, who face the problem of being a 'minor-major' party – maintaining a national profile while having realistic ambitions in only a small minority of seats). Equally, parties will usually spend only a modest amount of time working their own safest seats (though it's important not to make voters feel taken for granted – a problem that seems to have affected Labour's vote in both its former industrial heartland seats in the north of England and, far more seriously, in Scotland – so some visible presence will be necessary if only to forestall unpleasant surprises on polling day). As with everything else about elections conducted under

FPTP, the overwhelming majority of resources are concentrated on 'target' seats: those seats parties are either defending on modest majorities, or those they hope to capture from their opponents on realistically achievable swings.

So far, so straightforward. But targeting doesn't end with the identification of target seats – that's just where it begins. Campaigning within target seats is itself conducted according to the iron law of targeting. For the great majority of people who aren't political activists themselves and may take little or no interest in politics generally, their principal or, indeed, only contact with political parties comes at election time in the form of a ring on the doorbell or (increasingly, as patterns of work and leisure change and parties find that old-style house-to-house delivers ever-diminishing voter contact returns) a telephone canvassing call. But this 'canvassing' has become something of a misnomer: to the extent that canvassing implies soliciting views and opinion, or even engaging in political debate, as a primary aim, the major political parties barely canvas at all. Of course, by engaging in some kind of conversation with voters, canvassing teams hoover up large amounts of voter opinion and information on a wide range of issues, from a wide variety of local-authority-related issues (rubbish collection, dog waste, planning gripes etc.) that canvassers note for follow-up by local councillors, to pressing personal or community concerns that need to be addressed by the local MP, as well as views on a range of other topics: opinions of the party leadership, or feelings about key issues of the day. But tellingly, the printed-out forms that canvassers use bearing voters' names and addresses sourced from the electoral register don't leave much space for this kind of general discursive feedback. (Hence the returns passed back to party organisers are frequently a mess of canvassers' crabbed handwriting, the consequence of trying to squeeze often complex reports into an ungratefully formatted space not really designed for it.) Because ultimately, that isn't what canvassers are concerned with. Their job is something much more specific, even reductive: voter identification.

The canvassers' foremost concern is to establish whether the individual standing before them – and the other members of that person's household – is likely to cast their vote for the canvasser's party, or for one of their opponents (and if so, which one, if the voter will say). Not to ask why, really, and still less to attempt to change minds: simply to grab the all-important voter ID data for tabulation by volunteer staffers working at the local party offices with the candidate and the party agent. Because political party membership, like other traditional forms of social belonging (the extended cohabiting family, union membership, churchgoing, community societies, working men's clubs etc.), has steadily declined over decades under pressure from longer and more flexible working hours, multiplying and often ephemeral leisure options and, less tangibly, the inexorable shift towards individualism and even social atomisation, from one election to the next parties have found their volunteer base steadily shrinking. (The Corbyn Labour Party has spectacularly reversed this trend, surging from around 200,000 under Ed Miliband to over half a million immediately before the 2017 election was called, many of these under the age of thirty – and this would prove to have a major impact on the 2017 election – but whether this proves sustainable over the long term remains to be seen. In March 2017 by contrast the Conservatives had around 150,000 members, a growing proportion of them elderly.) And many party members are, of course, members in name and Direct Debit only, playing little or no active part in party work. The growth in telephone canvassing has partly compensated for this downturn in bodies on the ground (because one volunteer can ring far more voters than the same individual could knock on doors in the same time). But it also becomes ever more imperative to make the most efficient possible use of the time spent 'on the knocker' by the reduced cohort of house-to-house canvassers. So the conversations canvassers are encouraged to have with voters are strictly regulated to maximise data-gathering and minimise the time spent doing so.

Far more important than voters' motives, sentiments and opinions, what social scientists call qualitative data – though, of course, these matter immensely to parties in the abstract, in order to be able to tailor national campaigns to voters' most urgent concerns: hence the growth of focus groups and other such public-opinion-aggregating formats – is the quantitative data on how that voter plans to vote in the upcoming election, how s/he voted last time, how likely s/he is to vote at all and so forth. Each of these all-important answers, if provided, has its own field and its own letter code for volunteers to enter on the canvas return. To ensure that the right voter ID questions are asked as time-efficiently as possible, canvassers have an outline script they are encouraged to stick to. Cynically, if a canvasser leaves a doorstep knowing that a voter is intensely concerned about (for example) the proposed closure of a local hospital but not having ascertained that that concern will translate into a vote for a particular party, the exercise has been a waste of time – however important the issue might be to the local community or even the country in the larger scheme of things.

To some extent, parties – very much depending on their human resources – gather this kind of data year-round through a variety of local campaigning activities that bring voters into their orbit (a street stall collecting names on a petition against that hospital closure, for example). The Fixed-Term Parliaments Act notionally allows parties to pace their data-gathering efforts over time, because the date of the next election is written into law (though Theresa May demonstrated how little an obstacle the legislation really poses to a majority government that wants to hold an election at a time of its own convenience). But the biggest voter ID effort, of course, takes place at election time, when paper members tend to want to do something to justify their party subs and eager or curious volunteers appear at local party offices. Ideally, over the course of a five- to seven-week campaign, an adequately resourced party campaign will manage at least two complete canvases of the constituency – that is, every registered voter will have had their doorbell rung or their phone number called twice before election day. (Meaning the attempt to contact the voter has been made: it doesn't mean, of course, that all voters have been reached by the campaign even once. Depending on the demographic makeup of the seat in question, voter contact rates even on the same amount of campaign resource can vary wildly from very sketchy to near-comprehensive.)

Once a resident has been successfully contacted, boxing him or her into a discernible voter category is a relentless and insistent process. And always, getting an answer as quickly as possible matters more even than what the answer is, and far more than trying to persuade a voter to commit, still less change their mind. For party organisers, the triage of canvas returns is brutal. Not unreasonably, anyone who refuses to answer is marked down as an 'Against'. But so, very often, is anyone who insists they will vote Labour (or Conservative, or Lib Dem or whatever) but who has a track record from previous elections of voting for another party, or not voting at all. Canvassers (and often candidates) tend to be idealistic and optimistic about voters; organisers and agents are typically professional cynics. Voters may have many motivations for telling a canvasser what they want to hear: the most obvious being allowed to return undisturbed to their dinner or TV show. To hardened party hacks, actions – in this case, past voter behaviour – speak far louder than words. And did you think that choice, deliberated and discriminating, was what democracy was all about? Think again. The value of a 'don't know' canvassing response – never particularly high – depreciates dramatically as the campaign draws on. By the last week of a campaign, an 'Undecided' is usually re-categorised simply as an 'Against' (but too polite to say so), or equally likely a non-voter. The chances of the party returning before Election Day to try to turn that 'Don't know' into a 'Yes' are negligible. Organisers' cynicism is fathomless: the lagging canvasser who, upon catching up to the rest of her group following an intense, protracted doorstep session and announces with pride that she has secured the conversion of a waverer or even an opponent, expecting high praise, may instead be met with rolling eyes. That impressionable voter so readily persuaded by ten minutes' conversation may be just as readily persuaded by the canvasser from the next party to knock on her door; or he may be a loner simply grateful for the attention and the company. In any event, the acquisition of a solitary debatable vote wasn't worth the ten minutes it ate up – time in which another dozen voters could have been identified in the neighbouring properties.

Of course, parties don't come to their election canvasses blind. Parties' voter ID programmes are palimpsests, layering responses year on year upon one another – all the while drilling down to the solid, reliable (and reliably turning out to vote) supporters, the ones within the final concentric circle that gets activated in the final days of the campaign with leaflet runs targeted solely at identified supporters and, above all, on election day itself. Come polling day, any chatter about policy or values is for the birds. GOTV (Get Out The Vote) is the only game in town. Voter ID returns are used to print out 'knocking-up' sheets of Labour (or Conservative, Lib Dem, SNP etc.) 'promises', complete with voter numbers from the electoral roll. The lists compiled by polling-station tellers – the people on chairs who ask you for your voter number on your way in or out of the polling station – are periodically relayed to ward committee rooms where those who have voted are crossed off the list of promises while party workers are despatched to plague those who haven't with serial entreaties, growing ever more urgent with the passing hours till polls close to seal the deal and vote. A successful polling-day operation is one that sees its list of promises – virginal at the start of the day – mostly or even entirely (this happens only very rarely even in the best-run and -staffed campaigns) scored through with confirmed turnouts.

Everybody in the PA team knew this way of working. At one time or another, they'd all pounded the pavements and climbed the stairwells on behalf of their 'parties of origin' (as some PA staffers started to call their own parties). And, at one time or another – because the PA, by its nature, attracted those who were temperamentally inclined to question the received wisdom and the standard model – they'd all probably also felt how mechanical, how arid – how instrumental – the process had become. Of course, practical politics demands a disciplined and robust system for recording and rallying one's support. But, at some time in the last few decades – perhaps with the triumph of managerial politics under New Labour – the process seemed to have become disconnected from the values it notionally served. Was this really how democracy was really supposed to work?

> Good morning, I'm calling on behalf of Severus Snape, your local Labour candidate in the general election next week. Have you decided which way you'll vote yet?
> [SCRIPT: 'If 'yes', go to:'] You have? Are you likely to be supporting Labour?
> [SCRIPT: If 'yes', go to:] That's great! Many thanks for your support. Just a reminder that this is likely to be a very close fight so every vote will count. Thanks again.

And enter the appropriate letter code in the requisite box and on to the next doorbell…

The Progressive Alliance was preserved from this way of politics as data collection by a simple truth: they didn't have the resources, human or technological, to do it. Top-level targeting – the identification of key seats – was easy enough: from the local PA clusters, the seats where Greens had stood down, and other potential progressive wins (or progressive tragedies), a list pretty much wrote itself. But without any previous campaigns or canvas returns, there was no existing database of progressive-inclined voters to draw on; no pool of prior support to return to, confirm and check off on a list. To build such a database would take weeks of hard slog by armies of volunteers that Compass simply didn't have. In many cases, the best PA could do was to identify (for example, from recent local election results) areas of, say, strong Liberal Democrat support in a Labour-leaning seat vulnerable to the Tories, and start ringing on doorbells without any prior assumptions or data – without even knowing the resident's name (as a third-party campaign the PA was legally entitled to access the electoral rolls, but in the main they didn't do so). They were, compared to everything they'd grown used to over years of party work, flying blind, shooting in the dark.

But this ostensible major drawback, in fact, proved liberating. Freed from the tyranny of voter ID-as-we-know-it-Jim, the PA volunteers had no choice but to talk, honestly and openly, to voters. Having tossed away the comfort blanket – or was it a straitjacket? – of party label, with all their accompanying baggage (for good and ill: party 'brands' in the twenty-first century may have become increasingly diluted and vacuous, yet they still signal certain core values to which activists and voters alike continue to relate), PA workers had to undertake very different kinds of conversations with whoever answered the door. They had to introduce themselves, explain what had motivated them to be knocking on strangers' doors, convey the core principles of the Progressive Alliance – which most voters, not being dedicated *Guardian* readers, had never heard of – and explore with voters the ramifications of such a choice for their community and their democracy. The conversation might last a few seconds – not wearing a party badge was no guarantee you wouldn't get the door slammed in your face – or minutes at a time: the unheard-of, precious minutes of engagement that a standard party voter ID outing could never afford. Frances Foley, who ventured onto the streets of Clive Lewis's seat in Norwich South, testified to the energised feeling she got from approaching a front door on the basis of nothing but a Green poster in the window, armed with only her convictions and an eagerness to engage in a genuine debate. She spoke for many others. And, in Norwich, as elsewhere, Green voters tended to be better-informed than most about the Progressive Alliance, and – somewhat to their own leaders' chagrin, as we've seen – well-disposed towards it even in seats where the Greens decided to stand a candidate.

As with so much in the 2017 PA campaign, it was only by un-learning the habits and routines of the old politics that the new politics could start to take shape. Treating voters not as data points to be rounded off, rounded up and knocked up come polling day, but as human beings with values, concerns, consciences and sensibilities of their own, was another step on the road to that new politics.

Barnstorming

Over the second half of the campaign, PA acquired an American accent in the shape of Claire Sandberg: a slight, softly spoken veteran of Bernie Sanders's insurgent campaign for the Democratic presidential nomination in 2016. The introduction was made by Paul Hilder – the same Paul Hilder who, as co-founder (with David Cameron's former advisor Steve Hilton) of the new politics platform Crowdpac, had warned the political establishment that 'the new politics is coming' apparently in support of Arron Banks's efforts to create the Regressive Alliance. In fact, Hilder was a long-time associate at campaigning organisations such as change.org and Avaaz, and a vocal proponent of the idea that digitisation was transforming political campaigning in ways that went far beyond the application of new technological solutions to traditional ends, and saw the potential for opening up new forms of movement-based activism and opportunities for democratic renewal – views that made him a natural ally for Compass. Having met Sandberg during his own work 'feeling the Bern', Hilder was keen to blend the dynamism he saw infusing popular grassroots politics on both sides of the Atlantic with the large-scale practical campaigning experience acquired from Sanders's presidential run – which he believed had 'chang[ed] the laws of political physics'.

Sandberg's sojourn in the UK – dividing her time between Compass and the Corbyn-supporting Labour affiliate Momentum – focused on disseminating the 'barnstorm' model developed during the Sanders campaign. Part town hall debate, part training session, part revival meeting, the barnstorm aimed to mobilise volunteers and maximise their contribution by generating collective buy-in at the meeting to the principle of actively campaigning for the cause, and to organise and schedule that campaigning at that very same event. The format was that volunteers, having been introduced to one another and to the principle of the progressive alliance, would role-play canvassing in their local neighbourhood and then sign up to do so for real in the next few days, committing to work on specified days and locations in small groups. For Compass, which had a good-sized subscriber base but little track in the realm of active doorstep campaigning, this was the ideal means in a very limited window to translate interest and enthusiasm into boots on the ground.

All the PA/Compass team were old hands at the business of knocking on complete strangers' doors and asking them about their political preferences. If you've been doing it for years, it's often hard to recall how daunting the prospect may have seemed when you undertook to do so for the first time. Would your elector slam the door in your face? Shout at you? Tell you to get lost? Set the dogs on you? The PA team had experienced all of these (perhaps not the dogs) and their hides had thickened over time, as canvassers' skins must. But there was no guarantee many, or any, of the people who showed up at a PA barnstorm would have any of that experience; and there was no time to hand-hold them though their first forays into voter contact. The hope was that by assigning volunteers to teams ideally three-strong or larger – affinity groups, US radicals might have called them – novice canvassers would collectively support one another through the experience (and also be less likely to flake out, knowing that by doing so they were would be letting others down). The key was to generate a human wave of enthusiasm for the idea at the barnstorm itself and not to allow that energy to dissipate, as it invariably would, over subsequent days – but to get volunteers to commit, there and then, to hitting the streets and working to deliver the change they wanted.

It was all very un-English, Frances Foley thought, when she first met Sandberg for a quick-and-dirty training session. In particular, she wondered whether the raise-your-hands-and-testify ethos, rooted in a particular American tradition of participative voluntarism that went far back before the 1960s to the forms of religious enthusiasm on which the first colonies were founded, would translate to the UK's more reserved, 'after you, no, please, I insist' culture. The first version of the canvasser's script Sandberg devised (which would be used for the role-plays at the barnstorms and subsequently on the doorstep) was distinctly 'American' – liberally peppered with exclamation points, interjections like 'Beautiful!' and the like – and clearly needed some diplomatic editing if it wasn't to put people off.

Beyond these cultural hazards, though, the idea at the heart of the barnstorm spoke directly to the PA's core values. In truth, everyone knew that sending out a few dozen volunteers (if you were very lucky and successful) more or less at random onto a few streets in a given constituency, however marginal, was unlikely to make an enormous difference to the result. But that had never been the only objective. Had it been so,

the script – which asked open-ended questions (as any advocate or market researcher will tell you, always to be avoided
whenever possible) and invited voters to engage in potentially
extended conversations about the issues that mattered to them,
and whether they felt existing political arrangements addressed
those concerns – would have been a woefully inefficient use of
precious time, just as the non-targeted nature of the canvassing
was a poor use of volunteer resources. (In fact, Frances Foley
came to feel that Compass had never satisfactorily resolved the
question of how much ground campaigning the PA planned
to do, and where such activities stood in the already-strained
organisation's priorities.) Rather, by engaging respondents in
the first instance not as 'voters' but as concerned, engaged individuals with a wish to make themselves heard and a right to
be heard but, in all likelihood, hugely frustrated by the sheer
difficulty in getting heard – in other words, as citizens – the
script exemplified the Compass commitment to a deeper conversation as part of a rebooting of democracy itself.

And it worked. With some inevitable hiccups along the way,
and on a small scale – and even at that scale, involving as it did
running or supporting barnstorms in locations as far-flung as
Brighton, Hastings, Carlisle, Lewes, Norwich, Oxford and Cardiff as well as Kilburn and (of course) Richmond, Compass's
resources were stretched to breaking point. It quickly became
apparent that some of Sandberg's expectations – coming from
the vastly better-resourced, more ambitious and frankly more
professional environment of a US presidential campaign –
needed adjusting to the framework of what was possible for
an organisation like Compass. But it worked. People came,
they spoke and they put their hands up and their bodies on
the line (or at least on the doorstep). The very first barnstorm

in Carlisle, a Tory-held marginal and the kind of seat Labour had to win if it was to make significant inroads into May's majority – and also as far from London as you could get and still be in England – was predictably chaotic, with an inescapably improvisational feel. All the same, drawing some sixty people to a volunteer mobilisation drive for a still ill-understood third-party cause at three days' notice (WhatsApp groups came into their own in situations like this) was cause for considerable satisfaction. And with each barnstorm, the system improved. It transpired, for example, that offering people a shallower incline of voter engagement – running street stalls or voter registration drives (particularly important in university cities like Brighton and Norwich, and ultimately of course so critical to the outcome of the election), rather than insisting that everyone hurl themselves right away at complete strangers' front doors – was a good way to harness enthusiasm without scaring people away.

For Foley, the barnstorms and the associated door-to-door campaigning, beyond building volunteer networks and capacity for the next election, lent the PA campaign a sense of realness for both voters and the core PA members: something that the largely web-based campaign in the London office lacked. Initially, Foley worried – and she still worried – that every day she herself was on the road to run a barnstorm was a day she couldn't easily stay abreast of what was happening in the national campaign. But, by the end of the campaign, she came to feel that the value of the chance encounters with voters counterbalanced a day's absence from the office. From the outset, while making the utmost use of technology the PA had sought to strike a balance between online and 'real-world' activity, and was determined to avoid charges of encouraging or enabling empty 'clicktivism'. SmallAxe is grounded in the real-world principles of community organising, with many of its key workers graduates in one way or another from Citizens UK, the UK's largest community organisers' network. There was a deep scepticism on the team about the value of purely online activity. Alongside every website update the question was asked, how will this help in the real world? The default volunteering options in NationBuilder were changed from 'I can do social media', 'I'm good with tech', and so on, to 'I can knock on doors', 'I can run a stall' and the like.

Once on the doorstep – and this is an experience familiar to many campaigners – Frances Foley felt her own belief in the PA's cause deepen as her advocacy was reflected back to her by voters' reactions. Working on the streets, the Progressive Alliance concretised itself as it demonstrated the strength of its supporters' convictions, engaged voters who were immediately curious at the absence of the usual party rosettes and the reflex responses (positive or negative) they triggered, and was evidently more agile and adept than the parties because not tethered to any overriding party line. Foley recalls talking to a Lib Dem voter in Norwich who was somewhat reluctant to surrender his vote there to Labour, and telling him that she herself planned to vote Green, while just a few miles up the road in Norman Lamb's seat Norfolk North the PA were recommending a vote for the Liberal Democrats. For Foley and other PA volunteers like her, feeling themselves to be part of a campaign working all across the country for different people of different parties in different seats was an important step in the realisation of a progressive ideal that had genuinely started to transcend sectional party loyalties. Whether the Norwich Lib Dem was persuaded, and whether he did indeed cast his ballot for Clive Lewis, only he can know (though given the nearly 60 per cent decline in the Lib Dem vote locally on polling day, it's a fair bet). But, in that conversation, and the many dozens like it that took place around the country in the final weeks of the campaign, the Progressive Alliance palpably started to become more than the sum of its sometimes ragtag parts.

Other countries

The Progressive Alliance was overwhelmingly an English affair. In fact, it was largely a southern English affair: of the PA's thirty-one target seats in the last phase of the campaign, over half the total were south of Watford, with seven in London and another nine on the south coast. This wasn't due to any south-eastern chauvinism on the PA's part: it simply reflected the existing network of contacts available to Compass at the start of the campaign and the compressed time frame for a very small and overstretched team to develop and activate more. It was actually very much to the PA team's credit that in the end they managed to run ground campaigns as far afield as Carlisle, Norwich and Cardiff.

But the geographical slant did mean that the PA perforce essentially overlooked developments in the other constituent parts of the United Kingdom that not only turned out to have a crucial impact on the outcome of the election as a whole (and its aftermath), but also highlighted both problems and openings for the PA's analysis and strategy going forward.

Scotland

Even before the election was called, for example, the PA had tacitly agreed that Scotland was too tough a nut to crack. Partly this was the resources issue; partly, too, a recognition that the different contours of the political landscape north of the border massively complicated the already vexed electoral calculus for progressive alliances. As soon as Nicola Sturgeon put a second independence referendum, in her own words, 'on the table', she ensured that votes in the ensuing election campaign in Scotland would be cast in good measure on the question of the Union, which partly sheared across left–right party lines just as Brexit (itself of course a massive issue in Scotland, too) did in the rest of the UK. Even as clear evidence emerged of a significant Conservative recovery in Scotland – above all, local election results that were as gratifying for the Conservatives as they were disastrous for Labour – the idea of Labour (or the Lib Dems) in any way supporting the SNP to forestall the Tory advance was, frankly, for the birds. Even amongst the large number of Labour voters who were sympathetic to or simply uninterested in the independence issue, opposition was mounting on other grounds to the now decade-long SNP hegemony (never mind that Nicola Sturgeon's Holyrood administration wasn't on the ballot in 2017). The SNP were in everyone's sights (bar perhaps the – pro-independence – Scottish Greens, who stood just three candidates and were accused by the other parties of seeking to sustain the SNP).

As the campaign developed, this aspect became ever more pronounced, with Sturgeon enduring awkward questioning in televised debates on devolved matters including education and (from a nurse reduced to using a food bank) NHS funding. At the start of the campaign, the PA had somewhat blithely assumed that (given the Tories' long Scottish deep freeze, failing to return more than a single MP at any election in a quarter of a century) any movement in Scottish seat distribution would be amongst progressive parties, i.e. Labour or the Lib Dems making small gains at the SNP's expense – which therefore wouldn't affect the overall reckoning of anti-Tory forces at Westminster. By polling day, with growing evidence that there was a palpable appetite amongst voters to give the SNP a bit of a proverbial kicking for a variety of motives, this assumption was looking very shaky.

And so it proved. Both the Lib Dems (making net gains of three seats from the SNP) and Labour (benefiting from a late surge to put their dismal local election performance behind them with six gains) recovered from their 2015 nadir; but the night's clear winners – even as the SNP retained their overall majority with thirty-five of Scotland's fifty-nine seats – were the Conservatives, who finished with twelve new MPs, their strongest performance since 1983. These twelve seats – which included the scalps of former SNP leader Alex Salmond in Gordon and the SNP's Westminster leader Angus Robertson in neighbouring Moray – would ultimately prove absolutely vital to Theresa May's ability to cling to power while the Scottish Tory leader Ruth Davidson, whose energetic and positive campaign was favourably contrasted to May's wooden and defensive one, was one of the night's big winners and instantly propelled herself into the running as a potential future Tory leader. (Labour's Kezia Dugdale also received unfavourable comparisons to Davidson, with some arguing that a less negative, SNP-focused Scottish Labour campaign channelling the gathering enthusiasm for Jeremy Corbyn could have performed a good deal better than it did.) The gigantic swings to the Conservatives in some of these seats (over 20 per cent in Gordon) and against the SNP almost everywhere, rolling back the 2015 SNP tsunami and transforming many of their retained seats into marginals (eight with majorities below 1,000, a further six below 2,000)[38] was a reminder of the sheer volatility

---

38 The SNP held Glasgow South West with a majority over Labour of sixty; Glasgow East with a majority of seventy-five; and Fife North East with a majority over the Lib Dems, after three recounts, of two votes.

of the contemporary UK electorate – a factor with important if ambiguous implications for PA strategy.[39] The result also ensured that whenever the next election was called – and probably for the first time in living memory – almost every Scottish seat would be in play, with enormous potential repercussions for the composition of the UK government.

Wales

The election in Wales, unlike those in Scotland and Northern Ireland, fairly closely matched the general trend of the election in England. At the outset, Labour – defending twenty-five of the forty Welsh seats – faced the same problems in its Leave-voting Welsh strongholds as in similar former industrial areas in northern England. As gruesome for Labour as the polls were generally at the start of the campaign, it was particularly shocking when one poll not only put the Tories ahead in Wales but did so by fully 10 per cent, a political earthquake in the historically solidly Labour principality. An additional factor in the Welsh-speaking parts of the principality was the challenge from Plaid Cymru – which though it had supported Labour administrations in Cardiff since devolution, co-operating well enough in the Welsh Assembly, remained hostile, almost contemptuous rivals with Labour on the ground. Labour and Plaid were for the most part competing for the same ground. Indeed, Dwyfor Meirionnydd was the only one of the three Plaid-held seats where the Conservatives had finished second in 2015, but Plaid's majority of over 5,000 was secure enough not to need Labour's help even had it been on offer. Ceredigion was a rare Lib Dem–Plaid marginal with Labour nowhere. As far as the

PA was concerned, these four seats were all progressive-held and likely to remain so however they swung in the election (as it happened, Labour came within ninety-two votes of unseating Plaid in the heavily Welsh-speaking constituency of Arfon in the far north-west, while Plaid took Ceredigion, leaving Wales without a Liberal MP for the first time in living memory). But the relationship between Labour and Plaid, in particular, threw up a depressingly familiar pattern: the hostility between the parties ensuring that, although Plaid's limited support outside the Welsh coast might in many cases have made a significant difference in a number of Labour–Tory marginals, there was little prospect of any such alliance.

In the unitary elections in early May, Labour's vote held up rather better than expected, with the party staying slightly ahead in terms of the popular vote in Wales. The swing of approximately 2 per cent to the Tories since the previous general election would not be sufficient to gain the Tories any seats in Wales if applied evenly – consistent with the Conservative vote nationally somewhat underperforming their headline opinion poll figures. Even Labour's most vulnerable seat, Wrexham (traditionally a Labour stronghold, but where a mixture of boundary and social change have gradually strengthened the anti-Labour vote) was set to see the party squeak narrowly home. Notwithstanding, the Tories persisted with their aggressive targeting of Labour seats, not just Wrexham, but all of the other seats in the north, both Newport seats, Bridgend and two of Labour's three Cardiff city seats. This last was the basis on which Compass identified the same three Cardiff seats – West, South & Penarth (both Labour) and the Tory marginal North – as its only non-English targets.

As the polls turned, in line with but outstripping the

nationwide trend – successive Welsh polls putting Labour first 9, then 10, then 11 per cent ahead of the Tories (better than its 2015 result) – Labour losses started to seem much less likely, and thoughts turned to what just weeks before had seemed the remote possibility of actually gaining seats. Gower, which Labour held from the First World War until the Tories shockingly snatched it with a majority of just twenty-seven in 2015, was Labour's number one target seat in the whole of the UK, and Vale of Clwyd had also been lost only narrowly in 2015. Labour ended up taking both these seats, but also took the middle-class constituency of Cardiff North from the Tories on a substantial swing. In Ynys Mon (Anglesey), where more than one report during the campaign placed it third behind Plaid and the Tories, Labour increased its tiny 2015 majority twenty-fold to over 5,250.

As in its traditional formerly industrial strongholds elsewhere in the country, Labour was less than totally convincing in the valleys, where the swing ran at around 2 per cent, but still won everywhere without difficulty. At the same time, however, it recorded its strongest performances in urban areas, notably Cardiff where every one of the city's four seats recorded a swing of 6 per cent or higher – enough to win the PA target Cardiff North with a majority of over 4,000.

Northern Ireland

As always, the election in Northern Ireland was conducted in virtual isolation from the rest of the country. By long convention, the main UK parties do not field candidates in the province, whose parties line up (apart from the non-sectarian Alliance) on sectarian lines. However, not only would the 2017 election in the province prove profoundly consequential for the UK as a whole, it was also the outstanding example of a 'progressive tragedy' nationwide. In Northern Ireland, uniquely, an electoral pact amongst parties that at Westminster would either have joined a progressive coalition or, at the very least, opposed a Conservative government, was actively under discussion amongst party leaders during the campaign. Its failure had unpredictable but far-reaching consequences not only for Northern Ireland but for the country.

When the election was called, Sinn Féin and the moderate nationalist SDLP proposed a pact with the Alliance and the Green Party in three Belfast seats, South (where the SDLP were defending a majority of only 906), North (where the DUP's Westminster leader Nigel Dodds was vulnerable to Sinn Féin) and East (also held by the DUP and a potential target for the Alliance, with the nationalist parties nowhere). The basis for a pact was clear, and importantly transcended sectarian questions: the DUP was the only Ulster party to have campaigned to leave the EU – whereas Northern Ireland as a whole voted 56 per cent Remain. Since the referendum, the status of the Eire–Northern Ireland border – the UK's only land boundary with the EU 27 – had become a focal point of the forthcoming negotiations (the EU listing it as one of their four priorities for a quick resolution). The prospect of a return to a guarded – let alone fortified – border in the island of Ireland was regarded with dismay by all sides. So there was a clear cross-community interest in weakening the DUP's representation at Westminster.

But the pact never came about. Partly this was because the Alliance were reluctant to lend their support to Alasdair McDonnell, already announced (without prior consultation with the other parties) as the SDLP's candidate in South Belfast, on account of his pro-life stance on abortion, and partly because they were also reluctant to risk their non-sectarian reputation by supporting Sinn Féin in North Belfast. The upshot was that the contest in those seats rehearsed the familiar 'progressive tragedy' picture from elsewhere in the UK – the Alliance losing in a multi-party fight in Belfast East, Sinn Féin unable to unseat the DUP in North, and the SDLP losing in South.

As a consequence, the Northern Irish cohort at Westminster now comprises ten DUP members and the independent Unionist Lady Sylvia Hermon (the sole anti-Brexit MP). Sinn Féin nearly doubled their number in the Commons with two gains from the SDLP and one from the Ulster Unionists. But though the republicans are fiercely opposed to Brexit, of course Sinn Féin will not actually be 'in' the Commons at all as they remain adamantly committed to their abstentionist policy and will not take their seats. Thus the Remain majority of Northern Irish voters – most of all the nationalist community, who overwhelmingly opposed Brexit – have only a single MP to represent their views in the Commons chamber, and that vote alone on the Brexit deal, while the DUP conspire with the Tories to deliver a hard Brexit. For the UK as a whole, the outcome of the failure of the progressive pact in Belfast was the election of three more DUP votes for preserving Theresa May in government – effectively adding four to the Tories' majority.[40]

As the New Statesman's Patrick Maguire commented dolefully, 'there is no measure by which this election was a good one for progressive, pro-European politics – nor for co-operation between them.' The consequences of the failure of the anti-Brexit

---

40 Not six, as one of the MPs potentially elected under the pact would have been a Sinn Féin MP in Belfast North: each Sinn Féin MP elected lowers the threshold for an overall majority, effectively making it easier for the Tories to stay in office.

parties in Northern Ireland to strike a deal have already been far-reaching, and not only for Northern Ireland itself.

A thousand flowers

As the campaign entered its final week, an unseasonably damp month of May gave way to a sunny, warm June – 'election weather' in the eyes of many older hands, especially those who had cut their teeth in the long sunlit days of 1997 when every door seemed to open onto a Labour promise and it seemed indeed that things not only could, but would, get better. The day before the election, Neal Lawson sat in his tidy, sunny Teddington garden (like so many in the PA team, this son of proletarian south London had latterly relocated to the green, well-tended far south-western suburbs) and reflected on the tumultuous last seven weeks. Over the last fortnight of the campaign, Lawson had taken a step back from the daily grind of the campaign and sought to take a longer view of what had happened, what the PA had achieved – and failed to – and where to go from here.

In so many ways, it had been the strangest of campaigns. At the outset, the Tories' seemingly predetermined crushing victory recalled Thatcher's 1980s landslides – but at least then the question of whether the SDP–Liberal Alliance could 'break the mould' of British politics had added interest to the contest. As of 18 April, progressives had only a slow-motion car crash to look forward to – or a doomed trudge to the slaughterhouse. The first reversal of expectations was Theresa May's unexpected utter incompetence as a campaigner – a performance whose robotic opening came to seem positively Kennedy-esque compared with the subsequent levels of ineptitude. May made Gordon Brown seem like a natural. Was the nadir her assertion to Andrew Marr that people (including NHS nurses) turned to food banks for 'complex reasons?' (A stupefied Marr responded that people used food banks because they didn't have enough to eat.) Perhaps; but there were plenty of alternatives. And around her, the vaunted, feared Tory election-winning machine that just two years earlier had ground Ed Miliband and Nick Clegg to mincemeat simply ground to a halt. The party apparently had no strategy for communicating with the British people beyond the rancid – yet somehow flaccid and increasingly irrelevant – hysterics of its newspaper allies/overlords, and the sinister undertones of entitlement bordering on authoritarianism in May's election announcement seemed to have infected the manifesto, devoid of anything as vulgar as content – bar, of course, the disastrous dementia tax. Even the terrorist outrages in Manchester and London, each of which stayed campaigning nationwide for days at a time (making it three times in a year, following Jo Cox's murder during the referendum campaign, that political violence had marred British democracy) and which most observers assumed would play to traditional Tory strengths on national security (while highlighting Jeremy Corbyn's ambiguous track record on terrorism and extremism), failed to redound to May's credit as her own lengthy period overseeing (and cutting) police numbers and funding at the Home Office came under hostile scrutiny.

Meanwhile, those pesky polls – if they could be trusted – started to indicate the most dramatic shift in public opinion during an election campaign in modern polling history. The Tories' twenty-point lead halved, then halved again. The Labour Manifesto appeared not to be the second-longest suicide note in history, but a document whose robust optimism and sheer novelty – especially to those raised since nationalisation and redistribution became dirty words in the neoliberal consensus

– resonated and outweighed what economists disdained as its profligate, old-fashioned and Pollyannaish promises. Televised news footage in the last days of the campaign showed a relaxed and energised Jeremy Corbyn – visibly liberated from the strains of managing his hostile, disputatious party (which, in fact, largely avoided public divisions for the entire seven weeks) and his weekly purgatory at PMQs – addressing enthusiastic crowds larger than anyone could recall in modern electioneering as he promoted the Manifesto fashioned (defence policy aside) in his own image.[41] Far from trying to keep Corbyn away from voters' eyes, Labour had deliberately – and perversely, as it seemed – set out to make the election as 'presidential' as possible a context between himself and the Prime Minister: and, against all expectations, he seemed to be getting the better of the battle.

And yet, strangest of all, it was hard to find anyone who thought any of this had made much of a difference. Yes, May was an unanticipated gift to the opposition. And true, by polling day, expectations of a landslide Conservative victory had receded. But reports from Labour MPs on the doorstep – usually unattributed, but repeated on every platform, not just in the Tory press – were still almost universally gloomy. The local elections results had been appalling for Labour and, despite a slight improvement in vote share, poor also for the Lib Dems. Moving towards polling day, tales of traditional Labour voters recoiling from Corbyn and predictions of swathes of lost seats remained very much the norm. The cover of the *New Statesman*'s pre-election edition – 'The Labour Reckoning' – depicted

---

41 By common consent, Corbyn's quite rare missteps during the campaign typically came when he was forced to defend Labour's official policy of retaining Britain's so-called independent nuclear deterrent, which he was universally known to oppose.

Corbyn, John McDonnell and Diane Abbott cowering as the Tory fireball hurtled towards them, an extinction-level event. Nobody apart from the most fervid Corbynites put much faith in the long-promised upsurge of young voters eager to revenge themselves on their elders for Brexit, the highest university tuition fees in Europe (which Labour promised to abolish) and the prospect of a lifetime being fleeced by private landlords.

As for the Progressive Alliance, inevitably Lawson had both regrets and satisfactions. There was plenty to be pleased about, like building from scratch an organisation able to organise and direct targeted campaigns in seats across the country. Compass's efforts had established the term and the concept of a progressive alliance firmly in the political lexicon and the mainstream of debate. *The Guardian*'s election editorial endorsing Labour also endorsed at least the principle of PA: 'it should be embraced as an idea, though one whose time has not yet come'; *The Guardian* and *The Mirror* had both run eve-of-poll tactical voting guides. The PA had generated a political brand that had attracted hundreds of thousands of unique visitors to the PA website and to use the VoteSmart tool. By the end of the campaign, through much trial and error, the website was the central node of a highly sophisticated system. Within the final fortnight before polling, Claire Sandberg had pulled some strings back in the US and persuaded NationBuilder to enable the prohibitively expensive premium features that PA needed to maximise its functionality. Casual visitors were now being funnelled into any one of a number of carefully planned user journeys: these included donating, volunteering their time, hosting an event, and sharing their VoteSmart recommendation on social media, with all of these harvesting an email address to receive campaign updates. Visitors from specific email campaigns were greeted by customised pages addressing the issue at hand; visitors from the PA's own targeted advertising campaigns were encouraged to make the most of their influencer status; and visitors from barnstorms were guided into the hosting funnel, where they could download the hosting toolkit, see who had RSVPed to their events, and add new ones, just like that. Meanwhile, ethical design company ClearHonestDesign, who had joined the PA team after the initial launch, developed a highly shareable series of entertaining, eye-catching and informational graphics, interactive mini-sites and memes to generate discussion around the idea of PA and drive users back to the main PA site. (The 'Doom Loop' video, a simple recursive animation showing May, Johnson and the rest of the Tory crew parading in endless succession to the crack of doom and scored to the *Star Wars* Imperial March, was a particular favourite.)

And at the very least, the PA had demonstrated that contrary to reports, the British left could indeed organise a piss-up in a brewery.

The biggest regret, obviously, was that the PA had ultimately been unable to break the logjam of institutionalised resistance to change in the established parties. Whether from habit, fear or sheer bloody-mindedness, neither Labour nor, for the most part, the Lib Dems had been willing even to sit down and discuss what they, and the country, might gain from working together instead of against one another. Worse still, as the Godalming Three could testify, they had actively sought to persecute those who dared to think of breaking through, or breaking down, the stockade around the turf the parties so stridently claimed and so anxiously protected. There had been some glowing exceptions to this rule: Penny Rivers in SW Surrey; Greens canvassing alongside Lib Dems wearing orange-green rosettes in Oxford West & Abingdon. That's what Lawson had imagined happening all over the country, and it hadn't. But, maybe even here, there was a gain too: because the truth was that if PA – at least in the arm's-length form of tactical voting – was happening on a massive scale, and if it made a difference, it would have happened not because of the parties (Greens aside) but despite them; and not even because of Compass, not on its own. Lawson knew that Compass was too small, too under-resourced, too new at this kind of work and not national enough in its reach to have changed the way people thought and used their vote in the space of seven short weeks. But if people showed that they could think it through for themselves, work the system, force change upon those unwilling to embrace it, then that would be possibly an even bigger win than if it were the Progressive Alliance driving that change.

Most know the line from *Field of Dreams*: 'If you build it, he will come.' It had become the clarion call of all those who dared to dream absurd, quixotic dreams and start out on improbable journeys in the face of scepticism or mockery or 'hard-edged realism'. Less often recalled is the film's closing scene when Ray Kinsella (Kevin Costner), having realised that the catcher in the baseball team materialising from his cornfield is his own dead father, turns wonderingly to Shoeless Joe Jackson with a sudden insight: 'It was you.' To which Joe simply replies, 'No, Ray. It was you.'

The PA had never wanted to force change, but had hoped to catalyse it. They didn't want to be change makers, but to help others see that change was indeed possible. As Lawson thought deep thoughts in his garden, back in the PA offices Frances Foley felt that was exactly what was happening. The last few days of the campaign had seen a sudden flood of workers pouring into the War (and Peace) Room as volunteers from the online activist network Avaaz and elsewhere arrived to help towards the PA to help with phone banking. All around the country, Compass members' phones started buzzing with friendly invitations to help get out the vote in the nearest PA target seat. Demand had stripped the PA offices of leaflets. Reports were coming into Foley of self-generated PA activities in parts of the country that the PA hadn't had the time or resources to work themselves – such as Chipping Barnet where Compass member Nick Mahony organised his own cross-party campaign group with over 100 volunteers and tricolor rosettes. As the PA website had suggested, people were Hosting Their Own barnstorms, downloading window bills and flyers to print at home, working their own streets. A thousand flowers were blooming.

To tell the truth, nobody quite knew what was happening Out There. Was Corbyn simply preaching to crowds of the long-converted, as most commentators insisted, or did the numbers presage a subterranean wave of cresting support for Labour? Would all the traffic on all the tactical voting and vote-swap sites deliver a coherent statement of the popular will, or a cacophony of disaggregated dissent that would let the Tories off the hook yet again?

Neal Lawson didn't pretend to know more than anyone else – though, like most of those in the PA team, his money was on a Tory majority in the region of fifty or thereabouts. He was focusing on drafting his post-election communiqué to Compass members. Currently it began, 'On June 9th thousands if not millions of people will feel lost and let down – they will be looking for answers, explanations and a new way ahead…' That was the best guess, anyway.

CHAPTER EIGHT

AND IN THE END...

...in the end, of course, nobody knew anything.

As Big Ben struck ten and the TV companies released the results of the exit poll, many of the assumptions undergirding British politics were shredded upon the instant. By the small hours of Friday 9 June, Theresa May had been deprived of her already small existing majority – those April visions of an epochal Conservative landslide now the faintest and most ironic of memories. Jeremy Corbyn's Labour had not only avoided the widely predicted catastrophe, but soared to its largest share of the popular vote since 2001 and gained seats (a net twenty-nine) in a UK-wide election for the first time since the Blair landslide of 1997 (though, on 262 seats, Labour remained far behind the Conservatives and further still from taking office). And – in an almost separate contest in Scotland underlining the extent to which Scottish political culture had detached itself from that of England and Wales – the briefly monolithic hegemony of the SNP ended as the party surrendered a quarter of its votes and a third of its seats to the Conservatives (their eleven net gains ultimately supplying the crucial parliamentary margin that would keep May in office, if not in power), Labour and the Liberal

Democrats in an apparent fightback by the parties of the Union. Labour's remarkable 10 per cent increase in vote share on the meagre 30 per cent achieved under Ed Miliband in 2015, fuelled as it seemed in equal measure by huge turnout amongst younger voters determined to revenge the generational imbalance of the Brexit referendum, by a general hostility to the vacuous and mean-spirited campaign waged by the Tories and, perhaps most importantly of all, by a rejection, finally after seven long years, of the austerity policies inflicted by the Tories on ordinary Britons while billionaires and tax evaders thrived, was achieved on the basis of an unashamedly expansionist, redistributive and, indeed in some respects, old-fashioned social-democratic manifesto – overturning the thirty-year post-Thatcher consensus that anything but a pro-market, at best stealthily reformist platform, would inevitably doom centre-left parties in the post-industrial Western consumerist democracies.

Elections, by their very nature, produce winners and losers. The 2017 general election was unusual in producing, across the board, results in which ostensible winners were simultaneously losers, and vice versa. The PA's Roger Wilson summed it up neatly in a post-election email: 'We fought a very big battle on a complex medieval landscape, won major advances, and suffered some major wounds on our side, too.' If you wanted an allegorical representation of a country that many felt was teetering on the verge of chaos and was, without question, deeply divided and unsure of its priorities and direction, this *Game of Thrones*-esque outcome was right on the money.

The biggest losers, obviously, were the Conservatives, who ended Theresa May's ill-starred, tone-deaf campaign fourteen seats down on their 2015 tally and eight short of an overall majority. Given their starting-point of a seemingly unassailable twenty-plus-point poll lead and an internally divided and floundering opposition under the least popular leader in recent memory, this was the unlosable election the Conservatives somehow, through arrogance and incompetence, contrived to throw away. Yet, on another reckoning, the Tories 'won' this election: they remained by far the largest party (fifty-six seats ahead of Labour), within reach of a manageable majority with the support of the DUP (proffered within minutes of the publication of the exit poll) and increased their national vote share (for the third election running) to over 42 per cent – a level not seen since Margaret Thatcher's second landslide in 1987.

Labour, meanwhile, delivered unanticipated gains in never-before-held seats such as Canterbury, Portsmouth South and (the final – result not announced until Friday afternoon after three full recounts; the narrowest – a Labour majority of just twenty; and to the outside world the most improbable of all) Kensington, took upon themselves the air of victors. Corbyn's barnstorming, feel-good campaign of straight talking, mass meetings (derided as unrepresentative echo chambers of the already-converted) and extravagant Old Labour spending commitments surged across the finish line on a wave of first-time-voter engagement, delivering a net gain of twenty-nine seats and a 40 per cent vote share – approaching Tony Blair's level in his own second landslide in 2001. Yet at the same time, and for all Corbyn's slightly absurd 'government-in-waiting' posturing in the days after the election, Labour had for the third successive time failed to win power or indeed come anywhere very close to it: in fact, its final tally of 262 seats was barely up on Gordon Brown's disastrous campaign of 2010. It was, in large part, the abysmal poverty of expectations with which Labour entered the campaign (and conversely, the sky-high expectations of the Tories) that allowed the party to present – and truly perceive – what was by historic standards a fairly bruising defeat as at the very least a moral victory.

In Scotland, the SNP's problem was the opposite: an overwhelming victory – winning thirty-five of Scotland's fifty-nine Westminster seats, and a vote share of 37 per cent, ten points ahead of its nearest challenger – that felt very much like a defeat, coming as it did barely two years after the nationalists swept almost all before them in the SNP deluge of 2015. Having lost big SNP beasts like former leader Alex Salmond and the SNP's leader in the Commons Angus Robertson, with clear evidence of tactical voting by anti-independence voters against the SNP – provoked by Nicola Sturgeon's demand for a second independence referendum in the aftermath of Brexit (a prospect shelved indefinitely after this result) – and the principal beneficiaries the hated Tories (marginalised in Scottish politics ever since the Thatcher era), the SNP saw its authority and its claim to speak on behalf of the Scottish people massively reduced.

The unsatisfactory ambiguity of the election results extended to the smaller parties, too. For the Liberal Democrats, 2017 represented at best incremental progress following their immolation in 2015. With twelve MPs (an increase of 50 per cent on 2015, as Tim Farron announced to some amusement – 50 per cent increases being much easier to come by when you start in single figures), at least the party could now throw off the jibe that its parliamentary caucus could fit inside a suburban people carrier (they'd need to upgrade to a small minibus.) But Scotland's gift of three unexpected additional seats, courtesy of the SNP's sharp decline, put a comforting gloss on a picture of general stasis. The Liberal Democrats' national vote share, in fact, marginally declined from 2015, and while the party could welcome back sorely missed marquee names such as Vince Cable and Jo Swinson, it endured the defeat of its former leader and deputy Prime Minister Nick Clegg in Sheffield (cue much Labour glee), the reduction of Farron's own majority in Cumbria to three figures and the loss, however narrow, of its famous by-election gain in Richmond Park. In Southport, the Lib Dems not only lost the seat to the Tories but fell back into third place behind Labour. Beyond the statistics, the Liberal Democrats seemed oddly irrelevant to the national conversation: having bet the proverbial farm on a surge of passionate Remain sentiment, Farron found that 'the 48 per cent' obstinately refused to rally to his call. In this Brexit-election-that-wasn't, Labour's much-pilloried vagueness on the defining issue of the times seemed if not to find favour with both Leave and Remain voters, then at least to be sufficiently elastic not to deter voters attracted to the party, perhaps, for other (primarily economic) motives. Across the former Lib Dem fiefdom of the rural south-west of England – above all in heavily pro-Brexit Cornish seats – the party's devout pro-Europeanism clearly repelled voters, and the Lib Dems not only failed to win back any of the seats lost to the Tories in 2015, but saw themselves overtaken by Labour as the Tories' principal challenger in seats such as St Austell & Newquay and Truro & Falmouth (in the latter, a Lib Dem seat until 2015, the party now lies in third place, 13,000 votes behind Labour). Personally, Farron had a miserable campaign, dogged by questions around his evangelical Christian convictions and his apparently illiberal views on gay rights and abortion that he failed to address to the satisfaction of numerous metropolitan Lib Dem voters who, in turn, abandoned his party for Labour. Farron's leadership lasted just days beyond the election results.

But it was the Green Party – trailblazers for the Progressive

Alliance as a concrete political reality and very much one of this book's protagonists – whose ambivalence about the outcome of the 2017 general election ran deepest. Not for nothing did Caroline Lucas – in a *Guardian* comment piece co-written with Labour's Clive Lewis the week after the election – describe it as 'a bittersweet election'. For the Greens, it was bittersweet to the max. On the one hand, the party's generous and principled decision to stand down its candidates in so many key marginals paid dividends, in that ten of those were won from the Conservatives by Labour or the Lib Dems. And the party leadership's calls for cross-party collaboration to maximise the anti-Tory vote certainly encouraged Green votes in other tight marginals to lend their votes to Labour (especially) or the Lib Dems and in so doing contributed to progressive victories elsewhere. Yet the absence of any reciprocity on the part of the Greens' notional progressive allies – bar the Lib Dems' standdowns in Skipton and in Lucas's own seat of Brighton Pavilion, where she was returned with an almost doubled majority[42] – ensured that the Greens' sacrificial virtue was forced to be its own reward. Across the country, the party's vote halved – a fact that would have material consequences in terms of the ensuing distribution of Short money. And such was the scale of the swing to Labour in many of the seats the party took from the Tories – delivering majorities that often dwarfed the local Green vote in 2015 – that the significance of the Green's contribution to progressive successes was often lost in the flood and hard to quantify. In Brighton Kemptown, next door to Caroline

---

42 Entirely predictably, Labour obstinately insisted on fielding a candidate in the seat, who though posing no danger to Lucas nonetheless came second with over 15,000 votes. In his concession speech, he insisted that Pavilion 'would be Labour again' in the future.

Lucas's seat, where the Greens stood down their local candidate, Labour easily overturned the Conservatives' slim 2015 majority of just 690. In that year, the Greens polled 3,187 votes – making the seat Exhibit 'A' in that election's list of 'progressive tragedies'. In 2017, however, on a swing approaching 11 per cent Labour won a majority of almost 10,000, more than three times the notional Green contribution (the small Lib Dem vote in Kemptown held firm). Across the south and London in particular, as Labour marginals transformed into safe seats and already-solid Labour seats racked up outlandish majorities, this pattern was repeated. In some places, the Greens simply chose the 'wrong' seat to stand down their candidate: in Southampton Test, the party stood down while Labour held the seat with a majority of 11,500; next door in Southampton Itchen, the 725 votes cast for the Greens would have been more than enough to swamp the Tories' eventual miniscule majority of thirty-one. But this is hindsight pure and simple: the Greens, like everyone else in this confounding election, had no crystal ball nor even a sense of the unfolding numbers on the ground as the campaign progressed.

If the Greens' contribution to Labour victories in London and the south was easy to overlook, in seats held and targeted by the Liberal Democrats the picture was both clearer and more disappointing. Of thirteen seats where Green candidates stood down in favour of a Lib Dem, the party held two (including outgoing leader Tim Farron's seat in Westmorland and Lonsdale, almost certainly saved by the loan of 1,800 Green votes from 2015) and gained two, Twickenham and Oxford West & Abingdon (Vince Cable probably didn't need the Greens' help, but Layla Moran's tight victory by 816 votes in Oxford was equally clearly delivered by Bernie Sanders's Green brother Larry, who polled 2,500 votes for the Greens in 2015, migrating next door to the safe Labour seat of Oxford East where his 1,800 votes posed no threat to Labour's eventual majority of over 23,000). Elsewhere, most notably in the south-west, Green stand-asides could do little to compensate for the Lib Dems' fundamental weaknesses in their former strongholds, in several of which as noted above they suffered the indignity of falling into third place behind Labour, sometimes by wide margins.

The Greens' contribution to PA victories was most palpable in Labour-held or targeted seats in the North of England and Wales. (The Lib Dem targets Harrogate and Southport repeated the pattern of the party's regional weakness from the south-west.) In fact, here PA recorded its most impressive triumphs and justified itself in the most inarguable terms – partly, perhaps, because it was here that the conventional wisdom on the election (a defensive campaign against Tory advances in traditionally Labour seats where the working-class vote was peeled off by Brexit) was closest to the mark, and accordingly it was here that the assumptions on which the PA selected its targets proved most relevant and robust. Across the north, where there was a swing to Labour it was much weaker than in London and the south. Although larger cities like Sheffield and Leeds saw shifts to Labour as big as London, Manchester, Liverpool and Bristol, throughout the region's smaller conurbations and former industrial areas there was a marked swing in the opposite direction, especially notable in former mining areas like Ashfield (an 8.86 per cent swing to the Tories, reducing Gloria De Piero's majority to just 441 from nearly 9,000 in 2015) and Bolsover (7.7 per cent, though this still left Dennis Skinner with a majority of well over 5,000). The story underlying these figures was that a majority of UKIP's 2015 vote, largely comprised of ex-Labour votes, did indeed as May had calculated transfer to the Tories: but not all of it, with what appeared on average between a quarter and a third breaking back towards Labour. Given the size of Labour's historic majorities in many of these seats, the UKIP component wasn't enough to shift more than four seats to the Conservatives (their only English gains of the night from Labour), in the classic heartland Labour seats of Mansfield, Middlesbrough South & Cleveland East, Derbyshire North East and Walsall North. The Greens ran a candidate in only one of these (Derbyshire North) but in all four the swing from Labour to Conservative was marked enough to easily overcome the impact of Green tactical voting. Elsewhere in the region, however, that impact was evident and in some cases decisive. The 1,600 Green votes in 2015 in Derby North made Labour's recapture of the seat by just over 2,000 votes this time very much more comfortable: a story repeated in High Peak (1,800 Green votes last time, a 2,300 Labour majority in 2017) and Warrington South (1,765 Green votes in 2015, Labour majority 2,549 in 2017).

Of the fourteen PA (Green stand-aside) seats across the region, Labour gained six and held another six, with the Tories gaining none and successfully defending just two (Ed Balls's former seat in Morley & Outwood, and Copeland, a Conservative by-election gain in February 2017 that fuelled predictions of Labour's terminal condition and very likely helped prompt May's fateful decision to call the general election just seven weeks later). Complicating the analysis a good deal were the sixty seats (in addition to Compass's published list of Progressive Alliance seats) where the Greens stood in 2015 but not in 2017 – some of which were public or non-public stand-asides for alliance reasons, while others were uncontested for a variety of other reasons. In at least two of these, Bishop Auckland

(Green vote in 2015: 1,545; Labour majority in 2017 502) and, spectacularly, Newcastle-Under-Lyme (Green last time 1,246; Labour 2017: majority thirty!) there can be little doubt that Green votes saved Labour seats. (Newcastle-Under-Lyme was also apparently the campaign's most vivid example of PA trumping the Regressive Alliance: UKIP's stand-aside donated the best part of 7,200 votes to the Tories. Paul Farrelly MP has reason to be very grateful indeed to the Progressive Alliance, if indeed that's what it was.) By the same token, Crewe & Nantwich, regained by Labour after ten years with a postage-stamp-sized majority of forty-eight, could have been the belle of the PA's ball. But, though the seat was listed on the PA website as a Green stand-down, in fact the Greens hadn't stood a candidate in the seat since the 2008 by-election. That candidate won 359 votes – enough, in the 2017 circumstances – but whether this could be chalked up to the Progressive Alliance was debatable.

The Progressive Alliance contribution

On Election Night itself, the PA headquarters was surely amongst the calmest of places in British politics. Neal Lawson was making the rounds of election parties, observing the non-plussed, sometimes chaotic reactions to the stupefying – and initially, to many, simply incredible – exit poll. ('What a mess' was his first reaction to the poll – which, had the poll been exactly correct, would have prevented any plausible Commons bloc from forming even the slimmest majority.)[43] Frances Foley was at home enjoying the first night in weeks when she had nothing and nobody to organise. In the PA offices, from which on polling day most – bar the original innermost Compass circle and a

---

43 Though, given Sinn Féin abstentionism, DUP support would still have given the Tories a tiny overall advantage.

handful of phone canvassers – had joined the Momentum army of Labour activists flooding crucial marginals (many of which, especially in London, proved not to be marginal at all) as well as supporting other progressive parties in their key target seats, an air of almost monkish calm prevailed. Outside at around 1 a.m., a small band of twentysomethings paraded down Fleet Street chanting 'Corbyn! Corbyn!' Inside, sustained by pizza, Chuck Dreyer and Rich Williams quietly and painstakingly transferred each constituency result as it was announced into a sprawling Google spreadsheet devised by Dreyer and Roger Wilson. It tabulated not only raw numbers, but whether the seat in question was an 'official' PA seat (i.e. a seat where a Green or Liberal Democrat candidate had stood aside), a Compass target seat or one where a specific tactical vote had been recommended by the VoteSmart tool; in which of these cases the progressive candidate had prevailed; and, equally importantly, those seats to be classified as 'progressive tragedies' – seats where the combined centre-left vote share exceeded the actual Conservative majority (of which much more later). Most valuable of all, the tool allowed for number-crunching analysis that could determine whether PA activity was associated with discernible trends (for example, higher than average turnout or a larger than average swing towards the principal progressive party standing). This would be crucial in the post-match analysis for making the case that the Progressive Alliance had, indeed, made a difference.

The swing to Labour across England and Wales was around 2.4 per cent. But this top-line figure as always concealed very striking regional disparities. In London, for example – an area of particular interest to PA given the intensity of their effort in numerous constituencies in the capital – the swing to Labour averaged over 6.5 per cent.[44] Even here there were notable disparities between the anaemic swings Labour achieved in some East London and especially south-eastern/Kent borders seats (0.1 per cent in Erith & Thamesmead; 0.48 per cent in Bexleyheath & Crayford; 0.8 per cent in Old Bexley & Sidcup – not coincidentally, seats that unlike most of the capital had a majority Leave vote) and its extravagant gains elsewhere. Some of the latter were, surprisingly, in already safe Labour seats such as Hammersmith (over 11 per cent) and West Ham (10.8 per cent). Others were in apparently safe Tory seats where hardly anyone bar – and, by reliable reports, sometimes including – the local candidates had been paying much attention, such as Putney where a 10.2 per cent swing almost defeated Education Secretary Justine Greening, or most eye-catchingly, Kensington where a 10.6 per cent swing elected Corbynite Emma Dent Coad by the thinnest of margins. But the two biggest Conservative–Labour swings in London[45] transpired in Hampstead & Kilburn (12.3 per cent) and Ealing Central & Acton (12.2 per cent), transforming both in a single night from ultra-marginals to seemingly safe Labour seats boasting majorities well over 13,000. Both of these, of course, were seats where the Greens had stood aside – Ealing Central the first such to be announced – as well as PA targets in the campaign's final phase where barnstorms had been run and volunteers concentrated. In fact, PA's four London Labour–Tory targets all exceeded the average swing and four of them ranked in Labour's top ten swings city-wide (Harrow West came fourth on 10.85 per cent, Brentford & Isleworth tenth on 9.5 per cent). In all of them, small and

---

44 Excluding the five Lib Dem–Tory battleground seats in the south-west suburbs.
45 The biggest swing to Labour in London was won at the expense of the Lib Dems – a 15.1 per cent swing in Hornsey & Wood Green, a Lib Dem seat until 2015.

apparently highly vulnerable Labour majorities grew beyond all expectations.

Nobody could blame Compass for claiming these results, as they subsequently did in press statements, as 'their' victories. Politics isn't a trade that encourages or rewards undue modesty, and it would have been unnaturally self-denying of the PA not to want to claim their fair share of the night's unexpected successes. But, in truth, it was more complicated than that. The large swing to Labour across most of London meant that the PA's actual contribution was measurable, but not decisive. Given Labour's advances not only in the key marginals into which political parties invest the bulk of their campaigning resources, and which would therefore be expected to exceed the nationwide swing, but also in both lightly worked seats like Kensington, Putney, Chelsea & Fulham and Enfield Southgate and in already safe (and thus equally unworked) seats like Hammersmith, West Ham and Holborn, the results in the London PA target seats were not obviously exceptional. In fact – in a pattern that would be repeated across the country – as the results came in Compass realised that its efforts, if by no means wasted, had been directed towards the wrong places. Stephen Clark, the longstanding Labour member and Compass co-ordinator for the west/south-west London cluster, afterwards bitterly regretted continuing to direct volunteers into Ealing and neighbouring Brentford when, as it turned out, Labour had probably already piled up more than enough votes by teatime to make the seats safe. PA foot soldiers sent across the river to Richmond Park, by contrast, could surely have dug up the fewer than four dozen Sarah Olney needed to hold on to her seat.

None of this is to the PA's discredit. As a small organisation with limited resources – and no formal co-operation from the parties on whose behalf they were working – Compass could hardly have been expected to recognise trends on the ground that professional organisers, pollsters and pundits all failed to spot. For the PA, the first task of this election campaign had been to get the concept of a progressive alliance on the map. This they had unquestionably achieved. The second had been to make a measurable difference in the outcome. And the results would suggest that here too PA had been successful, delivering larger-than-average swings in their four Labour–Tory targets.

The same pattern is visible in the PA's two Lib Dem–Tory target seats in the south-west London cluster. Twickenham was won back by Vince Cable; its neighbour Richmond Park very narrowly lost. The intervening by-election makes calculating the swing in Richmond Park misleading, but given that historically sensational by-election gains driven by anti-government protest votes have tended to revert to political form at the ensuing general election, to have reduced Goldsmith's majority from 23,000 in 2015 to just forty-five was a remarkable achievement. Vince Cable's swing in winning Twickenham – with PA support – was 8.99 per cent; Ed Davey's in winning Kingston & Surbiton – where the Greens ran a candidate and which wasn't a PA target – was 5.71 per cent.

As any statistician will tell you, correlation is not the same as causation: just because two things happen together doesn't mean that one causes the other. But, even if Compass can't (or shouldn't) claim outright that 'it was the PA wot won it' (or, in Richmond Park, came near as dammit), the evidence is persuasive that PA, and above all PA targeting, made a material difference. (In the only London PA seat not to be also a PA target, Eltham, the swing to Labour was only 3.7 per cent – though again, other trends such as Labour's weaker overall performance in eastern London need to be factored in.)

Across the country as a whole, analysis shows that the Progressive Alliance enhanced the chances of progressive parties wherever it played a part. The average swing across England and Wales from the Conservatives to the leading progressive party (not just Labour) was only 0.9 per cent. In the thirty-six Green stand-aside seats,[46] the swing was nearly 3.5 per cent. (In the eight PA seats that were also PA target seats – i.e. where canvassing, barnstorms and other focused activity took place – the average swing was an eye-catching 7.14 per cent, but this reflects the very large swings in the London and south coast seats. The small swings to Labour in Oldham East & Saddleworth and Workington – both in areas where the general trend was in the other direction – may be more revealing.)

Progressive tragedies, real and imaginary

If the evidence supports the claim that the Progressive Alliance made a measurable difference, especially in those seats that were actively targeted in the final weeks of the campaign, what about the seats where it could have made a difference but no alliances were arranged – the 'progressive tragedies'? (Bear in mind the Green leadership's 'stand firm' announcement to Green candidates shortly before the filing deadline, which by Caroline Lucas's office's estimation prevented up to fifty-plus further stand-asides.)

In the days after the election, Compass went public with the eye-catching claim that in up to sixty-two seats held or gained by the Tories, a progressive alliance – that is, an across-the-board pact amongst centre-left parties, not simply individual

---

46 In fact, thirty-five for the purposes of this calculation: Richmond Park has been excluded as the intervening by-election distorts the 2015/2017 swing comparison (19.5 per cent!).

stand-asides – could have delivered victory for a progressive candidate. These seats ranged from St Ives, with a healthy notional
progressive majority for Liberal Democrat Andrew George of
6,986, all the way to Filton & Bradley Stoke, which delivered an
improbable progressive micro-majority – Labour + Lib Dem +
Green – of precisely thirty-two. In their post-election *Guardian*
piece, Caroline Lucas and Clive Lewis – while celebrating the
PA's achievements both in the 'transactional' business of maximising progressive votes and in establishing a framework for
a more 'responsive, open and collaborative' politics – lamented
the 'waste' of progressive votes in '62 progressive tragedies' and
the often narrow failure to elect progressive candidates in seats
where a distant, thus in electoral terms irrelevant – but still sizeable – third- or fourth-party showing diverted enough votes to
hand victory to the Conservatives. Perhaps nowhere was the
'bittersweet' tang of the election from a progressive perspective
sharper than in Richmond Park – ground zero for the Progressive Alliance the previous year – where Sarah Olney failed to
defend her by-election gain against Zac Goldsmith, who had
turned up once again like a bad penny, by the narrowest of margins after two recounts: forty-five votes out of over 80,000 cast
on an astonishingly high turnout of over 79 per cent. In itself,
to come so close to repeating a sensational by-election victory
(given the tendency of general election results to return to the
mean as voters choose a government rather than registering a
protest vote, Goldsmith's enormous majority in 2015, and the
additional campaign resources he could draw on this time as
an 'official' Conservative candidate) was a remarkable achievement. Yet Olney – an MP for barely six months – could hardly
be blamed for casting a bitter eye on the nearly 6,000 votes
(9 per cent) for Labour's Cate Tuitt (as in the by-election, the

Greens once again stood down their candidate, the redoubtable Andrée Frieze). Remarkably, Labour's vote was down just 1,600 votes on its 2015 showing – which in itself had been the party's best showing in years as erstwhile Lib Dem tactical voters revolted against the party's role in the Coalition government. But as Olney and Goldsmith duked it out with over 28,000 votes each and a wafer-thin margin between them, for anyone except the most diehard tribalist Labour's performance was supremely irrelevant – to everything bar the result, not only here but, insofar as every single Tory MP would be a precious asset to May as she struggled to preserve her administration, nationally too. Such diehard tribalists still abounded: Labour's candidate in Wells, yet another Liberal Democrat target seat where Labour's 7,000-odd votes helped preserve a Conservative MP (albeit with a healthy majority of some 9,500 votes, far from Olney's forty-five), was entirely unrepentant, telling *The Guardian* 'it's not my job to prop up the Lib Dems'. Results such as Richmond Park – where the relative resilience of the Labour vote was achieved despite almost no active campaigning being undertaken, certainly not by the candidate herself,[47] as party members concentrated their efforts on the nearby (former, as it turned out) super-marginals of Brentford & Isleworth and Ealing Central & Acton – are strong arguments for PA insofar as they evidence that if a major party fields even a 'paper' or token candidate, that candidate will attract a minority share of the vote generally consistent with the party's historic performance in that seat, national swings, voter habit etc. In the opinion of the Richmond Park CLP chair, Labour's votes were

---

47 She did, however, apparently find time to report local Labour members guilty of supporting the Progressive Alliance to the party's disciplinary authorities. As of the time of writing, no members have yet been expelled as a result of her actions.

mostly 'new voters' unknown to the party, enthused by Jeremy Corbyn and eager to be part of the Labour surge. Still, it seems likely that at least some voters who supported Olney in the by-election switched back to Labour in the general. It would be interesting to know their motives. This minority vote may well be more than enough – as it was in Richmond Park – to make the difference between victory and defeat for the main progressive candidate.

Another source of after-the-fact angst for PA supporters was the survival, sometimes by very narrow margins, of high-profile Tories in seats where the Regressive Alliance played a role – that is, where UKIP did not stand a candidate against Tory Leavers like Iain Duncan-Smith in Chingford and Theresa Villiers in Chipping Barnet but the PA failed to step up to the plate: Villiers's tiny eventual majority of 353, for example, would easily have been annihilated by the 1,406 votes secured by the Green candidate. In part, this reflected the general – and understandable – failure on the PA's (and everyone else's) part to realise that this was an offensive, not a defensive, campaign: that Tory seats were there for the taking. Equally, however, it reflected an adversarial political culture where, despite the PA's best efforts, communication and collaboration remained very much the exception rather than the rule.

So the chagrin in PA circles at missed opportunities to deliver not just incremental progress, however welcome, but radical change to British society was altogether understandable. But, to the extent at least that this frustration derived from an analysis of the election results, there are persuasive arguments that, on the contrary, the outcome of the election was, if not the best possible result achievable, still a good one in light of political realities. To make this argument involves reassessing the basis

for the 'profound sense of frustration and dismay' eloquent-
ly expressed by Lewis and Lucas, and, while we're about it,
correcting the somewhat abstract – abstracted, that is, from
political realities – headline number of '62 winnable seats'. In the
first place, the figure of sixty-two includes Scottish seats where
the combined progressive (SNP, Labour, Lib Dem etc.) votes
outstripped the winning Conservative – but, for the reasons
already discussed in the previous chapter and briefly rehearsed
below, this seems an even more problematic assumption. Strip
out the Scottish seats and the headline number of 'progressive
tragedies' reduces to forty-nine Seats in England and Wales.
Thirty-nine or forty of these seats could have been won by
Labour, seven or eight by the Liberal Democrats[48] and one by
a liberal independent candidate (Claire Wright in Devon East).
This generates an obvious headline: that, in place of the actual
combined UK total of 314 progressive MPs, Britain could in fact
have elected 363 – an emphatic outright Commons progressive
majority of seventy-six. On this basis, Labour's total seat count

---

48 The ranges given here reflect the fact that in a handful of seats the third-placed
party in 2015 leapfrogged the runner-up to place second behind the Tories in 2017:
thus, identifying the 'natural' PA challenger is not completely straightforward. In
St Albans, for example, the Liberal Democrats overtook Labour on an 8.71 per cent
swing. Between them, Labour and the Lib Dems polled over 31,000 votes – far
outstripping Anne Main's victorious 24,571 for the Conservatives. Based purely on
the 2015 results, however – when, to complicate matters further, the combined progressive vote fell some 1,000 short of Main's tally – Labour, who outpolled the Lib
Dems by over 2,500 votes, would have been the likeliest progressive nominee. On
the other hand, the Lib Dems have a much larger group on the St Albans council:
seventeen to Labour's seven. This seat well illustrates that even with goodwill on
all sides, the road map for progressive alliances is by no means always clear. Given
the imbalance between Lib Dem and Labour gains nationwide from (theoretical)
PA, a case could probably have been made to give the Lib Dems the nod in the seat
– which the 2017 result would tend to bear out. The case in the south-west is also
complex: here, following the Liberal Democrats' 2015 wipe-out in their traditional
heartland – and in a region that leant strongly to Leave – in 2017 Labour polled unexpectedly strongly to overtake the Lib Dems as the Tories' principal challenger in
Cornish seats such as Truro & Falmouth and St Austell & Newquay. For a complete
list of the forty-nine English & Welsh 'progressive tragedies', see Appendix B.

alone would have risen from its actual 262 to 301/302 while the number of Conservative MPs would plummet to 269.

But this top-line figure relies on an improbable calculus: it projects a 100 per cent transfer of votes actually cast for different progressive parties onto a single 'progressive' candidate. This is an obviously unrealistic outturn that doesn't even try to factor in, for example, different levels of voter consent from different parties. The *en bloc* compositing of all 'progressive' votes stacked up against the Tories doesn't actually bear very much scrutiny, and only in part because it includes manifestly fanciful outcomes in seats such as Filton & Bradley Stoke. 'If every progressive voter,' claimed Lucas and Lewis, 'had placed their X tactically to defeat the Tories then Jeremy Corbyn would now be prime minister with a majority of over 100.' Yes, but would those voters do this? Is either of these outcomes – defeating the Tories let alone electing a Corbyn government – in fact a universal and primary aspiration across all categories of 'progressive' voters?

Bearing in mind that – absent open primaries and joint candidacies, etc., which as discussed in previous chapters would likely transform the political landscape but are very far from being a realistic prospect anytime soon – PA invites tactical voting by supporters of smaller parties, and that furthermore these are actual voters, not just numbers on a returning officer's report, it might be worth making some informed guesstimates about how real voters are likely to behave. In other words, is there a possibly more realistic – however inevitably speculative – way to model voter behaviour in the event of PA than the idea of 100 per cent transfer? Keep in mind, too, that from Compass's perspective only eight of these 'tragedies' needed to switch from the Conservatives' column to prevent a Conservative government, even with DUP support. Does a more astringent/robust analysis deliver those eight seats, or more?

We will have to venture away from the deceptive simplicity of spreadsheets alone and try to factor into these projections the messy – and far less easy to predict or define – stuff of voters' ideology and self-perceptions. Insofar as such matters are inherently unpredictable or at least unreliable, translating them into numbers should always invite a high degree of scepticism. But one thing we do know is that the assertion that 100 per cent of 'progressive' voters would unhesitatingly line up behind a single candidate is simply not true. Even in the Richmond Park by-election, 1,500 voters still chose Labour. So, with a degree of caution and common sense, we can make some provisional estimations, for the sake of argument at least, that could bring us closer to a realistic outcome.

It may not be unreasonable, for example, to transfer as much as 90 per cent or even 95 per cent of the Labour vote to a Labour-supported Lib Dem PA candidate: the Richmond Park by-election, where Labour's vote collapsed through tactical voting despite the party's explicit opposition to PA, could be cited in support of this, and these percentages seem all the more persuasive in the context of an open, explicit, authorised and democratically achieved pact. This is because very few Labour supporters are likely to prefer a Tory to a Liberal Democrat, and the same, perhaps in even higher proportions, would probably be true for Green and Plaid Cymru voters, both of whom for (different) ideological reasons have a strong animus against the Conservatives and which as much smaller parties are probably more ideologically homogeneous than Labour. But there would surely be a much larger proportion of Lib Dem voters who would baulk at voting for a Labour PA candidate, even with their own party's official endorsement, and who would transfer their votes instead to the Conservatives. The Liberal Democrats' unreliable history of alternately casting themselves firmly as a centre-left party (under Paddy Ashdown for much of the 1990s and under Charles Kennedy in the 2000s), as 'equidistant' between the two larger parties and (in the 2010–2015 Coalition) as enthusiastic junior partners in an emphatically right-wing government certainly reflects political expediency and opportunism, but also the complexion of their core vote, much but by no means all of which identifies itself as centre-left.[49] Although the collapse of their vote in 2015 indicated that many Lib Dems (and an overwhelming proportion of their 'borrowed' Labour tactical voters) were repelled by their collaboration with the Tory 'enemy', at least some Liberal Democrats are equally hostile to Labour – certainly when, as currently, Labour is led from the left. So, though putting a number on it inevitably remains arbitrary and heavily speculative, shifting a sizeable minority – say 30 per cent – of the Lib Dem vote to the Tories in the event of a notional PA agreement to withdraw a Lib Dem candidate in favour of Labour seems a not unreasonable hypothesis. (In reality, of course, beyond the usual multitude of local factors there would also in this event surely be some voter abstentions and even in some seats independent Liberal/Labour candidacies – the kind of factors no purely mathematical model can ever really take into account.)

The '49/62-gains' model also fails to take into account the impact of UKIP withdrawal: if PA were ever to become a nationwide fact on the ground, the Regressive Alliance (already a feature of the 2017 election that clearly made a difference, most

---

49 See Chapter Five, note 23.

obviously in the Conservative gains by narrow margins – with UKIP not fielding a candidate and endorsing the Tories – of the heavily Leave traditional Labour seats of Middlesbrough South and Stoke South) would surely rematerialise forcefully to counter it. UKIP might well no longer exist as a national party by the time of the next general election, but if it does it's reasonable to assume it would seek to counter the impact of PA; and even in its reduced state, the UKIP vote could have a measurable impact on outcomes – not least because for modelling purposes one can transfer UKIP's vote 100 per cent to the Tories, on the basis that the rump 2017 UKIP vote, unlike its inflated 2015 share, is very likely to be monolithically right-wing.

Consider then the following – obviously entirely speculative, but at least defensible – premises for one such 'smart PA' model:

- that in the absence of a Labour candidate, 90 per cent of Labour voters would support a Lib Dem candidate (and 10 per cent the Conservatives);
- that in the absence of a Lib Dem candidate, 70 per cent of Lib Dem voters would support a Labour candidate (and 30 per cent the Conservatives);
- that in the absence of a Plaid candidate, 95 per cent of Plaid voters would support a Labour candidate (and 5 per cent the Conservatives);
- that in the absence of a Green candidate, 100 per cent of Green voters would support a Labour or Lib Dem candidate.

This reflects the political reality discussed above that, for example, Lib Dem voters do not necessarily uniformly regard themselves as centre-left, especially when the Labour Party advances a firmly left-wing (and union-friendly, a touchstone issue for many Lib Dems) platform: so positing 30 per cent of Liberal Democrats as 'soft Tories' seems reasonable based on observation, experience and common sense. By contrast, independence aside (and the independence issue is less highly charged in Wales than it is in Scotland) supporters of Plaid – an avowedly socialist party – would seem to have little objection to a Labour candidate, especially Corbyn-led Labour. Similarly, Labour voters can, will and have voted en masse for Lib Dems in the past (the Richmond Park by-election the most obvious example). Allocating even a small fraction of Labour and Plaid vote fractions switching to the Tories may seem unlikely on ideological grounds but is worth including if only to acknowledge the heterogeneity and hence unpredictability of voting blocs.

A really granular analysis would try to take into account conditions in individual seats: for example, it's obviously extremely unlikely that UKIP would actually stand aside or recommend a vote for strongly Remain Tories such as Amber Rudd in Hastings & Rye, let alone Anna Soubry in Broxstowe, but for the purposes of this argument this model imagines they would do so. Of course it is equally unlikely that in seats where the progressive parties swapped places in 2017 but the former second-placed party retains a very significant vote share, e.g. St Albans, Colchester, Southport or the new Con–Labour marginals in Cornwall, that the now third-placed party would simply consent to stand aside.

Scottish seats are excluded from this model altogether. As discussed in the previous chapter, the 2017 results and the ample evidence of pro-unionist/anti-SNP (not necessarily the same thing, but complementary) tactical voting in Scotland, the prospect of a Scottish PA, for Westminster at least, is dead in the water. Indeed, if Labour and the Lib Dems were to reach any agreement north of the border, it would in all likelihood be for one or other to stand aside to fight the SNP, as much as or more than the Tories. The SNP remain firm and potentially crucial progressive allies *after* any election – hence the reduced figure of forty-nine still offers ample scope for a progressive coalition government (including thirty-five SNP that's a bloc of 337–342, or a working majority of approximately thirty-five to forty given Sinn Féin abstentionism) – but not realistically before. (Incidentally, not allying with the SNP will also arm English progressives against the 2015-style 'SNP puppet' argument: 'see, we're fighting them tooth and nail!')

As unscientific as this obviously is, it may be that it reflects realities on the ground somewhat better – and thus more usefully for thinking forwards – than a 100 per cent vote transfer model. The results in all the forty-nine 'progressive tragedies' in England and Wales, and the outcomes under the suggested 'smart PA' model, are included as Appendix C to this book. The headline from the 'smart PA' analysis is that its methodology achieves not forty-nine but 'only' nineteen additional progressive gains: thirteen for Labour and six for the Lib Dems. This would create a progressive parliamentary 'bloc' (excluding the SNP for the moment) of not 279 MPs (262 Labour, eleven Lib Dem, four Plaid and one Green), as actually achieved in 2017, but 298 (275 Labour, seventeen Lib Dem, the others as before); then factoring in the support of the thirty-five SNP members (as previously noted, reliable members of a progressive coalition after an election even if, probably, a pre-election pact proved unachievable) we reach a total of 333 progressive MPs, a modest but functional overall majority of sixteen (effectively twenty-four with Sinn Féin abstentionism). The initial hurdle of eight seats to keep the Conservatives out of office is handily cleared: the Conservatives would remain the largest party but would be reduced to 299 seats, their lowest total since 2005.[50]

This may well be a conservative prediction inasmuch as, with a nationwide pact in place, parties standing down candidates would be actively working to persuade their voters to turn out to support the progressive candidate. Moreover, even if – as is certain to be the case – not all of these possibilities translate into actual wins, the mere fact of PA would enhance progressive chances generally because the Tories would have to defend up to four dozen more seats – seats they simply lack the (human) resources to fight; whereas the 2017 election proved that the ground game is where the Labour Party in particular can excel. (Although conversely Labour activists in particular might need to spend more time in their unwinnable home seats like Richmond Park to explain to their voters why they've chosen not to stand and are recommending a vote for the Lib Dems.) Or it may be optimistic, in that there would certainly be at least a handful of candidacies from diehard party members willing to run spoiling campaigns to defend the purity of their beliefs, candidacies which could make a difference in tight races.

Most of this is speculation. But one thing remains clear: even on the cautious model applied here, an authentic progressive alliance of the type mooted but not achieved in the 2017 election would create not just the possibility but the probability of a non-Conservative government; would indeed make continuing Tory rule all but impossible. So the next vital question is, how

---

50 Incidentally, this projection delivers an outcome that is as far as the two main parties are concerned somewhat more proportional than the reality: Labour's total of 279 representing 43 per cent of Commons seats (against the party's actual 40 per cent share of the 2017 popular vote), the Tories' 299 equalling 46 per cent of seats (against 43 per cent of votes).

much closer did Compass's efforts in the 2017 election bring the likelihood of building such an alliance in the future?

Beyond the numbers

In Neal Lawson's view, one particular dimension of the 2017 result imperilled not just the prospects for PA but the chance of a progressive victory at the next election: the unexpected return of two-party politics. In 2017, Labour and the Conservatives won 83 per cent of the popular vote (87.5 per cent in England) between them, compared to just 67 per cent in both 2015 and 2010. This was by far the highest combined share for the two main parties since 1970. The ideological polarisation of the two parties, as well as the presidential personalisation of the contest, seemed to have rejuvenated a previously moribund political structure. Smaller parties, though they could still play a hugely significant political role (as the DUP quickly demonstrated), were starved of political oxygen and squeezed by tactical voting in the majority of seats where they were not realistically competitive.

The risk, in Lawson's view, was that the understandable focus on Labour's dramatic surpassing of (very low) expectations would miss the real meaning of the of this hard-to-parse result. Within days of the election, Labour politicians and sympathetic commentators had calculated that the party would require a further nationwide swing of just 1.63 per cent to become the largest party; to achieve an outright majority would need a further 2 per cent (3.57 per cent).[51] Though these targets are hardly gimmes given Labour's overall swing in 2017 of about 2.8 per cent, they are evidently achievable within historical parameters

---

51 Labour's sixty-four target seats to achieve a majority are listed, in order of swing required, at http://www.electionpolling.co.uk/battleground/targets/labour

and realistically achievable enough for Labour to assume that it can sustain the politics-as-usual – with a left-wing twist – model that brought it, albeit qualified, success this time. Labour might well look at the 'smart PA' analysis above and decide that if the difficult and controversial process of getting to PA would net it only twice as many seats as the Lib Dems, the party's resources would be better used attacking Tory-held marginals and finishing the job begun in 2017 on its own.

This struck Lawson as a dangerous delusion for a host of reasons. In the first place, as many people were quick to point out, it seems very unlikely indeed that the Conservative campaign next time will be as inept as it was in 2017, or that whoever leads it – it surely won't be Theresa May – will be as deeply alienating to voters. The rare nay-saying Labour voices post-election, like former shadow Chancellor Chris Leslie, were largely embittered Blairites venting their anger at the comprehensive discrediting of their project. As such, they could easily be disregarded – and were. But Leslie was right in at least one respect: when he observed that this election was more winnable for Labour than anyone (including him) had realised. The next one will surely be tougher and the Tories – whose reputation as a ruthless vote-harvesting machine is not misplaced, whatever happened in 2017 – are unlikely to be caught napping again.

There are other reasons why Labour's current conviction that 'one more heave' will deliver a Labour majority government may be misplaced. Again, as has been pointed out by a number of commentators, the misleading polls created a context which may have had significant implications for how ballots were cast. Wanting to rein in the potential elective dictatorship of a Tory landslide, voters may well have preferred to elect a local Labour MP precisely because they saw little likelihood of a

Labour government (and Labour candidates indeed pressed this view on the doorstep – 'vote for me, you don't have to worry about Jeremy Corbyn becoming Prime Minister'). Whether such voters will stick with Labour next time, if they face the traditional straight choice between Labour and Conservative – and with Labour's economic programme, no longer a novelty, surely facing much more detailed scrutiny than it received in 2017 – is unknowable.

Indeed, given the many unknowns around the next election – timing, context (not least, of course, the state of the Brexit negotiations) and personalities – another of Labour's assumptions may be mistaken. Naturally, given that the party advanced in most areas, sometimes spectacularly, the party's focus is currently squarely on the many Tory marginals, mostly in the south of England, that now lie temptingly within its grasp: seats like Amber Rudd's in Hastings & Rye (majority now just 346), Theresa Villiers's in Chipping Barnet (353) and Anna Soubry's in Broxtowe (863) are only the highest-profile of fourteen Conservative-held seats with majorities below 1,000; a further thirteen have majorities less than 2,000. Winning these seats alone would bring Labour to the brink of power. Add in the ten Scottish seats where Labour now lie within 2,000 votes of the SNP (seven of these within 1,000) and Labour would be confident at the very least of being able to form and run a minority government, even if it chose not to enter a formal coalition. But in contemplating this tantalising prospect, Labour would do well to remember its classical mythology: Tantalus's fate was to be tormented eternally by having the objects of his desire withdrawn at the very moment of their consumption. And, more colloquially, that what's sauce for the goose is sauce for the gander. For, although the 2017 election overall reduced the number of marginal seats, it added to the number of ultra- (and ultra-ultra-) marginals, and Labour has as almost as many to defend as its opponents. Labour now holds nineteen seats with majorities below 1,000 – ten of them gains from the Conservatives this time – and a further five below 2,000. The mistaken assumption this time around was that this was a defensive campaign for Labour where the object was to hang on to as much of what it already held as possible. As things turned out, Labour stood to make many more gains than it did – certainly enough to prevent the Conservatives being able to form a government – had they only appreciated that the Tories were in retreat and campaigned accordingly. Next time, the opposite may be true: Labour may focus on gaining Tory marginals only to find (as in 2015) that its own soft underbelly is under attack. The swing towards the Tories in northern and Midlands seats has created several Labour ultra-marginals – seats like Ashfield, Barrow & Furness (majority 209, down from over 5,000 in 2010), Bishop Auckland and the ultra-ultra marginals Dudley North (majority 22, down from 4,181 in 2015) and Newcastle-Under-Lyme (30, down from 650 in 2015, 1,552 in 2010) – which are the tip of a potentially perilous iceberg of northern Labour seats at least as vulnerable to a Tory advance as their southern counterparts are to Labour.

Underlying all these numbers is the question of voter volatility: the single biggest factor that should give Jeremy Corbyn's self-styled Labour 'government-in-waiting' some pause as it waits for the apples from the rotten Tory tree to drop into its grateful lap. Labour strategists make the assumption that the unexpectedly large majorities racked in up in formerly marginal seats, mostly in London and the south, has indeed made those seats as safe for Labour as they appear on paper. Majorities of

15,560 (Hampstead & Kilburn), 13, 807 (Ealing Central & Acton) or 11,503 (Southampton Test) would on historical precedent be regarded as altogether secure. But if recent elections have demonstrated anything, it is that voter loyalty in the traditional sense – rooted, regional, durable, communal and familial – is eroding fast. The same trends that have transformed society at large – individualism, consumerism, mobility – is changing voting patterns too. Increasingly, voters do not head to the polls self-identified and pre-recorded as Labour, Conservative etc. – as if these choices were encoded in their electoral DNA – but to make the choice that in their view now, today, offers the best likelihood of achieving and preserving their, their families' and the country's wellbeing. In such a context, voting choices become less of a cultural reflex, less reliable, more malleable, more discriminating and more active. How someone voted in 2017 may only be a rough guide to how they will vote in 2022, or whenever the next election is called. Of course, voters compare their choice today to the one they made two or five years ago, and weigh up whether their hopes on that occasion have been fulfilled or disappointed when deciding how to vote. But there is less and less reason to assume that simply because someone – or many thousands of people – voted for a given party in one election, that party starts the next election with those votes 'in their column'. If British democracy ever worked that way, it is fast ceasing to do so.

If proof were needed of this growing volatility, a glance at Scotland – where Labour and the Tories are now hungrily eyeing those newly marginal Scottish seats – supplies it. In a single night in 2015, voters stripped Labour of all but one of its Scottish seats – its invincible firewall throughout the Thatcher– Major years. The abandonment of Labour seemed definitive and tectonic. Recovery from the abyss would be a generation-al project. Yet, just two years later, those same voters handed Labour an electoral lifeline. The extraordinary swings that handed dozens of Labour seats to the SNP were corrected by less colossal, but, by historical standards, still notable swings back in the other direction (swings in seats gained by the Con-servative were even larger). The thumping majorities amassed by the SNP last time proved not fortresses but castles in the air. Who's to say that Labour's apparently indomitable new south-ern fastness in Croydon Central, say, or Brentford & Isleworth or Brighton Kemptown may not be just as vulnerable? Perhaps the recovery of two-party politics is itself such an optical illu-sion, a function of voter volatility, not the 1970s reset some in Labour may imagine it to be.

If this provisionality is indeed the new normal, this above all should make Labour think again about PA. Because, even if party loyalty is weaker than ever before and only getting weaker, the underlying values that motivate voters' choices are unlikely to be weakened in the same way. Put simply, people may change the party they vote for but, in doing so, they are unlikely to feel they have fundamentally changed their outlook on the world. If you believe in social justice, a more sustaina-ble economic model, the peace movement and redistribution of wealth, you might at one time or another vote Labour, or Liberal Democrat, or Green, or Plaid if you live in Wales, or SNP if you live in Scotland, and that choice may change from one election to another for a host of reasons: but you will retain your core values regardless of the colour of the rosette you wear. Increasingly, this distinction between the values in which we ground ourselves, and the tribes by which we no longer do, is becoming normative. On election night 2017, shortly before the exit poll was announced, Neal Lawson and Frances Foley found themselves in a conference call with Luke Walter and Jana Mills of SmallAxe. Though the purpose of the call was to discuss practical arrangements for communicating the Progressive Alliance/Compass response to the election result (which all still assumed would be an increased Tory majority though not a landslide – the consensus was around 50/60),[52] the conversation turned naturally to people's reflections on the day itself, and somehow everyone ended up sharing how they themselves had voted. Foley, though with deep Labour roots, had voted Green because she lived in safe-as-houses Holborn & St Pancras and wanted to signal her appreciation for what the Greens had done and given during the campaign. A lifelong Labour supporter, Lawson was registered to vote in (what had been) the Lib Dem–Labour marginal Bermondsey & Old Southwark and though he preferred Labour didn't think it mattered unduly which of the two main progressive parties won. Walter and Mills, both Green supporters, had both voted Labour as their own seats were regarded (wrongly as it proved) as Labour–Tory marginals. Crossing party lines was something they were able to do without any stress or reluctance. 'Progressive' had become a far more meaningful, relevant concept than party. On the day after polling day, Foley received an email from Green Party member Peter Alan, who had run the PA campaign independently of Compass in the Green stand-aside seat of High Peak (and from where, coincidentally, the fateful pro-alliance motion at the Greens' spring conference had been moved) saying, simply,

---

52 About half an hour before the exit poll was released, the author received a text message from a friend with good London Labour connections advising him that 'senior Labour figures' were predicting a May majority of 70–100. Presumably the same Labour seers who foresaw a hung parliament in 2015…

'We did it!' It was Labour who gained the seat on a 7 per cent swing: but in that expanded 'we', Foley felt, all of the work and the hopes of the Progressive Alliance were encapsulated.

In such an expanded and expansive political culture, Lawson was sure that the unexpected revival of two-party politics in 2017 was the system's supernova moment – a final starburst before dwindling to a red (or blue) dwarf. In the future, it would be the shared commitment to progressive values – not outdated appeals to party loyalty, still less kneejerk ticking the box you've always ticked – that will bind progressive voters to candidates who embody those values. The Progressive Alliance was grounded in shared values, not party labels. As such, it offers a potentially more sustainable basis for a progressive coalition than any single party does or can. And the trust engendered by seeing parties overcome their differences to work together in a common cause will bind voters more firmly than ever to that cause. Voters moreover can be confident that candidates, knowing they represent not one sectional interest but a broad-based coalition, will be responsive and accountable to that broad base of support.

At present, Labour is taking the line that there was a progressive alliance at the 2017 election – and it was the Labour Party. This view has been expressed by many senior figures from all wings of the party. In a way, this is a backhanded compliment to the PA: it testifies to the potency of the concept, and the anxiety to domesticate or co-opt it. It's also one of those statements which is both true and dangerously misleading at the same time. It's true in that, very clearly, Labour both grew its own vote, notably through an upsurge in the turnout of voters aged below thirty (turnout was up about 2 per cent on 2015), and benefited from a tremendous amount of tactical voting by

supports of other parties. The halving of the Green vote in particular – attributable partly, of course, to the reduced number of
Green candidates but also to the attrition of the Green vote nationwide as Green voters supported Labour – makes this very
plain. But it's misleading in that it assumes, or affects to, that
these votes reflected conversion from the Green programme to
Labour's, support for the manifesto policies, etc. They didn't,
or not predominantly so. They reflected rather Green voters'
shared determination to resist Conservative domination and
the recognition that Labour was, in the overwhelming majority
of winnable seats, the only progressive party with the capacity
to make this resistance real.

And they also reflected the 'permissions structure' created by
the Progressive Alliance and the Green Party (and the National
Health Action Party, Women's Equality Party and, to an extremely limited degree, the Liberal Democrats) that told voters
it was OK to pool their support behind a progressive candidate
from another party, because the times demanded urgent action
and Britain's dysfunctional system wouldn't allow the expression of that urgency in any other way.

The real truth of the 2017 election is not that Labour *is* the
Progressive Alliance, but that Labour *needs* the Progressive Alliance – and that Labour cannot afford to take the Progressive
Alliance for granted. Because the hard truth is that the outcome
of this election may have made delivering PA harder rather
than easier.

For the Green Party, this election has been a traumatic experience, however much moral high ground they can claim. The
party has a less clear road map for its own future than before.
Whereas on paper, at least, before 8 June there might have been
a handful of Green target seats, there now isn't a single one (bar

the very debatable instance of the Isle of Wight.) In one sense, this eliminates a problem for a progressive alliance – namely that the Greens are no longer a realistic threat to Labour in any of their former target seats as none of these are any longer winnable. In another, however, it creates one: for it's not at all unreasonable for the Greens to ask why they should continue to act the good guys while, by so doing, consigning their important voice to political irrelevance. If there is to be, as many expect, another election sooner rather than later, and the question of a progressive alliance is once again on the table, it will be an unwelcome irony as far as the Greens are concerned that Labour and the Lib Dems – the parties that have thus far disgraced themselves by their indifference to PA – are much better placed to gain by it than the party culturally best disposed towards PA. Life is indeed very unfair. It is hardly surprising that a number of local Green parties have proposed motions for the Greens' 2017 conference withdrawing the party's support for electoral alliances. How Caroline Lucas and Jonathan Bartley, whose leadership has been so strongly identified with the PA/Compass cause, will respond if such a motion passes remains to be seen.

The appointment of Vince Cable as leader of the Liberal Democrats could open up new pathways. The rank hypocrisy of Tim Farron, who had the gall to recommend tactical voting only insofar as it benefited the Lib Dems, would have made the party under his continuing leadership a very difficult sell for PA going forward. By contrast, not only has Cable spoken frequently and publicly enough (often on Compass platforms) in favour of PA that it would hard for him to withdraw entirely from this position, but his own re-election in Twickenham was facilitated by the Greens and the Progressive Alliance. Were the Lib Dem conference in September (three weeks before the Greens' conference) to pass a similar motion to the one endorsed by the Greens in April – i.e. to sanction local parties entering into discussions about electoral alliances – this would mark another significant step towards the mainstreaming of PA.

At which point, of course, Labour would be left holding the bag.

Given the experiences of 2017 it is hard, realistically, to see Labour reversing its obdurate stance on PA any time soon – especially while the party is still in its post-election mood of self-congratulation/ecstatic relief. Hopefully, thoughtful voices within the PLP will be willing, now the election is over, to speak out forthrightly to make the case for PA: perhaps, given that there isn't going to be a Labour leadership contest anytime soon, the influential Clive Lewis might be willing to speak less ambiguously on the issue. (His aforementioned post-election *Guardian* piece co-written with Caroline Lucas still lacked concrete suggestions for how the collaborative politics they espoused might actually be fostered within the Labour Party.) Motions will be going forward to the Labour Party conference proposing changes to 'Clause One' of the party's constitution – the clause that has been used to rule out any discussion of alliances. Lewis and others – especially perhaps MPs without leadership ambitions such as Jon Cruddas – might seize this as an opportunity to force their party to have the conversation it needs to.

If, however, Labour remains obstinately tribal, there may be another route to break the impasse: the adoption of electoral reform as a firm manifesto commitment by Labour. There is already sizeable and growing support within the party – support which importantly is not associated with any particular wing but has backers on the Corbynite left (Clive Lewis), the Blairite right (Steven Twigg) and across the ideological spectrum

(including, in the past at least, shadow Chancellor John Mc-
Donnell). Those MPs who owed their survival in good measure
to the Greens' sacrifice could best show their appreciation by
following through on the Greens' priority of electoral reform.
Some, like Tulip Siddiq, have already done so. More need to
come forward. Winning Labour for proportional representation will be a tough battle that its present leader has shown no
interest in, let alone appetite for: but it could be the defining
'Clause Four moment' of the next leader. Adopting PR would
effectively close the door on single-party majority government
in the UK – which is, of course, exactly why so many within
Labour will continue to oppose it. By the same token, its implic-
it acceptance of a future of post-electoral coalitions will make
continuing hostility to pre-electoral pacts a nonsensical contradiction. Because the Conservatives will never introduce PR, it
will take a final FPTP election to deliver a Commons majority
for electoral reform. A thoroughgoing countrywide progressive
alliance is the obvious means to ensure that majority. And in
that moment, the new politics will finally be born.

AFTERWORD BY NEAL LAWSON

All Together

All or nothing? It doesn't have to be this way.

It was so close. A few hundred votes in half a dozen seats and it would have been so different. Theresa May would have been finished and the Tories would have turned in on themselves. No one would know who the DUP are. Labour would have been the biggest party, but short of a majority. It would have needed to negotiate some kind of deal with the other progressive parties. As Deborah Orr of *The Guardian* wrote on the Saturday after election day, 'Victory for a progressive alliance was so close that I could almost taste it'.

But something was tasted over those seven weeks and two days between Theresa May announcing the election on 18 April and the polls closing at 10 p.m. on 8 June. It was the taste of a new politics, where collaboration trumped competition and values trumped party. And those who got lucky by getting to know about it, and made their luck by getting involved with it, will never forget it. It was the taste of the future of politics.

What were they doing? The 5,773 Labour voters in Richmond

Park on 8 June who voted Labour and as a consequence saw Zac Goldsmith, the hard-Brexit Tory candidate take back his seat from the Liberal Democrats by forty-five votes? And, come to think of it, what were the 2115 Green and Lib Dem voters doing in Southampton Itchen to let the Tories keep the seat by just thirty-one votes? This infuriating act was replicated in over sixty other seats where the Tory majority was less than the progressive party votes combined. Sixty-two seats where the progressive vote outweighed the Tory vote and would have seen a Progressive Alliance government if only people had seen sense.

Why would so many people 'waste' their vote and let the Tories in and condemn the country to, probably, another long period of Tory rule, only this time made much worse by the malign influence of the DUP? Why would they want a regressive alliance over a progressive alternative? Of course, they might not have known how close things were. But back in December 2016 at the Richmond Park by-election when the Progressive Alliance first sprung into public life, they knew and Labour polled fewer votes – 1,115 – than they had members. And, this time, there were a plethora of tactical voting sites telling progressives how best to keep the Tories out, while the polls had overwhelmingly been telling them to expect some kind of Tory landslide. Furthermore, the idea of a progressive alliance had slipped in to the blood-steam of political consciousness. All the signals were being sent.

At the same time as some voters were loading their electoral guns and shooting themselves and the country in the foot, candidates, activists and voters from all the progressive parties were doing the 'right thing'. In seat after seat, parties and people were putting the national progressive interest first and working and campaigning together to at least reduce any Tory landslide

and, at best, give life to a new politics of pluralism, collaboration and empathy. Old tribal barriers were being broken down
nationally and locally as party activists found that more actually unites than divides them.

So, how do we explain these two vastly different ways of
thinking and behaving over the course of the same election
campaign? For one group, the imperative to act co-operatively
overwhelmed their instinct for tribalism. For the others, what
was most important was to register support for 'their party'
regardless of the national consequences. And, in terms of Richmond Park, how could there be such a dramatic change between
the general election and the by-election just six months before?
For some, it seems it was a case of all or nothing. Much better,
it seems, to vote Labour, Green or Lib Dem even if it means
letting the Tories back in. It could all have been so different. It
needs to be and it will be.

The Progressive Alliance was, and is, so many different things
to so many different people. It was an instrumental fix against
the potential of a Tory landslide in a competitive political culture that is as binary as it is boneheaded. It was a fix against
an even bigger fix, that of the corrupting and toxic nature of
our electoral system – FPTP – that cheats the vast majority of
voters out of making their vote count. In the face of adversity,
the Progressive Alliance was the reorganisation of rusty deck
chairs on the democratic equivalent of the *Titanic*.

At the same time, it was the taste of the politics to come –
the politics of the twenty-first century. For a beautiful moment,
people from Labour, the Greens, the Lib Dems and no
official party worked together nationally and locally for a result
beyond party interest for the advancement of national progres-
sion. They began to experience the power of collaboration – not

just combined electoral strength, but the cultural and intellectual possibilities of pluralism and what happens when you start to trust, share, cross-pollinate, experiment and co-operate. They had started the process of prefiguring the good society we all felt we wanted to live in.

So, here is the question. Can the old party tribes become new? Can they change fundamentally and systemically their old command-and-control tribal culture and adopt an open and plural outlook? The evidence is messy. People can and do change. Their experiences hit up against their prejudices and they are forced to adapt for instrumental and intrinsic reasons. But can institutions change their culture – and, in particular, can Labour?

The Green Party acts in a plural way because the electoral system gives them no other option, and many of their members have belonged to other parties and have a plural spirit. The Women's Equality Party are plural because they were born of this age and see the goal of gender equality as more important than party advantage. At one level, you can understand why Labour struggles so hard with pluralism; it was born out of a single class and trade union movement and is cursed with the belief that somehow history is on its side. All you had to do was believe enough and socialism would happen. If it didn't, then it must be some traitor's fault – from your tribe or another. Given its class base and relative concentration of voting support, FPTP gives Labour an electoral benefit some of the time, but now FPTP gives the most benefit most of the time to the Tories. And yet, it is the dream of being all-powerful, undiluted and pure that drives the Labour tribalists on.

Perhaps the biggest disappointment is the Lib Dems, because it is harder to see why they behave in such a tribal fashion. A practice of equidistance in 2010, then over-the-top collaboration with the Tories, morphed into a politics of refusing any deals with anyone in 2017. What is the purpose of a third party – one that is less than 10 per cent of the vote – that can only influence the political system in collaboration with others? Why does it back proportional representation (PR) but not practise and prefigure the collaborative politics this inevitably entails?

These were some of the opportunities and challenges we faced going into the campaign. It was a campaign and an aftermath in which my heart, in turn, soared when people collaborated and was broken when they competed unnecessarily. I never truly thought Labour would broker a deal on seats and stand aside anywhere. As a corporate entity, it cannot admit to being fallible in some places – or that other parties have something more to offer. But I have probably never quite felt so low politically as when Labour accepted the sacrifice of Green candidates and progressive voters across the land but could not bring themselves to recognise and applaud this sacrifice: a party that preaches solidarity but practises selfishness. On the Friday morning after the election, the Labour leadership were crystal clear – MPs from other parties could vote for the Labour Manifesto or not – nothing was going to be negotiated, they had no voice or place regardless of the generosity they had just shown. They could take it or leave it. It was all or nothing.

Does it have to be this way?

Like everyone else, Compass was caught out by Theresa May's announcement of a snap election on the morning of 18 April. We were planning and working hard, but for an election in 2020. This meant a long-term commitment to building relationships and creating a collaborative culture. To make it worse, we were in the middle of a process of finding a brand for the Progressive Alliance – a brand that was emotional and aspirational, not simply functional. To say we were unprepared to run a national campaign is a dramatic understatement.

For Compass, the value the idea of a progressive alliance was always essentially intrinsic. It was about prefiguring a different form of politics and recognising that if you wanted a world that was social, liberal and green – and we did – then it would demand socialists, liberals and greens working together to make it happen. Labour can't help itself but be the party of labour – of jobs, money and growth – just as Greens can't help being the party of the environment and the Lib Dems the party of civil liberties and human rights. It would take an eco-system to deal with all the things that matter – not a one-party state. Furthermore, it would take civil society movements, social enterprises and citizens in their millions to establish and embed, not only a new economy, but a new society.

To us, a progressive alliance was never some soggy, centrist deal – it was and is a hegemonic project to transform society and make it much more equal, democratic and sustainable. In that sense, it was and is about more than just party politics and Westminster. Change for Compass was always going to come from the bottom up.

But on 18 April, we faced a choice: either to sit the election out because we didn't feel ready, or do everything we could in the time we had to stop the Tories and maybe help create the conditions for a progressive alliance government. We decided to act.

The result was truly bittersweet. So much generosity and a result that was so close, and yet a new politics that remains so tantalisingly necessary but just out of our grip. Given its new-found prominence, not least because of the Progressive

Alliance, it is Labour that needs to change most to realise the potential of the moment: but it finds change hard.

The closed, tribal Labour mind-set goes something like this:

If we elect enough of the right people who can be trusted to do enough of the right things then, and only then, will socialism be enacted from the top down. We cannot be wrong. History and morality is on our side. If there is no socialism, then that is because people have betrayed us. So we must get rid of the wrong people and replace them with right people. Anyone not on our side – truly on our side – must by definition be our enemy because they are standing in the way of our success. You are either totally with us or totally against us. It is all or nothing.

Obviously the Tories are our enemy and must be crushed, but the Liberal Democrats cannot be trusted either. The Greens are better, but why don't they just join us and along the way drop all the environmental nonsenses – it's about jobs and growth and redistribution, so that the workers' flat-screen TVs can be as big as their bosses'. The SNP has taken our birthright in Scotland – they are just tricky Tartan Tories – and Plaid Cymru would do the same in Wales given half a chance. They are all our enemies.

The old-right in the Labour Party are our enemies, too, and so, of course, are the Blairites – though we don't really mind using the same techniques to gain control of the party, but for left-wing motives, of course. We hate the soft-left more than anything because they just confuse things within the party. There is only one true left. But Socialist Action, the Labour Representation Committee, Workers Liberty, Left Unity and even the new upstarts in Momentum – none of them can really be trusted. If only we could elect enough of the right people to do enough of the right thing, then socialism would be inevitable.

Thus, the closed tribalists try to recreate a moment (that

never happened) when Labour, and Labour alone, could rule the world. Knock on the doors, deliver the leaflets, lift the scales from the eyes of the masses, put the real class heroes into office and then the revolution will happen – just like 1945, Labour's crowning and defining moment.

But 1945 didn't happen like that. Yes, it was the victory of a majority Labour government, but a Labour government built on a 100-year conversation between an incredible rich stream of thinkers, actors, academics, socialists, Methodists, co-operators, liberals, guild socialists and the rest. In particular, it was the inspiration of Beveridge and Keynes that gave us the post-war settlement. They, of course, were Liberals and supposedly our enemies.

And that was 1945 – a moment made possible because of the collectivist nature of the war and the emotional spirit it created. It was made possible by the sheer size and solidarity of the working class and the pressure to meet the political threat of the Soviet Union – which was the biggest factor in capital and the bosses agreeing to the post-war settlement. And it was made possible by the fact that social democracy in one country was still possible. In an age of class, deference, hierarchy, nationhood and an emerging Cold War, 1945 and the singular dominance of the Labour Party was still possible – just. But all the things that made Labour strong then have gone, and have been replaced by everything that makes Labour weak: globalisation, individualisation and consumerisation.

Today, the world is so much more complex. Simply electing a Labour government – even a majority one – cannot do justice to the challenges we face in the form of global finance, jobs being replaced by machines and climate change. Yes, Labour did amazingly well in the 2017 election to get 40 per cent and inspire so many young people to vote, but its coalition of voters was an odd mix secured against an atrocious Tory campaign. Many people voted Labour safe in the knowledge that it couldn't win and despite Jeremy Corbyn, rather than because of him. Of course, Labour could win a parliamentary majority, not least because of the political and economic chaos Brexit is likely to cause. But does it have a coalition inside and outside its ranks to govern successfully?

Because the tragedy is not just that Labour makes it much harder for itself to beat the Tories without a progressive alliance – it's that, even if it does win alone, it will find it hard if not impossible to govern with any great effect because it has failed to build a broad counter-hegemonic bloc to neoliberalism. This has to be negotiated now with a vast array of forces within and far beyond the Labour Party. This will be especially the case if the chaos of Brexit delivers a Labour victory, since it then becomes the turmoil in which it must try to govern.

So Labour must replace closed tribalism with the politics of a progressive alliance. The moment demands nothing less. We can and must fight against many things in our world – inequality, climate change, sexism, racism and more – but what we cannot fight is the culture of our age. To try is akin to turning back the waves. Unlike the hierarchies, elitism and command-and-control culture of the last century, the twenty-first century is increasingly open, co-operative and collaborative. If the twentieth century was epitomised by the rigid and impersonal structures of the Ford car plant, which gave workers the security of a job for life but a fixed and limited identity as an appendage to a machine, the twenty-first century is defined by the fluidity of digital culture. Today, it is our freedom to form and reform identifies, to like and share, to know, speak and be active – but with little security – that defines us.

In today's world, voters are like summer swallows: they form huge flocks that shift and split, land for a while and then just as quickly take off and change their shape and direction once more. In this world, you have to be open, responsive and connected. Pluralism, not purity, is the defining feature of success and influence. And it can be a progressive era simply because, as the world is increasingly flattened by technology, the capacity to be more egalitarian and democratic grows. Of course, the terrain, as ever, is contested. It can be monopolised and privatised, as it is by the likes of Google and Facebook. But unlike the hierarchies of the twentieth century, in which, at best, socialism was to be done to people, in this more accessible world we see the potential for politics for all of us. Now, we at least have the hope that we can bend modernity to our values. It is a moment full of possibility – if we get the politics right.

In the Progressive Alliance Campaign HQ and through our local groups, we started to test the limits of the old politics and the limitlessness of the new. Greens sacrificed their party interests in the national progressive interest; Labour campaigners welcomed them; voters sought our tactical voting site and they willingly put up posters saying 'I love the Greens but I'm voting Labour here' – so many stood up for a new way of doing politics. The genie will not go back in the bottle because it defines the collaborative culture of our age.

The next test of this politics will be whether the Labour Party can commit itself to electoral reform. This is the simple but politically transformative demand that everyone's vote counts equally. There are, of course, instrumental reasons for Labour to back PR – indeed, the existing FPTP system favours the Tories more than Labour – but that can't be the real rationale. What is the most important reason, however, is that it's simply the right thing to do. PR is democratic and democracy is really the only weapon in our armoury against the right. Adopting PR shows Labour is serious about transforming our country and economy because it is dedicated to transforming our democracy. When Labour backs PR, it shows it trust the people.

So the conversion of Labour to democracy is one of the next tests for the Progressive Alliance. In addition, we must do all the deep digging Theresa May so rudely interrupted on 18 April 2017. We have to help define more precisely what it means to be progressive and then set out that 'manifesto' of ideas to show the desirability and feasibility of a good society and the new economy and democracy that must underpin it. We must set up local groups across the country so people can collaborate more effectively. We must work out how the Greens in particular can benefit from the plural politics they do so much to support and we must campaign together on issues such as how to maintain the best possible relationship with Europe and how to fight against the onslaught of climate change. But, more than any of that, we have to give voice and meaning to the cacophony of individuals, groups and organisations that are inevitably springing up in the networked twenty-first century – groups that are practicing pluralism and collaboration as a matter of common sense because it is the culture of their age.

On 8 June 2017, the Regressive Alliance secured 14.5 million votes and Progressive Alliance 17 million. And yet it is the regressive party that rules. Simon Jenkins writing in *The Guardian* on the day of the election commented: 'The British left's inability to engineer a progressive alliance against the Tories speaks volumes for its feebleness. It lacks a hunger for power.' Writing on the same day in the same paper, Suzanne Moore said 'If Labour is re-energised after this – I would hope it becomes more open and flexible. It has to work with the SNP and other parties. It has to lose the macho tribalism and stop calling anyone who does not bow down to Corbyn a Tory. It has to be about inclusion, not exclusion.'

Being a Progressive means you start by believing the best in people and then building a society on that basis. It means knowing, as the late Polish sociologist Zygmunt Bauman reminded us, that the good society is simply one that knows it's not good enough. We need much greater equality, democracy and sustainability.

PA means that we are not all the same, but the values we hold in common mean we should fight for our values rather than fight each other. It means that if we want a world that is social, liberal and green, then we as socialists, liberals and greens are going to have to work together – not just for the instrumental benefit of beating the right, but because it's the only way to build a good society. The right fears the people and we trust them. We want to build a world based on the best in people, not the worst. And this is why, in the end, we will win.

The 2017 general election will, of course, be remembered for the speculator failure of Theresa May. It will be remembered, too, for Jeremy Corbyn and Labour inspiring so many young people in particular and, at last, posing an alternative to neoliberalism and austerity. But it will be the deep cultural changes to our body politic that will have the lasting and transformative effect. It was there in the Greens and in many Lib Dems. It was laid bare by the Labour candidates who went out of their way to attract support from other parties. It was there in the creativity and exuberance of so many Momentum activists and people of no party who simply wanted a better world and voted for it.

And it was there in the hearts and minds of everyone who made the Progressive Alliance possible.

In a hot hall on Monday 17 June, to a rally of 1,000 people to mark the formal launch of the Progressive Alliance, I made the following speech:

This election has rightly forced us into the instrumental job of deals and pacts. In the short term, we have to do everything we can to defeat the right and the awful regressive shift they are inflicting on our people and our planet. But these tactics exist just to support a wider and deeper strategy: the transformation of our society. We settle for nothing less than a world where the poor don't get poorer and where the planet doesn't burn. We will no longer accept the least worst political option that simply slows the rate of decline for our people and planet. We want a good society and we are going to create one.

We start from this simple insight: that when we die, we don't look back and long to have owned more things; we die wishing for more time for the people we love and doing the things we really love doing. We start by taking that insight and applying it to our lives and our society now – not when it is too late. We want more than consuming the things we didn't know we needed with money we don't have to impressive people we don't know.

Our lives are so short and so precious. We have to build a politics that allows all of us to flourish to our full capacity. We know we are always better when we collaborate and don't compete.

And we know that the only thing we can really change is ourselves. And when we change ourselves then that is when others decide to change – and then, in turn, the world changes.

Let each of us promise that we will wake up on the morning after the election knowing we did everything we could to stop the right, and let us vow that we are never going to go into another election where what we know that what is necessary, what is needed, what is desirable is simply unfeasible because of our political and democratic system.

We will take inspiration from the candidates and the campaigners who have stood aside across the country and stood up for a new politics because they know this is about something bigger than just them.

We will do what is right with a sense of determination, but with an equal sense of joy and fun.

We are learning from this campaign about the limits of the old politics and the limitlessness of the new.

We will stop waiting for others to do it all for us. We are going to do it for ourselves.

We are the people we have been waiting for.

All great political movements are born in exile.

This campaign is giving life to a new political movement: the Progressive Alliance.

I ended the evening, as I do in many of my speeches, quoting the Welsh socialist Raymond Williams who said 'To be truly radical is to make hope possible rather than despair convincing.' It is the job of the Progressive Alliance to be these true radicals.

POSTSCRIPT

If journalism is, as the saying goes, the first draft of history, then this book might perhaps be considered a first revised draft. And, like any such draft, it is liable to ongoing revision and indeed instant obsolescence in light of events. The five weeks, following Election Day on 8 June, over which the text was drafted have, in keeping with Harold Wilson's famous maxim that a single week is a long time in politics, already seen developments that meaningfully change the landscape for the Progressive Alliance going forward.

Following the loss of her government's majority in the election she called under the most favourable imaginable circumstances, Theresa May endured the swiftest and most thoroughgoing loss of political authority most observers could remember. The aura of indomitability with which she had been vested by the Tory papers prior to the election dissipated the instant the exit poll was announced and was swiftly substituted by the (perhaps equally unexamined) judgment that she was a brittle, limited and over-promoted politician, an accident waiting to happen that had duly done so. Opinion was divided on whether she would be forced out before the end of the year or whether – as most seemed to believe – she would be permitted to preside over her DUP-sustained zombie government until the Brexit negotiations conclude in 2019, whereupon a fresher face, perhaps less fully associated with the gruelling and in all likelihood unsuccessful Brexit process, could attempt a relaunch of the damaged Tory brand. Another premature election, should a Brexit crisis trigger a split between Tory Remainers and Eurosceptic zealots, remained a distinct possibility.

Much more importantly, some saw the election result as a watershed moment in British politics, marking the definitive rejection of the neoliberal settlement ushered in by Margaret Thatcher's victory in 1979. The public's disinclination to endorse the Tories' prescription of apparently perpetual ongoing austerity and the unexpected support for a Labour manifesto charting a dramatically different economic and social course, it was claimed, signalled a shift in the so-called 'Overton window' – the prevailing horizon of the politically thinkable. A total of 40 per cent voted for progressive taxation to support public services: the first time this had happened in over thirty years. The Grenfell Tower disaster two weekends after the election – apparently caused by cost-cutting measures, inadequate regulation and a callous disregard for the lives of some of Britain's poorest citizens in one of its wealthiest (Tory-run) boroughs – and the reaction to it seemed somehow to encapsulate the shift in prevailing attitudes. Theresa May's belated and hapless appearance at the site, cordoned from residents by security and officials, jeered by a hostile crowd, compared poorly to Jeremy Corbyn's apparently unaffected embrace of a grieving Grenfell survivor on his own (earlier) visit.

Corbyn's own soaring popularity meanwhile almost mirrored May's precipitate decline. Following his messianic appearance at

Glastonbury, where Corbyn quoted Shelley ('Ye are many/They are few') to an adoring audience of tens of thousands, the 'Oh, Jeremy Corbyn' chant (to the tune of the White Stripes's 2003 song, 'Seven Nation Army', via football supporters worldwide) became the soundtrack of the early summer. However unrealistic (given the parliamentary arithmetic) Labour's claims to be a 'government-in-waiting', momentum was clearly shifting in the party's direction. Having fashioned a new coalition of support and demonstrating the mass appeal of a programme grounded in such outdated concepts as common decency and the common good, and with his internal critics largely silenced by the election result, Corbyn and those around him seemed to have a rare and potentially historic opportunity to reorient British politics in a new and progressive direction.

Whether they could take it remained a very open question. With the possibility of a Corbyn-led government now a far more realistic prospect, Labour's positions on key issues inevitably came under increasing scrutiny – not least on Brexit, where even as the start of the government's formal negotiations with the EU instantly opened the predicted Pandora's Box of irreconcilable, unconsidered and unachievable positions, Labour's own all-things-to-all-voters stance in the election (for which a good proportion of its support amongst younger voters was widely credited) began to fray. By the end of July, open divisions between the position of Corbyn and his shadow Cabinet allies on the one hand, and still-influential PLP voices like Chuka Ummuna and Heidi Alexander on the other, on key issues such as membership of the single market and the customs union were being rehearsed on LabourList and on the *Guardian* opinion pages.

The potential fissiparousness of Labour's coalition meant

that, as suggested in this book's final chapter and Neal Lawson's Afterword, the justification for forging a progressive anti-Tory alliance, led by Labour but openly co-operating with others, remained as strong as before. But in the aftermath of the election such an alliance seemed if anything less likely. Vince Cable's unopposed election as Lib Dem leader placed a forth-right supporter of PA in charge of Britain's third party. But Cable's inaugural round of interviews made no mention of any such possibility, in fact explicitly ruling out 'realignments' of British politics and placing clear orange water between himself and Corbyn's 'Venezuelan economics' while reaching out to PLP anti-Brexit rebels. The Green Party, as previously discussed, faced its own reckoning with the consequences of its embrace of PA at the party's autumn conference, ahead of which Green opinion seemed to be hardening against a repetition of the 2017 experiment absent any meaningful reciprocity from the larger centre-left parties or at the very least a clear commitment on Labour's part to electoral reform. The PA's own Roger Wilson declared in an email that in his view the Greens should plan to contest every seat in forthcoming general elections unless there are meaningful gestures in return by other parties, and he undoubtedly spoke for many.

Could Labour change? Would it want to? A small hopeful sign was the passage in July of motions proposing an amendment to Labour's constitution giving CLPs discretion to choose whether or not to stand candidates, by both Surrey SW and (where it all began) Richmond Park. Less promisingly, in the latter case the motion – proposed by Mike Freedman – passed only on the outgoing chair's casting vote and was strongly opposed for the usual incoherent reasons by the local party's now-ascendant Corbynite fraction. So whether sanity will gain traction within

Labour's tribal cohorts remains very dubious. However there was at least one shining exception: the same Surrey SW CLP meeting that supported this constitutional amendment also unanimously passed a motion demanding the rehabilitation of the Godalming Three. A battle royal on this totemic issue was on the cards for Labour's autumn conference in Brighton.

For Compass, these backwards steps were a source of intense frustration: not least because the 2017 election, in which a new coalition started to come together around a progressive agenda, also revealed the unexpected vulnerability of the Tory base. The emergent coalition catalysed by Jeremy Corbyn, if it could be stabilised and consolidated, offers the chance to reduce the Conservatives almost entirely to a party of the shires and outer suburbs. That in itself would make a progressive contribution to British politics insofar as if they wish to avoid perpetual ir-relevance, the Tories would have to cater their programme to start addressing the concerns of voters in lost metropolitan and urban areas, and newly-empowered voters aged below thirty-five, and away from the reactionary *Mail*/Murdoch agenda.

But the challenge facing progressives that post-election summer was precisely how to hold that ground and build on it, rather than slipping backwards. After all, in the short term at least the outcome of the tumultuous 2017 election was the most right-wing political arrangement ever to govern Britain. The tantalising failure – judged, at least, by the yardstick of what turned out to have been achievable victory – of the Progres-sive Alliance faced Compass with a choice. One option was to continue to work, on the kind of elongated timescale originally anticipated in spring 2017 before May called the election, towards deeper understandings and electoral collaborative arrangements between parties and try to forge a fully functioning 'PA 3.0' for the next general election, in 2022 or before. The other was to refashion Compass itself as a kind of umbrella organisation within which a statement of radical progressive values that can secure mass support within and across all parties can be fashioned, forming the basis for an informal 'common programme' on the 1970s French model[53] out of which a fully fledged Progressive Alliance can emerge.

From their experience in the 2017 election, everyone in Compass knew that, as always, it wouldn't be tactical manoeuvres or instrumental politicking but the deep conversations about where progressives want British politics to go and how to get there that might deliver the outcomes they desired – and in the process perhaps throw up entirely new mechanisms for achieving these ends.

Watch this space.

---

53 See Chapter Six.

APPENDIX A

PROGRESSIVE ALLIANCES AT THE 2017 GENERAL ELECTION

The following are seats identified by Compass as Progressive Alliance seats (where one or more progressive parties stood aside in favour of another).

(** = progressive challenger change, i.e. the best-placed progressive party in 2015 was leapfrogged by another in 2017)

Constituency	Party standing down	On behalf of	Result	Swing to (from) leading progressive party (%)
Brentford & Isleworth	Green	Labour	Lab hold	9.48 Con to Lab
Brighton Kemptown	Green	Labour	Lab gain	10.79 Con to Lab
Brighton Pavilion	Lib Dems, WEP	Green	Green hold	5.45 Lab to Green
Bury North	Green	Labour	Lab gain	4.98 Con to Lab
Bury South	Green	Labour	Lab hold	0.64 Con to Lab
Carlisle	Green	Labour	Con hold	0.24 Con to Lab
City of Chester	Green	Labour	Lab hold	8.04 Con to Lab
Copeland	Green	Labour	Con hold	(5.21 Lab to Con)^A
Crewe & Nantwich	Green	Labour	Lab gain	3.67 Con to Lab
Derby North	Green	Labour	Lab gain	2.12 Con to Lab
Ealing Central & Acton	Green	Labour	Lab hold	12.21 Con to Lab
Eltham	Green	Labour	Lab hold	3.7 Con to Lab

Gower	Green	Labour	Lab gain	3.62 Con to Lab
Harrogate & Knaresborough	Green	Lib Dems	Con hold	(0.67 LD to Con)
Hartlepool	Green	Labour	Lab hold	1.77 Con to Lab
Hastings & Rye	Green	Labour	Con hold	4.39 Con to Lab
High Peak	Green	Labour	Lab gain	6.97 Con to Lab
Hyndburn	Green	Labour	Lab hold	1.30 Con to Lab
Ilford North	Green	Labour	Lab hold	8.50 Con to Lab
Isle of Wight	WEP	Green	Con hold	(0.20 Lab to Con)
Lewes	Green	Lib Dems	Con hold	(4.01 LD to Con)
Mid Dorset & North Poole	Green	Lib Dems	Con hold	(4.57 LD to Con)
Morley & Outwood	Green	Labour	Con hold	(1.57 Lab to Con)
North Cornwall	Green	Lib Dems	Con hold	(0.20 LD to Con)
North Norfolk	Green	Lib Dems	LD hold	(0.73 LD to Con)
Oldham East & Saddleworth	Green	Labour	Lab hold	1.95 Con to Lab
Oxford West & Abingdon	Green	Lib Dems	LD gain	9.05 Con to LD
Pudsey	Green	Labour	Con hold	4.11 Con to Lab
Richmond Park	Green	Lib Dems	Con gain	19.44 Con to LD[B]
Saffron Walden	Green	Lib Dems	Con hold	2.21 Con to Lab
Shipley	Green	WEP	Con hold	5.14 Con to Lab
Skipton & Ripon	Lib Dems	Green	Con hold	1.84 Con to Lab
South West Surrey	Green	NHA	Con hold	7.83 Con to NHA
Southampton Test	Green	Labour	Lab hold	7.90 Con to Lab
Southport	Green	Lib Dems**	Con gain	(7.63 LD to Con)
St Austell & Newquay	Green	Lib Dems**	Con hold	4.72 Con to Lab
St Ives	Green	Lib Dems	Con hold	2.25 Con to LD
Twickenham	Green	Lib Dems	LD gain	8.99 Con to LD
Warrington South	Green	Labour	Lab gain	4.37 Con to Lab
Westmorland & Lonsdale	Green	Lib Dems	LD hold	(8.39 LD to Con)
Workington	Green	Labour	Lab hold	(1.38 Lab to Con)
York Central	Green	Labour	Lab hold	10.45 Con to Lab

A   Result compared to 2017 by-election; swing calculated from 2015 General Election.
B   Result compared to 2016 by-election; swing calculated from 2015 General Election.

COMPASS/PROGRESSIVE ALLIANCE TARGETS AT THE 2017 GENERAL ELECTION

(** = progressive challenger change, i.e. the best-placed progressive party in 2015 was leapfrogged by another in 2017)

Constituency	Targeted result	Actual result	Swing to (from) leading progressive party (%)
Birmingham Northfield	Lab hold	Lab hold	2.31 Con to Lab
Birmingham Erdington	Lab hold	Lab hold	2.39 Con to Lab
Brentford & Isleworth	Lab hold	Lab hold	9.48 Con to Lab
Brighton Kemptown	Lab gain	Lab gain	10.79 Con to Lab
Cardiff North	Lab gain	Lab gain	6.10 Con to Lab
Cardiff South & Penarth	Lab hold	Lab hold	6.66 Con to Lab
Cardiff West	Lab hold	Lab hold	5.71 Con to Lab
Carlisle	Lab gain	Con hold	0.24 Con to Lab
Ealing Central & Acton	Lab hold	Lab hold	12.21 Con to Lab
Eastbourne	LD gain	LD gain	2.09 Con to LD
Eastleigh	LD gain	LD gain	(4.14 LD to Con)
Hampstead & Kilburn	Lab hold	Lab hold	12.27 Con to Lab
Harrow West	Lab hold	Lab hold	10.85 Con to Lab
Hastings & Rye	Lab gain	Con hold	4.39 Con to Lab
Hove	Lab hold	Lab hold	15.10 Con to Lab
Ilford North	Lab hold	Lab hold	8.50 Con to Lab
Isle of Wight	Green gain	Con hold	(0.20 Lab to Con)
Lancaster & Fleetwood	Lab hold	Lab hold	5.73 Con to Lab
Lewes	LD gain	Con hold	(4.01 LD to Con)
Norwich South	Lab hold	Lab hold	7.29 Con to Lab

Oldham East & Saddleworth	Lab hold	Lab hold	1.95 Con to Lab
Portsmouth South	LD gain	Lab gain**	9.38 Con to Lab
Richmond Park	LD hold	Con gain	19.44 Con to LD[C]
Southampton Itchen	Lab gain	Con hold	2.56 Con to Lab
Southampton Test	Lab hold	Lab hold	7.90 Con to Lab
Southport	LD hold	Con gain**	(7.63 LD to Con)
South West Surrey	NHA gain	Con hold	7.83 Con to NHA
Stalybridge & Hyde	Lab hold	Lab hold	1.37 Con to Lab
Twickenham	LD gain	LD gain	8.99 Con to LD
Wirral South	Lab hold	Lab hold	3.71 Con to Lab
Workington	Lab hold	Lab hold	(1.38 Lab to Con)

C Result compared to 2016 by-election; swing calculated from 2015 General Election.

'PROGRESSIVE TRAGEDIES' AT THE 2017 GENERAL ELECTION

(ENGLAND & WALES ONLY)

In all of these seats, the combined total vote for progressive parties in 2017 was larger than the actual winning Conservative vote, giving rise to a notional 'progressive majority' (PROG MAJ). The following analysis tabulates the results for each seat in 2017 and then projects a 'Smart PA' outcome and notional vote share based on the following assumptions:

- that in the absence of a Labour candidate, 90 per cent of Labour voters would support a Lib Dem candidate (and 10 per cent the Conservatives);
- that in the absence of a Lib Dem candidate, 70 per cent of Lib Dem voters would support a Labour candidate (and 30 per cent the Conservatives);
- that in the absence of a Plaid candidate, 95 per cent of Plaid voters would support a Labour candidate (and 5 per cent the Conservatives);

- that in the absence of a Green candidate, 100 per cent of Green votes would support a Labour or Lib Dem candidate.

(** = progressive challenger change, i.e. the best-placed progressive party in 2015 was leapfrogged by another in 2017)

ABERCONWY
Con 14,337
Lab 13,702
PC 3,170
LD 941
CON MAJ 635
PROG MAJ 3,476
Lab 13,702 + (95 per cent PC) 3,012 + (70 per cent LD) 659 = 17,373
Con 14,337 + (5 per cent PC) 159 + (30 per cent LD) 282 = 14,778
Smart PA LAB GAIN MAJ 2,595

BOLTON WEST
Con 24,459
Lab 23,523
UKIP 1,587
LD 1,485
CON MAJ 936
PROG MAJ 549
Lab 23,523 + (70 per cent LD) 1,040 = 24,563
Con 24,459 + (30 per cent LD) 446 + (100 per cent UKIP) 1,587 = 26,492
Smart PA CON HOLD MAJ 1,929

BRECON & RADNORSHIRE
Con 20,081
LD 12,043
Lab 7,335
PC 1,299
UKIP 576
CON MAJ 8,038
PROG MAJ 596
LD 12,043 + (90 per cent Lab) 6,602 + (95 per cent PC) 1,234 = 19,879
Con 20,081 + (10 per cent Lab) 733 + (5 per cent PC) 65 + (100 per cent UKIP) 576 = 21,455
Smart PA CON HOLD MAJ 1,576

BROXTOWE
Con 25,983
Lab 25,120
LD 2,247
UKIP 1,477
Green 681
CON MAJ 863
PROG MAJ 2,065
Lab 25,120 + (70 per cent LD) 1,573 + (100 per cent Green) 681 = 27,374
Con 25,983 + (30 per cent LD) 674 + (100 per cent UKIP) 1,477 = 28,134
Smart PA CON HOLD MAJ 760

CALDER VALLEY
Con 26,790
Lab 26,181
LD 1,952
UKIP 1,466
Green 631
CON MAJ 609
PROG MAJ 1,974
Lab 26,181 + (70 per cent LD) 1,366 + (100 per cent Green) 631 = 28,178
Con 26,790 + (30 per cent LD) 586 + (100 per cent UKIP) 1,466 = 28,842
Smart PA CON HOLD MAJ 664

CAMBORNE & REDRUTH
Con 23,001
Lab 21,424
LD 2,979
Green 1,052
CON MAJ 1,577
PROG MAJ 2,454
Lab 21,424 + (70 per cent LD) 2,085 + (100 per cent Green) 1,052 = 24,561
Con 23,001 + (30 per cent LD) 894 = 23,895
Smart PA LAB GAIN MAJ 666

CARMARTHEN WEST & PEMBROKESHIRE SOUTH
Con 19,771
Lab 16,661
PC 3,933
LD 956
UKIP 905
PROG MAJ 1,779
CON MAJ 3,110
Lab 16,661 + (95 per cent PC) 3,736 + (70 per cent LD) 669 = 21,066
Con 19,771 + (5 per cent PC) 197 + (30 per cent LD) 287 + (100 per cent UKIP) 905 = 21,160
Smart PA CON HOLD MAJ 94

CHEADLE
Con 24,331
LD 19,824
Lab 10,417
CON MAJ 4,507
PROG MAJ 5,910
LD 19,824 + (90 per cent Lab) 9,375 = 29,199
Con 24,331 + (10 per cent Lab) 1,042 = 25,373
Smart PA LIB DEM GAIN MAJ 3,826

CHELTENHAM
Con 26,615
LD 24,046
Lab 5,408
Green 943
CON MAJ 2,569
PROG MAJ 3,782
LD 24,046 + (90 per cent Lab) 4,867 + (100 per cent Green) 943 = 29,856
Con 26,615 + (10 per cent Lab) 541 = 27,156
Smart PA LIB DEM GAIN MAJ 2,700

CHINGFORD & WOODFORD GREEN
Con 23,076
Lab 20,638
LD 2,043
Green 1,204
CON MAJ 2,438
PROG MAJ 809
Lab 20,638 + (70 per cent LD) 1,430 + (100 per cent Green) 1,204 = 23,272
Con 23,076 + (30 per cent LD) 613 = 23,689
Smart PA CON HOLD MAJ 417

CHIPPING BARNET
Con 25,679
Lab 25,326
LD 3,012
Green 1,406
CON MAJ 353
PROG MAJ 4,065
Lab 25,326 + (70 per cent LD) 2,108 + (100 per cent Green) 1,406 = 28,840
Con 25,679 + (30 per cent LD) 904 = 26,583
Smart PA LAB GAIN MAJ 2,257

CITIES OF LONDON & WESTMINSTER
Con 18,005
Lab 14,857
LD 4,270
Green 821
UKIP 426
CON MAJ 3,148
PROG MAJ 1,943
Lab 14,857 + (70 per cent LD) 2,989 + (100 per cent Green) 821 = 18,667
Con 18,005 + (30 per cent LD) 1,281 + (100 per cent UKIP) 426 = 1,9712
Smart PA CON HOLD MAJ 1,045

CLWYD WEST
Con 19,541
Lab 16,104
PC 3,918
LD 1,091
CON MAJ 3,437
PROG MAJ 1,572
Lab 16,104 + (95 per cent PC) 3,722 + (70 per cent LD) 764 = 20,590
Con 19,541 + (5 per cent PC) 196 + (30 per cent LD) 327 = 20,064
Smart PA LAB GAIN MAJ 526

COLCHESTER
Con 24,565
Lab 18,888 **
LD 9,087
Green 828
CON MAJ 5,677
PROG MAJ 4,238
Lab 18,888 + (70 per cent LD) 6,361 + (100 per cent Green) 828 = 26,077
Con 24,565 + (30 per cent LD) 2,726 = 27,291
Smart PA CON HOLD MAJ 1,214

DEVON EAST

Con 29,306
Ind 21,270
Lab 6,857
LD 1,468
UKIP 1,203
CON MAJ 8,036
PROG MAJ 289
Ind 21,270 + (100 per cent Lab) 6,857 + (70 per cent LD) 1,028 = 29,155
Con 29,306 + (30 per cent LD) 440 + (100 per cent UKIP) 1,203 = 30,949
Smart PA CON HOLD MAJ 1,794

DEVON NORTH

Con 25,517
LD 21,185
Lab 7,063
UKIP 1,187
CON MAJ 4,332
PROG MAJ 2,731
LD 21,185 + (90 per cent Lab) 4,944 = 26,129
Con 25,517 + (10 per cent Lab) 706 + (100 per cent UKIP) 1,187 = 27,410
Smart PA CON HOLD MAJ 1,281

FILTON & BRADLEY STOKE

Con 25,331
Lab 21,149
LD 3,052
Green 1,162
CON MAJ 4,182
PROG MAJ 32
Lab 21,149 + (70 per cent LD) 2,136 + (100 per cent Green) 1,162 = 24,447
Con 25,331 + (30 per cent LD) 916 = 26,247
Smart PA CON HOLD MAJ 1,800

FINCHLEY & GOLDERS GREEN

Con 24,599
Lab 22,942
LD 3,463
Green 919
UKIP 462
CON MAJ 1,657
PROG MAJ 2,725
Lab 22,942 + (70 per cent LD) 2,424 + (100 per cent Green) 919 = 26,285
Con 24,599 + (30 per cent LD) = 25,637
Smart PA LAB GAIN MAJ 648

HARROW EAST

Con 25,129
Lab 23,372
LD 1,573
Green 771
CON MAJ 1,757
PROG MAJ 587
Lab 23,372 + (70 per cent LD) 1,101 + (100 per cent Green) 771 = 25,244
Con 25,129 + (30 per cent LD) 472 = 25,601
Smart PA CON HOLD MAJ 357

HASTINGS & RYE

Con 25,668
Lab 25,322
LD 1,885
UKIP 1,479
CON MAJ 346
PROG MAJ 1,539
Lab 25,322 + (70 per cent LD) 1,320 = 26,642
Con 25,668 + (30 per cent LD) 566 + (100 per cent UKIP) 1,479 = 27,713
Smart PA CON HOLD MAJ 1,071

HAZEL GROVE

Con 20,047
LD 14,533
Lab 9,036
Green 516
CON MAJ 5,514
PROG MAJ 4,038
LD 14,533 + (90 per cent Lab) 8,133 + (100 per cent Green) 516 = 23,182
Con 20,047 + (10 per cent Lab) 904 = 20,951
Smart PA LIB DEM GAIN MAJ 2,231

HENDON

Con 25,078
Lab 24,006
LD 1,985
Green 578
UKIP 568
CON MAJ 1,072
PROG MAJ 1,491
Lab 24,006 + (70 per cent LD) 1,390 + (100 per cent Green) 578 = 25,974
Con 25,078 + (30 per cent LD) 595 + (100 per cent UKIP) 568 = 26,242
Smart PA CON HOLD MAJ 268

LEWES

Con 26,820
LD 21,312
Lab 6,060
CON MAJ 5,508
PROG MAJ 552
LD 21,312 + (90 per cent Lab) 5,454 = 26,766
Con 26,820 + (10 per cent Lab) 606 = 27,426
Smart PA CON HOLD MAJ 660

MIDDLESBOROUGH SOUTH & CLEVELAND EAST

Con 23,643
Lab 22,623
LD 1,354
CON MAJ 1,020
PROG MAJ 334
Lab 22,623 + (70 per cent LD) 948 = 23,571
Con 23,643 + (30 per cent LD) = 24,049
Smart PA CON GAIN MAJ 478

MILTON KEYNES NORTH

Con 30,307
Lab 28,392
LD 2,499
UKIP 1,390
Green 1,107
CON MAJ 1,915
PROG MAJ 1,691
Lab 28,392 + (70 per cent LD) 1,749 + (100 per cent Green) 1,107 = 31,248
Con 30,307 + (30 per cent LD) 748 + (100 per cent UKIP) 1,390 = 32,445
Smart PA CON HOLD MAJ 1,197

MILTON KEYNES SOUTH

Con 30,652
Lab 28,927
LD 1,895
UKIP 1,833
Green 1,179
CON MAJ 1,725
PROG MAJ 1,349
Lab 28,927 + (70 per cent LD) 1,327 + (100 per cent Green) 1,179 = 31,433
Con 30,652 + (30 per cent LD) 567 + (100 per cent UKIP) 1,833 = 33,052
Smart PA CON HOLD MAJ 1,619

MORECAMBE & LUNESDALE

Con 21,773
Lab 20,374
LD 1,699
UKIP 1,333
Green 478
CON MAJ 1,399
PROG MAJ 778
Lab 20,374 + (70 per cent LD) 1,189 + (100 per cent Green) 478 = 22,041
Con 21,773 + (30 per cent LD) 510 + (100 per cent UKIP) 1,333 = 23,616
Smart PA CON HOLD MAJ 1,575

NORTHAMPTON NORTH

Con 19,065
Lab 18,258
UKIP 1,404
LD 1,015
Green 636
CON MAJ 807
PROG MAJ 844
Lab 18,258 + (70 per cent LD) 711 + (100 per cent Green) 636 = 19,605
Con 19,065 + (30 per cent LD) 304 + (100 per cent UKIP) 1,404 = 20,773
Smart PA CON HOLD MAJ 1,168

NORTHAMPTON SOUTH
Con 19,231
Lab 18,072
UKIP 1,630
LD 1,405
Green 696
CON MAJ 1,159
PROG MAJ 942
Lab 18,072 + (70 per cent LD) 984 + (100 per cent Green) 696 = 19,752
Con 19,231 + (30 per cent LD) 421 + (100 per cent UKIP) 1,405 = 21,057
Smart PA CON HOLD MAJ 1,305

NORWICH NORTH
Con 21,900
Lab 21,393
LD 1,480
Green 782
CON MAJ 507
PROG MAJ 1,725
Lab 21,393 + (70 per cent LD) 1,036 + (100 per cent Green) 782 = 23,211
Con 21,900 + (30 per cent LD) 444 = 22,344
Smart PA LAB GAIN MAJ 867

PENDLE
Con 21,986
Lab 20,707
LD 941
Green 502
CON MAJ 1,279
PROG MAJ 164
Lab 20,707 + (70 per cent LD) 659 + (100 per cent Green) 502 = 21,868
Con 21,986 + (30 per cent LD) 282 = 22,268
Smart PA CON HOLD MAJ 400

PRESELI PEMBROKESHIRE
Con 18,302
Lab 17,988
PC 2,711
LD 1,106
UKIP 850
CON MAJ 314
PROG MAJ 3,503
Lab 17,988 + (95 per cent PC) 2,575 + (70 per cent LD) 774 = 21,337
Con 18,302 + (5 per cent PC) 136 + (30 per cent LD) 332 + (100 per cent UKIP) 850 = 19,620
Smart PA LAB GAIN MAJ 1,717

PUDSEY
Con 25,550
Lab 25,219
LD 1,761
CON MAJ 331
PROG MAJ 1,430
Lab 25,219 + (70 per cent LD) 1,233 = 26,452
Con 25,550 + (30 per cent LD) 528 = 2,6078
Smart PA LAB GAIN MAJ 374

PUTNEY
Con 20,679
Lab 19,125
LD 5,448
Green 1,107
UKIP 477
CON MAJ 1,554
PROG MAJ 5,001
Lab 19,125 + (70 per cent LD) 3,814 + (100 per cent Green) 1,107 = 24,046
Con 20,679 + (30 per cent LD) 1,634 + (100 per cent UKIP) 477 = 22,790
Smart PA LAB GAIN MAJ 1,256

READING WEST
Con 25,311
Lab 22,435
LD 3,041
Green 979
CON MAJ 2,876
PROG MAJ 1,144
Lab 22,345 + (70 per cent LD) 2,129 + (100 per cent Green) 979 = 25,453
Con 25,311 + (30 per cent LD) 912 = 26,223
Smart PA CON HOLD MAJ 770

RICHMOND PARK
Con 28,588
LD 28,543
Lab 5,773
CON MAJ 45
PROG MAJ 5,728
LD 28,543 + (90 per cent Lab) 5,196 = 33,739
Con 28,588 + (10 per cent Lab) 577 = 29,165
Smart PA LIB DEM GAIN MAJ 4,574

ST ALBANS
Con 24,571
LD 18,462 **
Lab 13,137
Green 828
CON MAJ 828
PROG MAJ 7,856
LD 18,462 + (90 per cent Lab) 11,823 + (100 per cent Green) 828 = 31,113
Con 24,571 + (10 per cent Lab) 1,314 = 25,885
Smart PA LIB DEM GAIN MAJ 5,228

ST AUSTELL & NEWQUAY
Con 26,856
Lab 15,714 **
LD 11,642
CON MAJ 11,142
PROG MAJ 500
Lab 15,714 + (70 per cent LD) 8,150 = 23,864
Con 26,856 + (30 per cent LD) 3,493 = 30,349
Smart PA CON HOLD MAJ 6,485

ST IVES

Con 22,120
LD 21,808
Lab 7,298
CON MAJ 312
PROG MAJ 6,986
LD 21,808 + (90 per cent Lab) 6,568 = 28,376
Con 22,120 + (10 per cent Lab) 730 = 22,850
Smart PA LIB DEM GAIN MAJ 5,526

SOUTHAMPTON ITCHEN

Con 21,773
Lab 21,742
LD 1,421
UKIP 1,122
Green 725
CON MAJ 31
PROG MAJ 2,115
Lab 21,742 + (70 per cent LD) 995 + (100 per cent Green) 725 = 23,462
Con 21,773 + (30 per cent LD) 426 + (100 per cent UKIP) 1,122 = 23,321
Smart PA LAB GAIN MAJ 141

SOUTHPORT

Con 18,541
Lab 15,627 **
LD 12,661
UKIP 1,127
CON MAJ 2,914
PROG MAJ 9,747
Lab 15,627 + (70 per cent LD) 8,863 = 24,490
Con 18,541 + (30 per cent LD) 3,798 + (100 per cent UKIP) 1,127 = 23,46
Smart PA LAB GAIN MAJ 1,024

STOKE-ON-TRENT SOUTH

Con 20,451
Lab 19,788
LD 808
Green 643
CON MAJ 663
PROG MAJ 788
Lab 19,788 + (70 per cent LD) 566 + (100 per cent Green) 643 = 20,997
Con 20,451 + (30 per cent LD) 242 = 20,693
Smart PA LAB GAIN MAJ 304

SWINDON SOUTH

Con 24,809
Lab 22,345
LD 2,079
UKIP 1,291
Green 747
CON MAJ 2,464
PROG MAJ 362
Lab 22,345 + (70 per cent LD) 1,455 + (100 per cent Green) 747 = 24,547
Con 24,809 + (30 per cent LD) 624 + (100 per cent UKIP) 1,291 = 26,724
Smart PA CON HOLD MAJ 2,177

TELFORD

Con 21,777
Lab 21,057
LD 954
Green 898
CON MAJ 720
PROG MAJ 1,132
Lab 21,057 + (70 per cent LD) 668 + (100 per cent Green) 898 = 22,623
Con 21,777 + (30 per cent LD) 286 = 22,063
Smart PA LAB GAIN MAJ 560

TRURO & FALMOUTH

Con 25,123
Lab 21,331 **
LD 8,465
UKIP 897
Green 831
CON MAJ 3,792
PROG MAJ 5,504
Lab 21,331 + (70 per cent LD) 5,926 + (100 per cent Green) 831 = 28,088
Con 25,123 + (30 per cent LD) 2,539 + (100 per cent UKIP) 831 = 28,493
Smart PA CON HOLD MAJ 405

VALE OF GLAMORGAN

Con 25,501
Lab 23,311
PC 2,295
LD 1,020
UKIP 868
Green 419
CON MAJ 2,190
PROG MAJ 1,544
Lab 23,311 + (95 per cent PC) 2,180 + (70 per cent LD) 714 + (100 per cent Green) 419 = 26,624
Con 25,501 + (5 per cent PC) 115 + (30 per cent LD) 306 + (100 per cent UKIP) 868 = 2,679
Smart PA CON HOLD MAJ 166

WATFORD

Con 26,731
Lab 24,639
LD 5,335
UKIP 1,184
Green 721
CON MAJ 2,092
PROG MAJ 3,964
Lab 24,639 + (70 per cent LD) 3,875 + (100 per cent Green) 721 = 29,235
Con 26,731 + (30 per cent LD) 1,600 + (100 per cent UKIP) 1,184 = 29,515
Smart PA CON HOLD MAJ 280

WIMBLEDON
Con 23,946
Lab 18,324
LD 7,472
Green 1,231
UKIP 553
CON MAJ 5,622
PROG MAJ 3,081
Lab 18,324 + (70 per cent LD) 5,231 + (100 per cent Green) 1,231 = 24,786
Con 23,946 + (30 per cent LD) 2,241 + (100 per cent UKIP) 553 = 26,740
Smart PA CON HOLD MAJ 1,954

WORCESTER
Con 24,731
Lab 22,223
LD 1,757
UKIP 1,354
Green 1,211
CON MAJ 2,508
PROG MAJ 460
Lab 22,223 + (70 per cent LD) 1,230 + (100 per cent Green) 1,211 = 24,664
Con 24,731 + (30 per cent LD) 527 + (100 per cent UKIP) 1,354 = 26,612
Smart PA CON HOLD MAJ 1,948

INDEX